INTRODUCTION

This Snapshot guide, excerpted from my guidebook *Rick Steves' Croatia & Slovenia*, introduces you to Croatia's single best destination, the "Pearl of the Adriatic"—Dubrovnik. This magnificent medieval city, encircled by a stout wall and poking proudly into the sea, comes with an epic history and plenty of ways to idle away your vacation days. Climb steep steps to the top of the city's imposing stone walls, and stroll high above Dubrovnik's patchwork of red roof tiles. Promenade down the inviting main drag, dropping into an eclectic smattering of fine museums—history, art, folk life, war photography, and the Jewish and Orthodox faiths. Hit the beach and go for a swim in the crystal-clear waters of the Adriatic.

While there are many island and resort-town side-trips from Dubrovnik, this book emphasizes a diverse pair of neighboring countries that offer a more culturally stimulating look at the region. Mostar and Sarajevo, leading cities of Bosnia-Herzegovina, are a fascinating combination of Ottoman (Turkish) history, Muslim faith, welcoming locals, lingering war damage, and inspiring postwar reconciliation. Rugged, scenic Montenegro, just south of Dubrovnik, is an emerging Mediterranean hotspot—especially the historic old town of Kotor—but deep in its mountains, you'll find echoes of a bygone mountain kingdom.

To help you have the best trip possible, I've included the following topics in this book:

• **Planning Your Time,** with advice on how to make the most of your limited time

• **Orientation,** including tourist information (abbreviated as TI), tips on public transportation, local tour options, and helpful hints

• **Sights** with ratings:

▲▲▲—Don't miss
▲▲—Try hard to see
▲—Worthwhile if you can make it
No rating—Worth knowing about

• **Sleeping and Eating,** with good-value recommendations in every price range

• Connections, with tips on driving, buses, and boats

The **Understanding Yugoslavia** chapter offers a simplified explanation of the history of this complex part of Europe.

Practicalities, near the end of this book, has information on money, phoning, accommodations, transportation, and other helpful hints, plus Croatian survival phrases.

To travel smartly, read this little book in its entirety before you go. It's my hope that this guide will make your trip more meaningful and rewarding. Traveling like a temporary local, you'll get the absolute most out of every mile, minute, and dollar.

Sretan put—happy travels!

Rick Steves

DUBROVNIK

DUBROVNIK

Dubrovnik is a living fairy tale that shouldn't be missed. It feels like a small town today, but 500 years ago, Dubrovnik was a major maritime power, with the third-biggest navy in the Mediterranean. Still jutting confidently into the sea and ringed by thick medieval walls, Dubrovnik deserves its nickname: the Pearl of the Adriatic. Within the ramparts, the traffic-free Old Town is a fun jumble of quiet, cobbled back lanes; low-impact museums; narrow, steep alleys; and kid-friendly squares. After all these centuries, the buildings still hint at old-time wealth, and the central promenade (Stradun) remains the place to see and be seen. If I had to pick just one place to visit in Croatia, this would be it.

The city's sleepy charm is the result of its no-nonsense past. Busy merchants, the salt trade, and shipbuilding made Dubrovnik rich. But the city's most valued commodity was always its freedom—even today, you'll see the proud motto *Libertas* displayed all over town (see the *"Libertas"* sidebar).

Dubrovnik flourished in the 15th and 16th centuries, but an earthquake (and ensuing fire) destroyed nearly everything in 1667. Most of today's buildings in the Old Town are post-quake Baroque, although a few palaces, monasteries, and convents displaying a rich Gothic-Renaissance mix survive from Dubrovnik's earlier Golden Age. Dubrovnik remained a big tourist draw through the Tito years, bringing in much-needed hard currency from Western visitors. Consequently, the city never acquired the hard socialist patina of other Yugoslav cities (such as the nearby Montenegrin capital Podgorica, then known as "Titograd").

As Croatia violently separated from Yugoslavia in 1991, Dubrovnik became the only coastal city to be pulled into the fight-

Libertas

Libertas—liberty—has always been close to the heart of every Dubrovnik citizen. Dubrovnik was a proudly independent republic for centuries, even as most of Croatia became Venetian and then Hungarian.

In the Middle Ages, the city-state of Dubrovnik (then called Ragusa) bought its independence from whichever power was strongest—Byzantium, Venice, Hungary, the Ottomans, the Vatican—sometimes paying off more than one at a time. Dubrovnik's ships flew whichever flags were necessary to stay free, earning the derisive nickname "Town of Seven Flags." It was sort of a Hong Kong or Singapore of the Middle Ages—a spunky, trading-oriented statelet that maintained its sovereignty while being completely surrounded by an often-hostile mega-state (in Dubrovnik's case, the Ottoman Empire). Dubrovnik persevered partly because of the inherently corrupt nature of the Ottomans; always susceptible to bribery (or "tribute"), the sultans were more than happy to let Dubrovnik thrive...provided they got their cut.

As time went on, Dubrovnik's status grew. Europe's big-league nations were glad to have a second major seafaring power in the Adriatic to balance the Venetian threat; Dubrovnik emerged as an attractive alternative at times when Venetian ports were blockaded by the Ottomans. A free Dubrovnik was more valuable than a pillaged, plundered Dubrovnik.

In 1808, Napoleon conquered the Adriatic and abolished the Republic of Dubrovnik. After Napoleon was defeated, the fate of the continent was decided at the Congress of Vienna. But Dubrovnik's delegate was denied a seat at the table. The more powerful nations, no longer concerned about Venice and fed up after years of being sweet-talked by Dubrovnik, were afraid that the delegate would play old alliances off each other to re-establish an independent Republic of Dubrovnik. Instead, the city became a part of the Habsburg Empire and entered a long period of decline.

Libertas still hasn't died in Dubrovnik. In the surreal days of the early 1990s, when Yugoslavia was reshuffling itself, a movement for the creation of a new Republic of Dubrovnik gained some momentum (led by a judge who, in earlier times, had convicted others for the same ideas). Another movement pushed for Dalmatia to secede as its own nation. But now that the dust has settled, today's locals are content and proud to be part of an independent Republic of Croatia.

ing. Imagine having your youthful memories of good times spent romping in the surrounding hills replaced by visions of tanks and warships shelling your hometown. The city was devastated, but Dubrovnik has been repaired with amazing speed. The only physical reminders of the war are lots of new, bright-orange roof tiles. Locals, relieved the fighting is over but forever hardened, are often willing to talk openly about the experience with visitors—offering a rare opportunity to grasp the harsh realities of war from an eyewitness perspective.

Though the war killed tourism in the 1990s, today the crowds are most decidedly back—even exceeding prewar levels. In fact, Dubrovnik's biggest downside is the overwhelming midday crush of multinational tourists who converge on the Old Town when their cruise ships dock. These days the city's economy is based almost entirely on tourism, and most locals have moved to the suburbs so they can rent their Old Town apartments to travelers. All of this can make the Old Town feel, at times, like a very pretty but soulless theme park. Dubrovnik lacks the gritty real-world vibe of Split or the charming local vitality of Ljubljana. But, like Venice, Dubrovnik rewards those who get off the beaten path and stick around beyond the normal midday cruise-ship window. Europeans set up here for a full week or two to explore the entire region, and even busy Americans might want to build some slack into their Dubrovnik time for a wide array of worthwhile sidetrips (outlined in the Near Dubrovnik, Montenegro, and Mostar chapters).

Planning Your Time

While Dubrovnik's museums are nothing special, the city is one of those places that you never want to leave the real attraction here is the Old Town and its relaxing, breezy ambience. While Dubrovnik could easily be "seen" in a day, a second or third day to unwind (or even more time, for side-trips) makes the long trip here more worthwhile.

To hit all the key sights in a single day, start at the Pile Gate, just outside the Old Town. Walk around the city's walls to get your bearings (before it gets too hot and crowded), then work your way down the main drag (following my "Strolling the Stradun" self-guided walk). As you explore, drop in at any museums or churches that appeal to you. Ride the cable car to the top of Mount Srđ for the sunset, then descend to the Old Town for dinner. With a second day, spread out these activities, hit the beach, or take a boat excursion from the Old Port (Lokrum Island, just offshore, requires the least brainpower).

Dubrovnik also makes an excellent home base for day trips

into the surrounding area, including a dizzying array of island getaways, plus a pair of particularly striking international destinations: Bosnia-Herzegovina's Mostar and Montenegro's Bay of Kotor. I enjoy staying at least three or four nights, for maximum side-tripping flexibility.

Orientation to Dubrovnik

(area code: 020)
Nearly all of the sights worth seeing are in Dubrovnik's traffic-free, walled **Old Town** (Stari Grad) peninsula. The main pedestrian promenade through the middle of town is called the **Stradun;** from this artery, the Old Town climbs steeply uphill in both directions to the walls. The Old Town connects to the mainland through three gates: the **Pile Gate,** to the west; the **Ploče Gate,** to the east; and the smaller **Buža Gate,** at the top of the stepped lane called Boškovićeva. The **Old Port** (Gradska Luka), with leisure boats to nearby destinations, is at the east end of town. While greater Dubrovnik has about 50,000 people, the local population within the Old Town is just a few thousand in the winter—and even smaller in summer, when many residents move out to rent their apartments to tourists.

The **Pile** (PEE-leh) neighborhood, a pincushion of tourist services, is just outside the western end of the Old Town (through the Pile Gate). In front of the gate, you'll find the main TI, ATMs, a post office, taxis, buses (fanning out to all the outlying neighborhoods), a bus ticket kiosk, a cheap Konzum grocery store, and a DM pharmacy. This is also the starting point for my "Strolling the Stradun" self-guided walk.

A mile or two away from the Old Town are beaches peppered with expensive resort hotels. The closest area is **Boninovo Bay** (a 20-minute walk or 5-minute bus trip from the Old Town), but most cluster on the lush **Lapad Peninsula** to the west (a 15-minute bus trip from the Old Town). Across the bay from the Lapad Peninsula is **Port Gruž,** with the main bus station, ferry terminal, and cruise-ship port.

Tourist Information

Dubrovnik's main TI is just outside the Old Town's **Pile Gate,** at the far end of the big terrace with the modern video-screens sculpture (June-Sept daily 8:00-21:00; May and Oct daily 8:00-20:00; Nov-April Mon-Sat 8:00-19:00, Sun 9:00-15:00; Brsalje 5, tel. 020/312-011, www.tzdubrovnik.hr). There are also locations at **Port Gruž,** across the street from the Jadrolinija ferry dock (same hours except closes earlier in Nov-April, Gruška obala, tel.

DUBROVNIK

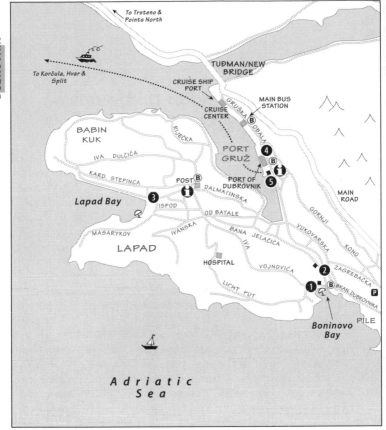

020/417-983); in the **Lapad** resort area, at the head of the main drag (June-Sept daily 8:00-20:00; May and Oct Mon-Fri 8:00-20:00, Sat-Sun 9:00-12:00 & 17:00-20:00; April Mon-Sat 9:00-12:00 & 17:00-20:00, closed Sun; closed Nov-March; Šetalište Kralja Zvonimira 7, tel. 020/437-460); on two of the Elaphite Islands, **Lopud** (Obala Iva Kuljevana 12, tel. 020/759-086) and **Šipan** (Luka b.b., tel. 020/758-084); and at the arrivals area of the **airport.**

All the TIs are government-run and legally can't sell you anything except a Dubrovnik Card—but they can answer questions and give you a copy of the free town map and two similar information booklets: the annual *Dubrovnik Riviera Info* and the monthly *The Best in Dubrovnik* (with a current schedule of events and performances); both contain helpful maps, bus and ferry schedules, museum hours, specifics on side-trip destinations, and more.

Sightseeing Pass: The heavily promoted **Dubrovnik Card**

Greater Dubrovnik

1. Hotels Bellevue, R & Lero; Launderettes
2. Youth Hostel
3. Lapad Resort Area
4. Jadrolinija Office
5. Nona Ana Catamaran & Tickets

covers local public transportation; admission to the City Walls (one time only), Rector's Palace, Rupe Museum, Maritime Museum, and a few other minor sights; and various discounts around town. If you're here for three days and plan to do a lot of sightseeing and take the bus a few times, this may add up—figure out what you want to see, and do the math (150 kn/24 hours includes unlimited transit, 200 kn/3 days includes 10 transit rides, 250 kn/7 days includes 20 transit rides, sold at TIs and many sights and hotels; it's cheaper if you buy it online, then pick it up at the TI when you arrive).

Arrival in Dubrovnik

As is the case throughout Croatia, you'll be met at the boat dock or bus station by locals trying to get you to rent a room *(soba)* at their house. If you've already reserved elsewhere, honor your reservation; if not, consider the offer (but be very clear on the location before you accept—many are nowhere near the Old Town).

Dubrovnik Essentials

English	Croatian	Pronounced
Old Town	Stari Grad	STAH-ree grahd
Old Port	Stara Luka	STAH-rah LOO-kah
Pile Gate	Gradska Vrata Pile	GRAHD-skah VRAH-tah PEE-leh
Ploče Gate	Gradska Vrata Ploče	GRAHD-skah VRAH-tah PLOH-cheh
Main Promenade	Stradun	STRAH-doon
Adriatic Sea	Jadran	YAH-drahn

By Bus: Dubrovnik's **main bus station** (Autobusni Kolodvor) is just beyond the ferry terminal along the Port Gruž embankment (about 2.5 miles northwest of the Old Town). It's straightforward and user-friendly, with pay toilets, baggage storage, and a helpful bus information window. To reach the Old Town's Pile Gate, walk straight ahead through the bus stalls, then bear right at the main road to the city bus stop, where you can hop on a bus (#1, #1a, #1b, #1c, #3, and #8) to the Pile stop. A taxi from the main bus station to the Old Town and most accommodations runs about 75 kn.

Alternate Bus Stop for Outbound Buses: For buses that are leaving Dubrovnik toward regional destinations to the south (such as the airport or Cavtat), there's another bus stop that's much closer to the Old Town, saving you the long journey out to the main bus station. The **"cable car" bus stop** (a.k.a. "fire station" bus stop) is just uphill from the Buža Gate, overlooking the old wall, right next to the bottom station of the cable car up to Mount Srđ.

By Car Ferry or Catamaran: The big car ferries arrive at Port Gruž, two miles northwest of the Old Town. On the road in front of the ferry terminal, you'll find a bus stop (#1, #1a, #1b, #1c, #3, and #8 go to the Old Town's Pile Gate; wait on the embankment side of the street) and a taxi stand (figure 70 kn to the Old Town and most accommodations). Across the street is the Jadrolinija office (with an ATM out front) and a TI. The fast *Nona Ana* catamaran from Mljet and Korčula also arrives near this big ferry dock.

By Cruise Ship: Some ships anchor just offshore from the Old Port, then send their passengers into the Old Town on tenders.

Others put in at Port Gruž, just beyond the bus station. To reach the Old Town, take a public bus or pay 80 kn for a taxi (described earlier, under "By Bus").

By Plane: Dubrovnik's small airport (Zračna Luka) is near a village called Čilipi, 13 miles south of the city. A bus meets arriving flights for most major airlines at the airport, and brings you to the Pile Gate just outside the Old Town, then continues to the main bus station (35 kn, 40 minutes). Legitimate cabbies charge around 210-250 kn for the ride between the airport and the center (though some cabbies charge as much as 300 kn; consider arranging your transfer in advance through your *soba* host; airport code: DBV, tel. 020/773-333, www.airport-dubrovnik.hr). The karstic **Đurović Cave,** which runs beneath the runway, may be open to the public; if you have extra time at the airport and want to go spelunking, ask around.

To get *to* the airport, you can take the same bus, which typically leaves from Dubrovnik's main bus station 1.5 hours before each Croatia Airlines or Austrian Airlines flight, or two hours before other airlines' international flights (the schedule is posted the day before—ask at the TI). Generally, this bus also stops at the "cable car" bus stop near the lower cable-car station just above the Old Town's Buža Gate; this can save you the hassle of going to the main bus station—but confirm the schedule at the TI.

Bad-Weather Warning: If you're planning to fly into or out of Dubrovnik, be aware that the airport is located right in the blast zone of the fierce Bora winds that periodically howl along the Dalmatian Coast (especially in the late fall). It's not uncommon for flights coming into Dubrovnik to be diverted to Split instead, with passengers forced to take a dull five-hour bus journey to their intended destination. Departing flights are usually less affected (though disruptions to incoming planes could, obviously, cause delays for departures as well). Personally, I've flown out of Dubrovnik a dozen times without incident, but it's not unheard of for travelers to be inconvenienced by this.

By Car: Coming from the north, you'll drive over the modern Tuđman Bridge (which most locals, mindful of their former president's tarnished legacy, call simply "the New Bridge"). Immediately after crossing the bridge, you have two options: To get to the main bus station, ferry terminal (with some car-rental drop-off offices nearby), and Lapad Peninsula, take the left turn just after the bridge, wind down to the waterfront, then turn left and follow this road along the Port Gruž embankment. Or, to head for the Old Town, continue straight after the bridge. You'll pass above the Port Gruž area, then take the right turn-off marked *Dubrovnik* (with the little bull's-eye). You'll go through a

DUBROVNIK

Dubrovnik at a Glance

▲▲▲Stradun Stroll Charming walk through Dubrovnik's vibrant Old Town, ideal for coffee, ice cream, and people-watching. **Hours:** Always open. See page 17.

▲▲▲City Walls Scenic mile-long walk along top of 15th-century fortifications encircling the city. **Hours:** July-Aug daily 8:00-19:30, progressively shorter hours off-season until 10:00-15:00 in mid-Nov-mid-March. See page 27.

▲▲▲Mount Srđ Napoleonic fortress above Dubrovnik with spectacular views and a modest museum to the recent war. **Hours:** Mountaintop—always open; cable car—daily June-Aug 9:00-24:00, Sept 9:00-22:00, April-May and Oct 9:00-20:00, Feb-March and Nov 9:00-17:00, Dec-Jan 9:00-16:00; museum—same hours as cable car. See page 43.

▲Franciscan Monastery Museum Tranquil cloister, medieval pharmacy-turned-museum, and a century-old pharmacy still serving residents today. **Hours:** Daily April-Oct 9:00-18:00, Nov-March 9:00-17:00. See page 33.

▲Rector's Palace Sparse antiques collection in the former home of rectors who ruled Dubrovnik in the Middle Ages. **Hours:** Daily May-Oct 9:00-18:00, Nov-April 9:00-16:00. See page 34.

▲Cathedral Eighteenth-century Roman Baroque cathedral and treasury filled with unusual relics, such as a swatch of Jesus' swaddling clothes. **Hours:** Church—daily 8:00-18:00, treasury—generally open same hours as church, both have shorter hours off-season. See page 36.

▲Dominican Monastery Museum Another relaxing cloister with precious paintings, altarpieces, and manuscripts. **Hours:** Daily April-Oct 9:00-18:00, Nov-March 9:00-17:00. See page 37.

tunnel, then turn left for *Grad/Old City*; individual big hotels are also signed from here.

This road passes a big parking garage (described later), then twists you around over the top of the Old Town, until you can see the lower station for the cable car. Here, you have two choices, which will determine which one-way loop you'll get stuck in: If you want to reach the Pile Gate (at the eastern end of the Old Town), make a sharp right turn just before the cable car (watch for *Grad/Old City* signs), then turn right again (passing the entrance to the "tennis court" parking lot) to curl around the back of the city wall and pop out at the Pile Gate (with another, very pricey parking lot), then back

▲**Synagogue Museum** Europe's second-oldest synagogue and Croatia's only Jewish museum, with 13th-century Torahs and Holocaust-era artifacts. **Hours:** May-mid-Nov daily 10:00-20:00; mid-Nov-April Mon-Fri 10:00-13:00, closed Sat-Sun. See page 40.

▲**War Photo Limited** Thought-provoking photographic look at contemporary warfare. **Hours:** June-Sept daily 10:00-22:00; May and Oct Tue-Sun 10:00-16:00, closed Mon; closed Nov-April. See page 40.

▲**Serbian Orthodox Church and Icon Museum** Active church serving Dubrovnik's Serbian Orthodox community and museum with traditional religious icons. **Hours:** Church—daily May-Sept 8:00-14:00 & 16:00-21:00 or 22:00, until 19:00 in shoulder season, until 17:00 in winter; museum—May-Oct Mon-Sat 9:00-13:00, closed Sun; Nov-April Mon-Fri 9:00-13:00, closed Sat-Sun. See page 41.

▲**Rupe Granary and Ethnographic Museum** Good folk museum with tools, jewelry, clothing, and painted eggs above immense underground grain stores. **Hours:** Wed-Mon 9:00-18:00, until 14:00 off-season, closed Tue year-round. See page 42.

Maritime Museum Contracts, maps, paintings, and models from Dubrovnik's days as a maritime power and shipbuilding center. **Hours:** Flex with demand, usually March-Oct Tue-Sun 9:00-18:00, until 16:00 in Nov-Feb, closed Mon year-round. See page 39.

Aquarium Tanks of local sea life housed in huge, shady old fort. **Hours:** Daily July-Aug 9:00-21:00, progressively shorter hours off-season until 9:00-16:00 Nov-March. See page 39.

up out of town toward Boninovo Bay and Lapad. Or, if you want to head east of the Old Town, continue straight past the cable-car station for a long, scenic drive above the Viktorija area, then (after looping down again) past luxury hotels and to the Ploče Gate.

If you're sleeping in or near the Old Town, **parking** is tricky. The handiest place to park long-term is the Old Town garage, which you'll pass on the right as you head toward the Old Town (10 kn/hour, 170 kn/day, cheaper Oct-May). From here, it's about a 10-minute downhill walk to the Old Town—and a much steeper, 20-minute hike back up. If you'd like to be closer to the Old Town, you can take your chances on finding a spot—on the street directly

behind and above the City Walls (pay at meter), or in one of the convenient but often-crammed pay lots: "the tennis court," right up against the wall, or the lot between the wall and the cable car (all options: 10 kn/hour, 170 kn/day). If you're desperate, the priciest option is the lot just behind the DM pharmacy near the Pile Gate (a hefty 30 kn/hour or 360 kn/day). Another option is to drive to this area near the Old Town to unload your bags, then leave your car at the Old Town garage (or at a cheaper, more distant one) for the duration of your visit. When in doubt, ask your *soba* host or hotel for parking tips.

If you're sleeping at Boninovo Bay, you'll have an easier time finding parking at or near your hotel—ask.

Helpful Hints

Festivals: Dubrovnik is most crowded during its Summer Festival, a month and a half of theater and musical performances held annually from July 10 to August 25 (www.dubrovnik-festival. hr). This is quickly followed by the Late Summer Festival, designed to continue the festivities into September. For other options, see "Entertainment in Dubrovnik," later.

Crowd-Beating Tips: Dubrovnik has been discovered—especially by cruise ships (nearly 800 of which visit each year, bringing a total of around 900,000 passengers—in 2013, one September day brought 16,000 passengers on six ships). Cruise-ship crowds descend on the Old Town roughly between 8:30 and 14:00 (the streets are most crowded 9:00-13:00). On busy days, try to avoid the big sights—especially walking around the wall—during these peak times, and hit the beach or take a siesta midday, when the town is hottest and most crowded.

No Euros: Dubrovnik's merchants can be stubborn about accepting only kunas—no euros. (While it's technically illegal for vendors to accept any payment other than kunas, this is rarely enforced.) Even some of the top sights—including the City Walls and the cable car to Mount Srđ—accept only kunas (or, sometimes, credit cards). Even if you're in town for just a few hours, visit an ATM to avoid hassles when it comes time to pay.

Wine Shop: For the best wine-tasting selection in a cool bar atmosphere, don't miss **D'Vino Wine Bar**. If you want to shop rather than taste, **Vinoteka Miličić** offers a nice variety of local wines; wry Dolores can explain your options, though she does tend to push Miličić wines (daily June-Aug 9:00-23:00, April-May and Sept-Oct 9:00-20:00, Nov-March 9:00-16:00, near the Pile end of the Stradun, tel. 020/321-777).

Internet Access: Most accommodations in Dubrovnik offer free Wi-Fi, and several cafés and bars around town provide Wi-Fi for customers. In the Old Town, the modern **Buzz Bar** has

free Wi-Fi and loaner laptops with the purchase of a drink (daily 9:00-24:00, Prijeko 21, tel. 020/321-025).

English Bookstore: The **Algoritam** shop, right on the Stradun, has a wide variety of guidebooks, nonfiction books about Croatia and the former Yugoslavia, novels, and magazines—all in English (July-Aug Mon-Sat 9:00-23:00, Sun 10:00-13:00 & 18:00-22:00; June and Sept Mon-Sat 9:00-21:00, Sun 10:00-14:00; shorter hours off-season; Placa 8, tel. 020/322-044).

Laundry: Hotels charge a mint to wash your clothes; *soba* hosts are cheaper, but often don't have the time (ask). The handy, fun, retro, self-service **Sanja and Rosie's Launderette** is just outside the Ploče Gate (cross the bridge and look left; 50-kn wash, 30-40-kn dry, clear English instructions, machines take bills, daily 8:00-22:00, put od Bosanke 2, mobile 091-896-7509, www.dubrovniklaundry.com). Two full-service launderettes are near the hotels at **Boninovo Bay,** a 20-minute uphill walk or five-minute bus trip from the Pile Gate (one at Pera Čingrije 8, the other at bana Jelačića 1, both closed Sat afternoon and all day Sun)—but unless you're staying in that area, Sanja and Rosie's is far more convenient.

Car Rental: The big international chains have offices at the airport; a few also have branches near the Port Gruž embankment where the big ships come in. In addition, the many travel agencies closer to the Old Town also have a line on rental cars. Figure €50-60 per day, including taxes, insurance, and unlimited mileage (at the bigger chains, there's usually no extra charge for drop-off elsewhere in Croatia). Be sure the agency knows if you're crossing a border (such as Bosnia-Herzegovina or Montenegro) to ensure you have the proper paperwork.

Travel Agency: You'll see travel agencies all over town. At any of them, you can buy seats on an excursion, rent a car, or book a room. The most established company is **Atlas,** just off the Stradun in the Old Town (Mon-Fri 9:00-21:00, Sat-Sun 10:00-13:00 & 16:00-20:00, Boškovićeva 5, tel. 020/442-574, www.atlas-croatia.com).

Best Views: Walking the **Old Town walls** late in the day, when the city is bathed in rich light, is a treat. The cable car up to **Mount Srđ** provides bird's-eye panoramas over the entire region, from the highest vantage point without wings. The **Fort of St. Lawrence,** perched above the Pile neighborhood cove, has great views over the Old Town. The **panoramic cruises** that loop around the Old Town are another fine choice. A stroll up the road east of the city walls offers nice views back on the Old Town (best light early in the day). Better yet, if you have a car, head south of the city in the morning for gorgeously lit Old Town views over your right shoulder; various turn-offs along

Game of Thrones in Dubrovnik

Fans of the HBO television series *Game of Thrones* may feel the tingle of déjà vu during their visit to Dubrovnik. Over the last few years, part of the series has been filmed here, generally between mid-August and mid-September. Many locals have been extras, and they've become accustomed to seeing Peter Dinklage strolling down the Stradun in full costume on his way to the set, or spotting King Joffrey at the next table when dining at their favorite *konoba*.

In the show, Dubrovnik often stands in for King's Landing, while the island of Lokrum was the site of the Qarth garden party. The Fort of St. Lawrence (filmed in various battle scenes) looks over a pleasant cove that becomes Blackwater Bay for the show's purposes. Other filming locations have included Trsteno Arboretum, the rock quarry, and Gradac park (where the royal wedding took place). Filming has also taken place in other parts of Croatia, most notably the fortified town of Ston and the city of Split. Of course, the fantasy-world locations on the show don't match the real-world locations exactly; digital effects are often added to dress things up.

GoT aficionados may want to take a guided tour of filming locations; check to see if a local company offers one, or book through the international tour company, Viator.com.

The city, hardly oblivious to this potential boost in tourist popularity, may open a *Game of Thrones* exhibition with costumes and props from the show. If you're a fan, ask around town for the latest—both star sightings and sightseeing.

this road are ideal photo stops. The best one, known locally simply as **"panorama point,"** is where the road leading up and out of Dubrovnik meets the main road that passes above the town (look for the pull-out on the right, usually crowded with tour buses). Even if you're heading north, in good weather it's worth a quick detour south for this view.

Updates to This Book: Check www.ricksteves.com/update for any significant changes that have occurred since this book was published.

Getting Around Dubrovnik

If you're staying in or near the Old Town, everything is easily walkable. But those sleeping on Boninovo Bay or the Lapad Peninsula will want to get comfortable using the buses. Once you understand the system, commuting to the Old Town is a breeze.

By Bus: Libertas runs Dubrovnik's public buses. Tickets, which are good for an hour, are cheaper if you buy them in advance from a newsstand or your hotel (12 kn, ask for *autobusna karta*, ow-toh-BOOS-nah KAR-tah) than if you buy them from the bus

driver (15 kn). A 24-hour ticket costs 35 kn (only sold at special bus-ticket kiosks, such as the one near the Pile Gate bus stop).

When you enter the bus, validate your ticket in the machine next to the driver (insert it with the orange arrow facing out and pointing down). Because most tourists can't figure out how to validate their tickets, it can take a long time to load the bus (which means drivers are understandably grumpy, and locals aren't shy about cutting in line).

All buses stop near the Old Town, just in front of the Pile Gate (buy tickets at the newsstand). From here, they fan out to just about anywhere you'd want to go (e.g., hotels on Boninovo Bay, Lapad Peninsula, and the ferry terminal and main bus station). You'll find bus schedules and a map in the TI booklet (for more information, visit www.libertasdubrovnik.hr).

By Taxi: Taxis start at 25 kn, then charge 8 kn per kilometer. The handiest taxi stand for the Old Town is just outside the Pile Gate. The biggest operation is Radio Taxi (tel. 0800-0970).

Tours in Dubrovnik

Walking Tours

Two companies—**Dubrovnik Walking Tours** (www.dubrovnik-walking-tours.com) and **Dubrovnik Walks** (www.dubrovnikwalks.com)—offer similar one-hour walking tours of the Old Town daily at 10:00 and usually also at 13:00 and 18:00 or 18:30 (90 kn). I'd skip these tours—they're pricey and brief, touching lightly on the same information explained in this chapter. However, both companies also offer themed tours, typically covering wartime Dubrovnik and the historic Jewish quarter, which may be worthwhile. Pick up their fliers locally or check online for details.

Local Guide

For an in-depth look at the city, consider hiring your own local guide. **Roberto de Lorenzo** and his mother **Marija Tiberi** are both warm people enthusiastic about telling evocative stories from medieval Dubrovnik, including some off-the-beaten-path stops tailored to your interests (500 kn/2 hours, mobile 091-541-6637, bobdel70@yahoo.com); ask about guided transfers to Bosnia-Herzegovina, Split, or beyond. **Štefica Ćurić Lenert** is a sharp professional guide who offers a great by-the-book tour and an insider's look at the city (550 kn/1.5 hours, other tour options explained on her website, reserve at least one day ahead, mobile 091-345-0133, www.dubrovnikprivateguide.com, stefe@ubrovnikprivateguide.com). If these guides are busy, they can refer you to another good guide for a similar price.

From Dubrovnik

Package Excursions

For information on tour boats and guided big-bus excursions from Dubrovnik to nearby destinations, see the next chapter.

Hire Your Own Driver

I enjoy renting my own car to see the sights around Dubrovnik. But if you're more comfortable having someone else do the driving, hire a driver. While the drivers listed here are not licensed tour guides, they speak great English and offer commentary as you roll, and can help you craft a good day-long itinerary to Mostar, Montenegro, or anywhere else near Dubrovnik (typically departing around 8:00 and returning in the early evening). They're flexible about tailoring the tour to your interests: Because there are lots of options en route to either Mostar or Montenegro, do your homework so you can tell them what you'd like to see (and not see; for example, I'd skip Međugorje to have maximum time in Mostar).

Friendly **Pepo Klaić,** a veteran of the recent war, is enjoyable to get to know and has a knack for making the experience both informative and meaningful (€250/day, €125 for half-day trip to nearer destinations, airport transfer for about €30—cheaper than a taxi, these prices for up to four people—more expensive for bigger group, mobile 098-427-301, www.dubrovnikshoretrip.com, pepoklaic@yahoo.com). **Petar Vlašić** does similar tours for similar prices, and specializes in wine tours to the Pelješac Peninsula, with stops at various wineries along the way (€30 airport transfers, €190-200 for 2-person trip to Pelješac wineries, €230 to Mostar or €250 to Montenegro including local guide, these prices for 1-3 people—more for larger groups, mobile 091-580-8721, www.dubrovnikrivieratours.com, info@dubrovnikrivieratours.com). **Pero Carević,** who runs the recommended Villa Ragusa guest house, also drives travelers on excursions (similar prices, mobile 098-765-634, villa.ragusa@du.t-com.hr).

If your destination is Mostar, likeable Bosnian driver **Ermin Elezović** will happily come pick you up for less than the Dubrovnik-based drivers (for up to 3 people: €120 for one-way transfer from Dubrovnik to Mostar with a few brief sightseeing stops en route, €240 for round-trip to Mostar with same-day return to Dubrovnik).

Recommended local guide **Roberto de Lorenzo,** listed earlier, also offers guided transfers to Mostar, Sarajevo, Split, and beyond, peppered with historical commentary en route.

Self-Guided Walk

▲▲▲Strolling the Stradun

Running through the heart of Dubrovnik's Old Town is the 300-yard-long Stradun promenade—packed with people and lined with sights. This walk offers an ideal introduction to Dubrovnik's charms. It takes about a half-hour, not counting sightseeing stops.

• *Begin at the busy square in front of the west entrance to the Old Town, the Pile (PEE-leh) Gate.*

Pile Neighborhood

This bustling area is the nerve center of Dubrovnik's tourist indus-try—it's where the real world meets the fantasy of Dubrovnik (for details on services offered here, see "Orientation to Dubrovnik," earlier).

Behind the modern, mirrors-and-LED-screens monument (which honors the "Dubrovnik Defenders" who protected the city during the 1991-1992 siege) is a leafy café ter-race. Wander over to the edge of the terrace and take in the imposing walls of the Pearl of the Adriatic. The huge, fortified peninsula just outside the city walls is the **Fort of St. Lawrence** (Tvrđava Lovrijenac), Dubrovnik's oldest fortress. Imagine how this fort and the stout walls worked together to fortify the little harbor—and the gate just behind you. You can climb this fortress for great views over the Old Town (30 kn, or covered by same ticket as City Walls on the same day).

• *Cross over the moat (now a shady park) to the round entrance tower in the City Walls. This is the...*

Pile Gate (Gradska Vrata Pile)

Just before you enter the gate, notice the image above the entrance of **St. Blaise** (Sveti Vlaho in Croatian) cradling Dubrovnik in his arm. You'll see a lot more of Blaise, the protector of Du-brovnik, during your time here—he is to Dubrovnik what the winged lion of St. Mark is to Venice.

Inside the first part of the gate, dead ahead you'll see another image of Blaise. Down the ramp to your left, look for the white **map** (next to the tourist map) that shows where each bomb dropped on the Old Town during the siege. Once inside town, you'll see virtually no

signs of the war—a testament to the townspeople's impressive re-silience in rebuilding so well and so quickly.

Passing the rest of the way through the gate, you'll find a lively little square surrounded by landmarks. The giant, round struc-ture in the middle of the square is **Onofrio's Big Fountain** (Ve-lika Onofrijea Fontana). In the Middle Ages, Dubrovnik had a complicated aqueduct system that brought water from the mountains seven miles away. The water ended up here, at the town's biggest foun-tain, before continuing through

the city. This plentiful supply of water, large reserves of salt (a key source of Dubrovnik's wealth, from the town of Ston), and a mas-sive granary (now the Rupe Granary and Ethnographic Museum, described later) made little, independent Dubrovnik very siege-resistant.

Tucked across the square from the church is the **Visia Du-brovnik Multimedia Museum,** showing a badly produced 3-D film about the city's history that isn't worth your 35 minutes or 75 kn (schedule posted at entry). In the evening, the theater shows first-run 3-D movies.

To the left as you come through the Pile Gate, a steep stairway leads up to the imposing **Minčeta Tower.** It's possible to enter here to begin Dubrovnik's best activity, walking around the top of the wall (described later, under "Sights in Dubrovnik")—but this walk ends near a better, less crowded entry point.

Next to the stairway is the small **Church of St. Savior** (Crkva Svetog Spasa). Appreciative locals built this votive church to thank God after Dubrovnik made it through a 1520 earthquake. When the massive 1667 quake destroyed the city, this church was one of the only buildings left intact—its Renaissance interior stands at odds against the predominantly Baroque styles in other town churches. And during the recent war, the church survived another close call when a shell exploded on the ground right in front of it (you can still see faint pockmarks from the shrapnel).

The big building on the left just beyond the small Church of St. Savior is the **Franciscan Monastery Museum.** This tourable building has a delightful cloister and one of Europe's oldest con-tinually operating pharmacies (described later; enter through the gap between the small church and the door of the big church).

Historically, the monastery's **Franciscan Church** was the house of worship for Dubrovnik's poor people, while the Domini-can Church (down at the far end of the Stradun, where our walk ends) was for the wealthy. Services were staggered by 15 minutes

to allow servants to drop off their masters there, then rush up the Stradun for their own service here. If you peek inside the church, you'll find a Baroque interior—typical of virtually all of the town's churches, which were rebuilt after the 1667 quake.

Looking up, notice the **bell tower** of the Franciscan Church—with its rounded top—which is integrated into the structure of the building. If your travels have taken you beyond Dubrovnik, you'll notice the difference from other Croatian towns, where church steeples follow Venetian convention: Set apart from the church, and with a pointy top. This is just the first of many contrasts we'll see between Dubrovnik and Venice—two powerful maritime republics who were rivals for control of the Adriatic.

Notice the stubby little, shin-high, mustachioed **gargoyle** embedded in the wall, just left of the Franciscan Church's door. You may see a commotion of tourists trying to balance on the small, slippery surface of the gargoyle's head. Tour guides enjoy spinning a variety of tall tales about this creature—if you can balance on one leg for three seconds, your fondest wish comes true—but these are a recent innovation. This legend began in the 1960s, when local teens tried to convince female tourists that balancing on the gargoyle and removing their blouse would grant them three wishes. (Why didn't I think of that in high school?) As for the gargoyle itself, it's simply a drain for rainwater. Why is it down here instead of up on the roofline? Perhaps simply to avoid deluging people who are on their way to church.

• *When you're finished taking in the sights on this square, continue along...*

The Stradun

Dubrovnik's main promenade—officially called the Placa, but better known as the Stradun—is alive with locals and tourists alike. This is the heartbeat of the city: an Old World shopping mall by day and sprawling cocktail party after dark, when everybody seems to be doing the traditional evening stroll—flirting, ice-cream-licking, flaunting, and gawking. A coffee and some of Europe's best people-watching in a prime Stradun café is one of travel's great $4 bargains.

When Dubrovnik was just getting its start in the seventh century, this street was a canal. Romans fleeing from the invading Slavs lived on the island of Ragusa (on your right), and the Slavs settled on the shore. In the 11th century, the canal separating

Dubrovnik's Old Town

<u>Other</u>
- ⑫ Sloboda Cinema
- ⑬ Jadran Cinema
- ⑭ Visia Dubrovnik (3-D Movies)
- ⑮ Vinoteka Miličić Wine Shop
- ⑯ Buzz Bar (Internet)
- ⑰ Algoritam Bookshop
- ⑱ Launderette
- ⑲ Atlas Travel Agency

Ragusa from the mainland was filled in, the towns merged, and a unique Slavic-Roman culture and language blossomed. While originally much more higgledy-piggledy, this street was rebuilt in the current, more straightforward style after the 1667 earthquake. The ensuing fire raged for three weeks and consumed much of the city.

The distinctively shaped doors—with shop windows built right in, to provide maximum view of goods, but minimum access—indicate that this was the terrain of the merchants...and it still is.

The austerity of Dubrovnik's main drag disappoints some visitors. Rather than lavish funds on ostentatious palaces, as in Venice, Dubrovnik seems eager to downplay its wealth. For much of its history, Dubrovnik paid a hefty tribute to the sultan of the Ottoman Empire to maintain its independent status. Flaunting wealth would have raised Ottoman eyebrows...and, likely, Ottoman taxes. Unlike its rival Venice, which then as now is desperate to impress, Dubrovnik embodies a restraint that reflects the tumultuous time and place in which it thrived. Venice was surrounded by Italians, Austrians, Germans—some allies, some rivals, but all Christian. Dubrovnik sat five miles from the frontier of the Ottoman Empire; leaving the city felt like leaving the known world and the safety of what we'd today call "Western Civilization." Dubrovnik was, culturally and spiritually, an island of European Christianity surrounded on all sides by something so very different.

Today, you probably feel surrounded on all sides by hordes of international tourists. Things are worst on days when several cruise ships drop anchor—and when excursions into town feel more like incursions. But try some attitude adjustment: For much of its history, the maritime republic of Dubrovnik has been a crossroads of merchants, sailors, and other travelers from around the world. While today they may be following their tour guides' numbered paddles rather than trading exotic spices, the legions of visitors are still part of the city's tapestry of history.

If you're here in the summer (June-Sept), you'll periodically hear the rat-a-tat-tat of a drum echoing through the streets from the Stradun. This means it's time to head for this main drag to get a glimpse of the colorfully costumed **"town guards"** parading through (and a cavalcade of tourists running alongside them, trying to snap a clear picture). You may also see some of these characters standing guard outside the town gates. It's all part of the local tourist board's efforts to make their town even more atmospheric.

• Branching off from this promenade are several museums and other attractions. At the end of the Stradun is a passageway leading to the Ploče Gate. Just before this passage is the lively Luža Square. Its centerpiece is the 20-foot-tall...

Orlando's Column (Orlandov Stup)

Columns like this were typical of towns in northern Germany. Dubrovnik erected the column in 1417, soon after it had shifted allegiances from the oppressive Venetians to the Hungarians. By putting a northern European symbol in the middle of its most prominent square, Dubrovnik decisively distanced itself from Venice. Whenever a decision was made by the Republic, the town crier came to Orlando's Column and announced the news. The step he stood on indicated the importance of his message—the higher up, the more important the news. It was also used as the pillory, where people were publicly punished. The thin line on the top step in front of Orlando is exactly as long as the statue's forearm. This mark was Dubrovnik's standard measurement—not for a foot, but for an "elbow."

• *Now stand in front of Orlando's Column and orient yourself with a...*

Luža Square Spin-Tour

Orlando is looking toward the **Sponza Palace** (Sponza-Povijesni Arhiv). This building, from 1522, is the finest surviving example of Dubrovnik's Golden Age in the 15th and 16th centuries. It's a combination of Renaissance (ground-floor arches) and Venetian Gothic (upstairs windows). Houses up and down the main promenade used to look like this, but after the 1667 earthquake and fire, they were replaced with boring uniformity. This used to be the customs office *(dogana),* but now it's an exhaustive archive of the city's history, with temporary art exhibits and a war memorial. The poignant **Me-** **morial Room of Dubrovnik Defenders** (inside and on the left) has photos of dozens of people from Dubrovnik who were killed fighting Yugoslav forces in 1991. A TV screen and images near the ceiling show the devastation of the city. Though the English descriptions are pointedly—if unavoidably—slanted to the Croat perspective, it's compelling to look in the eyes of the brave young men who didn't start this war...but were willing to finish it (free, long hours daily in peak season, shorter hours off-season). Beyond the memorial room, the impressive **courtyard,** which generally displays temporary exhibits, is worth a peek (25 kn, generally free after-hours).

To the right of Sponza Palace is the town's **Bell Tower** (Gradski Zvonik). The original dated from 1444, but it was rebuilt when it started to lean in the 1920s. The big clock may be an octopus, but only one of its hands tells time. Below that, the golden circle

The Siege of Dubrovnik

In June 1991, Croatia declared independence from Yugoslavia. Within weeks, the nations were at war (for more on the war, see the Understanding Yugoslavia chapter). Though warfare raged in the Croatian interior, nobody expected that the bloodshed would reach Dubrovnik.

As refugees from Vukovar (in northeastern Croatia) arrived in Dubrovnik that fall, telling horrific stories of the warfare there, local residents began fearing the worst. Warplanes from the Serb-dominated Yugoslav People's Army buzzed threateningly low over the town, as if to signal an impending attack.

Then, at 6:00 in the morning on October 1, 1991, Dubrovnik residents awoke to explosions on nearby hillsides. The first attacks were focused on Mount Srđ, high above the Old Town. First the giant cross was destroyed, then a communications tower (both have been rebuilt and are visible today). This first wave of attacks cleared the way for Yugoslav land troops—mostly Serbs and Montenegrins—who surrounded the city. The ragtag, newly formed Croatian army quickly dug in at the old Napoleonic-era fortress at the top of Mount Srđ, where just 25 or 30 soldiers fended off a Yugoslav takeover of this highly strategic position.

At first, shelling targeted military positions on the outskirts of town. But soon, Yugoslav forces began bombing residential neighborhoods, then the Pearl of the Adriatic itself: Dubrovnik's Old Town. Defenseless townspeople took shelter in their cellars, and sometimes even huddled together in the city wall's 15th-century forts. It was the first time in Dubrovnik's long history that the walls were actually used to defend against an attack.

Dubrovnik resisted the siege better than anyone expected. The Yugoslav forces were hoping that residents would flee the town, but the people of Dubrovnik stayed. Though severely outgunned and outnumbered, Dubrovnik's defenders managed to hold the fort atop Mount Srđ, while Yugoslav forces controlled the nearby mountaintops. All supplies had to be carried up to the fort by foot or by donkey. Dubrovnik wasn't prepared for war, so its citizens had to improvise their defense. Many brave young locals lost their lives when they slung old hunting rifles over their shoulders and, under cover of darkness, climbed the hills above Dubrovnik to meet Yugoslav soldiers face-to-face.

After eight months of bombing, Dubrovnik was liberated by

the Croatian army, which attacked Yugoslav positions from the north. By the end of the siege, 100 civilians were dead, as well as more than 200 Dubrovnik citizens who lost their lives actively fighting for their hometown (much revered today as "Dubrovnik Defenders"); in the greater Dubrovnik area, 420 "Defenders" were killed, and another 900 wounded. More than two-thirds of Dubrovnik's buildings had been damaged, and more than 30,000 people had to flee their homes—but the failed siege was finally over.

Why was Dubrovnik—so far from the rest of the fighting—dragged into the conflict? Yugoslavia wanted to catch the city and surrounding region off-guard, gaining a toehold on the southern Dalmatian Coast so they could push north to Split. They also hoped to ignite pro-Serb passions in the nearby Serb-dominated areas of Bosnia-Herzegovina and Montenegro. But perhaps most of all, Yugoslavia wanted to hit Croatia where it hurt—its proudest, most historic, and most beautiful city, the tourist capital of a nation dependent on tourism. It seems their plan backfired. Locals now say, "When Yugoslavia attacked Dubrovnik, they lost the war"—because images of the historic city under siege swayed international public opinion *against* Yugoslavia.

The war initially devastated the tourist industry. Now, to the casual observer, Dubrovnik seems virtually back to normal. Aside from a few pockmarks and bright, new roof tiles, there are scant reminders of what happened here more than two decades ago. But even though the city itself has been repaired, the people of Dubrovnik are forever changed. Imagine living in an idyllic paradise, a place that attracted and awed visitors from around the world...and then watching it gradually blown to bits. It's understandable if Dubrovnik's citizens are a little less in love with life than they once were.

It's clear that in the case of this siege, the Croats of Dubrovnik were the largely innocent victims of a brutal surprise attack. But keep in mind the larger context of the war: The cousins of these Croats, who were defending the glorious monument that is Dubrovnik, bombarded another glorious monument—the Old Bridge of Mostar (see page 165). It's just another reminder that the "good guys" and "bad guys" in these wars are far from clear-cut.

Dubrovnik has several low-key attractions related to its recent war, including the museum in the ruined fortress atop Mount Srđ and the Memorial Room of Dubrovnik Defenders in the Sponza Palace on Luža Square. Another sight, War Photo Limited, expands the scope to war photography from around the world.

shows the phase of the moon. At the bottom, the old-fashioned digital readout tells the hour (in Roman numerals) and the minutes (in five-minute increments). At the top of each hour (and again three minutes later), the time is clanged out on the bell up top by two bronze bell-ringers, Maro and Baro. (If this all seems like a copy of the very similar clock on St. Mark's Square in Venice, locals are quick to point out that this clock predates that one by several decades.) The clock still has to be wound every two days. Notice the little window between the moon phase and the "digital" readout: The clock-winder opens this window to get some light. The Krasovac family was in charge of winding the clock for generations (1877-2005). During the 1991-1992 siege, their house was destroyed—with the winding keys inside. For days, the clock bell didn't run. But then, miraculously, the keys were discovered lying in the street. The excited Dubrovnik citizens came together in this square and cheered as the clock was wound and the bell chimed, signaling to the soldiers surrounding the city that they hadn't won yet. If you have a Dubrovnik Card, you can climb up to the gallery next to the tower for a fine view of the Stradun (entrance in the passage; likely June-Sept only—as hours are in flux, check the posted information or ask the TI for details).

To the right of the Bell Tower, you'll see the entrance to the Sloboda movie theater (the rainy-day location for cultural events in the summer), and next to that, **Onofrio's Little Fountain** (Mala Onofrijea Fontana), the little brother of the one at the other end of the Stradun. The big building beyond the fountain is the **City Hall** (Vijećnica)—the only 19th-century building inside the Old Town. The terrace at the near end of City Hall is occupied by the **Gradska Kavana,** or "Town Café." This hangout—historically Dubrovnik's favorite spot for gossiping and people-watching—has pricey drinks and seating all the way through the wall to the Old Port. Just down the street from the Town Café is the Rector's Palace, and then the cathedral (for more on each, see "Sights in Dubrovnik").

Behind Orlando is **St. Blaise's Church** (Crkva Sv. Vlaha), dedicated to the patron saint of Dubrovnik. You'll see statues and paintings of St. Blaise all over town, always holding a model of the city in his left hand. According to legend, a millennium ago St. Blaise came to a local priest in a dream and warned him that the up-and-coming Venetians would soon attack the city. The priest alerted the authorities, who prepared for war. Of course, the prediction came true. St. Blaise has been a Dubrovnik symbol—and locals have resented Venice—ever since.

The church, like most churches in this city, was built following the 1667 earthquake and fire. And, while we've heard plenty on this walk about Dubrovnik's rivalry with Venice, there's no denying that the Venetians were some of Europe's top cultural trendsetters at that time. So Dubrovnik invited a Venetian architect to design the church dedicated to their favorite saint. That's why St. Blaise's looks like it would be right at home reflected in a Venetian canal...right down to its bulbous dome, which seems to have been transplanted here from the top of St. Mark's.

• *Your tour is finished. From here, you've got plenty of sightseeing options (all described next, under "Sights in Dubrovnik"). As you face the Bell Tower, you can go up the street to the right to reach the Rector's Palace and cathedral; you can walk straight ahead through the gate to reach the Old Port; or you can head through the gate and jog left to find the Dominican Monastery Museum. Even more sights—including an old synagogue, an Orthodox church, a modern exhibit of war photography, and the medieval granary—are in the steep streets between the Stradun and the walls.*

Sights in Dubrovnik

▲▲▲City Walls (Gradske Zidine)

Dubrovnik's single best attraction is strolling the scenic mile-and-a-quarter around the city walls. As you meander along this lofty perch—with a sea of orange roofs on one side, and the actual sea on the other—you'll get your bearings, peek down into secluded gardens, and snap pictures like mad of the ever-changing views. Bring your map, which you can use to pick out landmarks and get the lay of the land.

Cost: 100 kn to enter walls, also includes the Fort of St. Lawrence outside the Pile Gate (kunas or credit cards only—no euros).

Hours: July-Aug daily 8:00-19:30, progressively shorter hours off-season until mid-Nov-mid-March 10:00-15:00. Since the hours change with the season, confirm them by checking signs posted at the entrance (essential if you want to time your wall walk to avoid the worst crowds—explained below). The posted closing time indicates when the walls shut down, *not* the last entry—ascend well before this time if you want to make it all the way around. (If you want to linger, begin at least an hour ahead; if you're speedy, you can ascend 30 minutes before closing time.) Attendants begin circling the walls at the posted closing time to lock the gates. There's talk of

someday illuminating the walls at night, in which case the hours would be extended until after dark.

Entrances and Strategies: There are three entry points for the wall, and wall-walkers are required to proceed counterclockwise. The best plan is to begin at the far side of the Old Town, using the entrance **near the Ploče Gate** and Dominican Monastery. This entrance is the least crowded, and you'll tackle the steepest part (and enjoy the best views) first, as you climb up to the landward side of the wall with magnificent views across the entire Old Town and the Adriatic. If you're wiped out, overheated, or fed up with crowds after that, you can bail out halfway (at the Pile Gate), having seen the best—or you can continue around the seaward side. The other two entrances are **just inside the Pile Gate** (by far the most crowded; for this location only, you must buy your tickets at the desk across the square; if you begin here, you'll reach the Minčeta Tower—with the steepest ascent and best views—last) and **near St. John's Fort** overlooking the Old Port (next to the Maritime Museum).

Crowd Control: Because this is Dubrovnik's top attraction, it's extremely crowded. Your best strategy is to avoid the walls during the times when the cruise ships are in town. On days when the walls open at 8:00, try to get started around that time. The walls are the most crowded from about 9:00 until 11:00, when the cruise ships are docked. There's generally an afternoon lull in the crowds (13:00-14:00)—but that's also the hottest time to be atop the walls. Crowds pick up again in the late afternoon (around 17:00), peaking about an hour before closing time (18:30 in high season). During busy times, your best bet is to hit the walls around 8:30, or just before 17:00 (to avoid both the worst heat and the worst crowds).

Tips: Speed demons with no cameras can walk the walls in about an hour; strollers and shutterbugs should plan on longer. Because your ticket is electronically scanned as you enter, you can't leave and re-enter the wall later; you have to do it all in one go. If you have a Dubrovnik Card—even a multiple-day one—you can only use it to ascend the walls once.

Warning: The walls can get deliriously hot—all that white stone and seawater reflect blazing sunshine something fierce, and there's virtually no shade. It's essential to bring sunscreen, a hat, and water. Pace yourself: There are several steep stretches, and you'll be climbing up and down the whole way around. A few scant shops and cafés along the top of the wall (mostly on the sea side) sell water and other drinks, but it's safest to bring what you'll need with you. If you have trouble with the heat, save the walls for a cloudy day. In that hazy light, the red roof tiles seem more vivid, since they're not washed out by glaring sunshine.

Audioguide: You can rent an audioguide, separate from the

admission fee, for a dryly narrated circular tour of the walls (look for vendors near the Pile Gate entrance—not available at other entrances). But I'd rather just enjoy the views and lazily pick out the landmarks with my map.

Background: There have been walls here almost as long as there's been a Dubrovnik. As with virtually all fortifications on the Croatian Coast, these walls were beefed up in the 15th century, when the Ottoman navy became a threat. Around the perimeter are several substantial forts, with walls rounded so that cannonballs would glance off harmlessly. These stout forts intimidated would-be invaders during the Republic of Dubrovnik's Golden Age, and protected residents during the 1991-1992 siege.

❍ Self-Guided Tour: It's possible to just wander the walls and snap photos like crazy as you go. And trying to hew too closely to guided commentary kind of misses the point of being high above the Dubrovnik rooftops. But this brief tour will help give you bearings to what you're seeing, as you read Dubrovnik's unique and illustrious history into its street plan.

Part 1—Ploče Gate to Pile Gate: Begin by ascending near the **Ploče Gate** (go through the gate under the Bell Tower, walk along the stoutly walled passageway between the port and the Dominican Monastery, and look for the wall entrance on your right). Buy your ticket, head up, turn left, and start walking counterclockwise. Climbing stairs, you'll walk with Mount Srđ and the cable car on your right. After passing the Dominican Monastery's fine courtyard on the left, you're walking above what was the poorest part of medieval Dubrovnik, the domain of the craftsmen—with narrow, stepped lanes that had shops on the ground floor and humble dwellings up above. Standing above the Buža Gate (one of just three places where people can enter and exit the walled Old Town), you have a great view down narrow Boškovićeva street, with its many little stone ledges sticking out next to windows. (These were used to hang banners during the city's Golden Age.)

As you walk, keep an eye on the different-colored **rooftops** for an illustration of the damage Dubrovnik sustained during the 1991-1992 siege. It's easy to see that nearly two-thirds of Dubrovnik's roofs were replaced after the bombings (notice the new, bright-orange tiles—and how some buildings salvaged the old tiles, but have 20th-century ones underneath). The pristine-seeming Old Town was rebuilt using exactly the same materials and methods with which it was originally constructed.

The path you're on alternates between straight stretches and stairs; as you walk you're rewarded with higher and higher views.

Nearing the summit, you pass a juice bar (you can use the WCs if you buy a drink). At the very top, you enjoy the best possible view of the Old Town—you can see the rooftops, churches, and the sea. For an even better view, if you have the energy, huff up the steep stairs to the (empty) **Minčeta Tower.** From either viewpoint, observe the valley-like shape of Dubrovnik. It's easy to imagine how it began as two towns—one where you are now, and the other on the hilly island with the church spires across the way—originally separated by a sea-water canal. Notice the relatively regular, grid-like pattern of houses on this side, but the more higgledy-piggledy arrangement on the far side (a visual clue that the far side is older).

The sports court at your feet is a reminder that Dubrovnik is a living city—though it's not as vibrant as it once was. While of-

ficially 2,000 people live within these walls, most locals estimate the real number at about half that; the rest rent out their homes to tourists. And with good reason: Imagine the challenges that come with living in such a steep medieval townscape well into the 21st cen-tury. Delivery trucks rumble up and down the Stradun early each morning, and you'll see hardworking young men delivering goods on hand carts throughout the day. Looking up at the fortress atop Mount Srđ—seemingly custom-made for keeping an eye on a large swathe of coastline—the strategic position of Dubrovnik is clear. Independent Dubrovnik was not just this walled city, but an entire region.

Now continue downhill (you've earned it), noticing views on your right of the bustling Pile Gate area and the Fort of St. Lawrence (we'll reach better views of both of these soon). As the wall walk levels off, you'll pass an exit (on the left); if you're bushed and ready to head back to town, you can bail out here—but be aware that once you leave, you can't re-enter on the same ticket. Better yet, carry on straight for part 2.

Part 2—Pile Gate to Old Port: Pause to enjoy the full frontal view of the **Stradun,** barreling right at you. In the Middle Ages, lining this drag were the merchants, and before that, this was a canal. At your feet is Onofrio's Big Fountain, which supplied water

to a thirsty town. From here, you can see a wide range of church steeples representing the cosmopolitan makeup of a thriving medieval trade town (from left to right): Dominican, Franciscan (near you), the town Bell Tower, St. Blaise's (the round dome—hard to see from here), Serbian Orthodox (twin domed steeples), Cathedral, and (high on the hill) Jesuit St. Ignatius. Sit and watch the river of humanity, flowing constantly up and down one of Europe's finest main streets. Now do a 180 for a good view of the Pile Gate chaos, with a steady stream of buses lumbering up and down the hill, tethering the Old Town to Port Gruž and the Lapad resort zone.

Carry on through the guard tower and along the wall, climbing uphill again. Looking to the wall ahead of you, notice that—after we passed along a straighter, lower stretch—this wall is scampering up a mighty foundation of solid rock. We've left the canal that once separated the two parts of Dubrovnik, and now we're ascending what used to be a separate, very steep, rocky island.

On the right, across the little cove, is the **Fort of St. Lawrence,** which worked in concert with these stout walls to make Dubrovnik virtually impenetrable. (That fort is also climbable, and covered by the same ticket as the walls.) Climbing higher and looking to your left, into town, you'll see that this area is still damaged—not from the 1991-1992 siege, but from the 1667 earthquake. Notice that, unlike the extremely dense construction on the poorer far side of town, this area has more breathing space and larger gardens. Originally this was also densely populated, but after the quake, rather than rebuild, the wealthy folks who lived here decided to turn some former homes into green space. Grates cover the openings to old wells and grain stores that once supplied homes here—essential for surviving a siege.

As the walkway summits and levels out, you pass a drink stand. Farther along, at the picturesque little turret, is an artsy souvenir

boutique. You'll stroll past local residents' backyards, peering into their inviting gardens and checking the status of their drying laundry. Looking down to your right (outside the wall), you'll begin to see tables and umbrellas clinging to the rocks at the base of the wall. This is the recom-

mended Cold Drinks "Buža" II, the best spot in town for a scenic drink. (You can't enter from atop the wall—you'll have to wait until later.) On the horizon is the isle of Lokrum and—often—cruise ships at anchor, sending their passengers to and fro on tenders. After passing Buža, look down on the left to see the neighborhood kids' makeshift soccer pitch, wedged between the walls, and a little chapel—the best they can do in this vertical town. Soon you'll see the "other" Buža (technically Buža I) ahead; just above it, notice the little statue of St. Blaise, Dubrovnik's patron, enjoy some shade under the turret.

Rounding the bend, look left to see the facade of the Jesuit St. Ignatius Church. Notice that the homes in this area are much larger. These are aristocratic palaces—VIPs wanted to live as close as possible to the Cathedral and Rector's Palace, which are just below—and this also happens to be the oldest part of town, where "Ragusa" was born on a steep offshore island.

Continue around the wall, passing two more snack bars (the second with pay WCs) and more quake-ruined houses. Eventually you'll pop out at a high plateau, where *The City Walls—Continuation* signs lead down to the next part. From here, if you're bushed, you can bail out for the exit. (In the little plant-filled square at the bottom of these stairs is a sweet cat hospice, with a donation box for feeding some homeless feline residents.) But the final stretch of our wall walk is shorter than the other two, and mostly level.

Part 3—Old Port to Ploče Gate: Continuing along the wall, you'll pass near the entrance to the skippable Maritime Museum, then walk along the top of the wall overlooking the Old Port. Imagine how this heavily fortified little harbor (facing away from Dubrovnik's historic foes, the Venetians) was busy with trade in the Middle Ages. Today it's still the economic lifeline for town watch the steady stream of cruise-ship tenders injecting dose after dose of tourist cash into town. As you curl around the far side of the port, you'll see the outdoor tables of 360°, a cocktail bar/restaurant catering to high-rolling yachters. While it looks appealing, it's a very exclusive place that frowns on would-be visitors who dress like normal people. Gussied-up jet-set diners enjoy coming here for good but extremely expensive designer fare. (One local told me, "The food is great—just eat a hamburger before you go.")

Just past 360°, you come to the stairs back down to where you started this wall walk. Nice work. Now head on down and reward yourself with an ice-cream cone...and some shade.

The "Other" Wall Climb: Your ticket for the City Walls also includes the Fort of St. Lawrence just outside the Old Town (valid same day only). If you've already bought a 30-kn ticket there, show it when buying your main wall ticket and you'll pay only the difference.

Near the Pile Gate

This museum is just inside the Pile Gate.

▲Franciscan Monastery Museum
(Franjevački Samostan-Muzej)

In the Middle Ages, Dubrovnik's monasteries flourished. And, as a part of their charity work, the monks at this monastery took on the responsibility of serving as pharmacists for the community. Visiting here today, you'll stroll through a delightful cloister and walk through a one-room museum in the old pharmacy.

Cost and Hours: 30 kn, daily April-Oct 9:00-18:00, Nov-March 9:00-17:00, Placa 2, tel. 020/321-410.

Visiting the Museum: Enter through the gap between the small church and the big monastery. Just inside the door (before the ticket-seller), a century-old **pharmacy** still serves residents. Notice the antique jars, advertisements (including one of the first known aspirin ads), and other vintage pharmacist gear. By keeping this open, the monastery maintains one of the world's oldest continually operating pharmacies.

Explore the peaceful, sun-dappled **cloister.** Examine the capitals at the tops of the 60 Romanesque-Gothic double pillars.

Each one is different. Notice that some parts of the portals inside the courtyard are made with a lighter-colored stone—these had to be repaired after being hit during the 1991-1992 siege. The damaged 19th-century frescoes along the tops of the walls depict the life of St. Francis, who supposedly visited Dubrovnik in the early 13th century. If you look closely, in a few panels you may see two layers of (different) scenes; beneath the 19th-century frescoes, restorers have found even more precious fragments of some early 18th-century paintings; where possible, these are also being resurrected.

In the far corner stands the monastery's original medieval **pharmacy.** The Franciscans opened this pharmacy in 1317, and it's been in continual operation ever since. On display are jars, pots, and other medieval pharmacists' tools. Notice the row of old pharmacists' books from the 16th, 17th, and 18th centuries—expertise imported from as far away as Venice, Frankfurt, Amsterdam, and Bologna. The sick would come to get their medicine at the little window (on

the left side), which limited contact with the pharmacist and reduced the risk of passing on disease. On the right side, look for the glass case marked *venena*—where poisons were locked away and carefully doled out, with a record of who had what (if only modern gun dealers were so cautiously regulated).

Around the room, you'll also find some relics, old manuscripts, and a detailed painting of early 17th-century Dubrovnik. In the painting, notice that at the top of Mount Srđ—the highly strategic locale where Napoleon built a fortress that was key during the 1991 siege—is a chapel. Though Dubrovnik was always heavily fortified, they avoided putting a fortress on the mountaintop—fearing it might seem overly provocative to the Ottoman Empire that surrounded them, and upon whose favor they depended for their autonomy.

Leaving the museum room, turn right and walk to the end of this corridor. While you're walking upon tombs, look up to see one with privileged position, affixed high on the wall. The **Gučetić-Gozze** family donated vast sums to help rebuild the monastery after the devastating 1667 earthquake. As thanks, the Franciscans helped them get just that much closer to God when they passed on, offering them this final resting place that was elevated...in every sense.

Near Luža Square

These sights are at the far end of the Stradun (nearest the Old Port). As you stand on Luža Square facing the Bell Tower, the Rector's Palace and cathedral are up the wide street called Pred Dvorom to the right, and the Dominican Monastery Museum is through the gate by the Bell Tower and to the left.

▲Rector's Palace (Knežev Dvor)

In the Middle Ages, the Republic of Dubrovnik was ruled by a rector (similar to a Venetian doge), who was elected by the nobility.

To prevent any one person from becoming too powerful, the rector's term was limited to one month. Most rectors were in their 50s—near the end of the average life span and when they were less likely to shake things up. During his term, a rector lived upstairs in this palace. Because it's been plundered twice (most recently by Napoleon's forces, who stole all the furniture), this empty-feeling museum isn't as interesting as most other European palaces. What little you'll see was donated by local aristocrats to flesh out the pathetically empty complex. The palace collection, which requires a ticket and has good English explanations, is skippable, but it does offer a glimpse of Dubrovnik

in its glory days. Even if you pass on the interior, the palace's exterior and courtyard are viewable at no charge.

Cost and Hours: 70 kn, ticket also includes Maritime Museum and Rupe Ethnographical Museum, daily May-Oct 9:00-18:00, Nov-April 9:00-16:00, some posted English information, 7-kn English booklet is helpful, Pred Dvorom 3, tel. 020/322-096.

Visiting the Palace: The **exterior** is decorated in the Gothic-Renaissance mix (with particularly finely carved capitals) that was so common in Dubrovnik before the 1667 earthquake. Above the entrance is the message *Obliti privatorum publica curate*—loosely translated, "Forget your personal affairs and concern yourself with the affairs of state." This was a bold statement in a feudal era before democracy, when aristocrats were preoccupied exclusively with their self-interests.

Standing at the main door, you can generally get a free look at the palace's impressive **courtyard**—a venue for the Summer Festival, hosting music groups ranging from the local symphony to the Vienna Boys' Choir. During Dubrovnik's Golden Age, this courtyard was open to the public. People would wander in and out—gossiping, washing their laundry in the fountain, and bringing food to family members imprisoned in the cells. In the courtyard (and also visible from the door) is the only secular statue created during the centuries-long Republic. Dubrovnik republicans, mindful of the dangers of hero-worship, didn't believe that any one citizen should be singled out. They made only one exception—for Miho Pracat (a.k.a. Michaeli Prazatto), a rich citizen who donated vast sums to charity and willed a fleet of ships to the city. But notice that Pracat's statue is displayed in here, behind closed doors, not out in public.

If you pay to go **inside,** you'll start on the ground floor, where you'll see dull paintings, the green-stucco courtroom (with explanations of the Republic's unique governmental system), and one of the palace's highlights, the original bronze bell-ringers from the town Bell Tower (named Maro and Baro). Like antique robots (from the Renaissance, 1477-1478), these eerily lifelike sculptures could pivot at the waist to ring the bell. Then you'll see stonework that used to decorate city buildings. Iron chests (including a few with elaborate locking mechanisms) are displayed inside some poorly restored old prison cells, which supposedly were placed within earshot of the rector's quarters, so he would hear the moans

of the prisoners...and stay honest. Leaving the prison, you'll enter the courtyard described earlier, where you can get a better look at the Pracat statue.

On the mezzanine level (stairs near the main entrance, above the prison—notice the "hand" rails), you'll find a decent display of furniture, a wimpy gun exhibit, votive offerings (mostly silver), a ho-hum coin collection, and an interesting painting of "Ragusa" in the early 17th century—back when its stout walls were surrounded by a moat.

Head back down to the courtyard and ascend the grand stairway to the upper floor (using the staircase across from mezzanine stairs, near the Pracat statue—with more "hand" rails). Upstairs, you'll explore old apartments that serve as a painting gallery. The only vaguely authentic room is the red room in the corner, decorated more or less as it was in 1500, when it was the rector's office. Mihajlo Hamzić's exquisite *Baptism of Christ* painting, inspired by Italian painter Andrea Mantegna, is an early Renaissance work from the "Dubrovnik School" (see "Dominican Monastery Museum" listing, later). This area also often displays temporary exhibits.

Back in the courtyard, you can go up the smaller stairs to the Domus Christi collection of old pharmacist tools and pots.

Handy WCs are just off the courtyard next to the shop, through which you'll exit.

Nearby: Just to the left as you face the entrance of the Rector's Palace, notice the statue of Dubrovnik poet **Marin Držić** (1508-1567). This beloved bard's most famous work concerns "Uncle Maro," an aristocrat who's as stingy as he is wealthy. His son cleans out his savings account and goes on a bender in Rome...until his father gets wind of it and comes calling. The shiny lap and bright nose of this statue, erected in 2008, might lead you to believe it's good luck to rub his schnozz—and, sure enough, you'll see a steady stream of tourists doing just that. But the truth is that when the statue went up, local kids were drawn to his prominent proboscis, and couldn't resist climbing up on his lap and grabbing it. Tourists saw the shine and assumed they were supposed to do it, too. A legend was born.

▲Cathedral (Katedrala)

Dubrovnik's original 12th-century cathedral was funded largely by the English King Richard the Lionheart. On his way back from the Third Crusade, Richard was shipwrecked nearby. He promised God that if he survived, he'd build a church on the spot where he landed—which happened to be

on Lokrum Island, just offshore. At Dubrovnik's request, Richard agreed to build his token of thanks inside the city instead. It was the finest Romanesque church on the Adriatic...before it was destroyed by the 1667 earthquake. This version is 18th-century Roman Baroque.

Cost and Hours: Church—free, open daily 8:00 until Mass begins at 18:00; treasury—15 kn, generally open same hours as church; both have shorter hours off-season.

Visiting the Cathedral: Inside, you'll find a painting from the school of Titian *(Assumption of the Virgin)* over the stark contemporary altar, and a quirky treasury *(riznica)* packed with 187 relics. Examining the treasury collection, notice that there are three locks on the treasury door—the stuff in here was so valuable, three different VIPs (the rector, the bishop, and a local aristocrat) had to agree before it could be opened. On the table near the door are several of St. Blaise's body parts (pieces of his arm, skull, and leg—all encased in gold and silver). In the middle of the wall directly opposite the door, look for the crucifix with a piece of the True Cross. On a dig in Jerusalem, St. Helen (Emperor Constantine's mother) discovered what she believed to be the cross that Jesus was crucified on. It was brought to Constantinople, and the Byzantine czars doled out pieces of it to Balkan kings. Note the folding three-paneled altar painting (underneath the cross). Dubrovnik ambassadors packed this on road trips (such as their annual trip to pay off the Ottomans) so they could worship wherever they traveled.

On the right side of the room, the silver casket supposedly holds the actual swaddling clothes of the Baby Jesus (or, as some locals call it somewhat less reverently, "Jesus' nappy"). Dubrovnik bishops secretly passed these clothes down from generation to generation...until a nun got wind of it and told the whole town. Pieces of the cloth were cut off to miraculously heal the sick, especially new mothers recovering from a difficult birth. No matter how often it was cut, the cloth always went back to its original form. Then someone tried to use it on the wife of a Bosnian king. Since she was Muslim, it couldn't help her, and it never worked again. True or not, this legend hints at the prickly relationships between faiths (not to mention the male chauvinism) here in the Balkans.

▲Dominican Monastery Museum (Dominikanski Samostan-Muzej)
You'll find many of Dubrovnik's art treasures—paintings, altarpieces, and manuscripts—gathered around the peaceful Dominican Monastery cloister inside the Ploče Gate. As you climb the stairs up to

the monastery, notice that the spindles supporting the railing are solid up until about two feet above the ground. This was to provide a modicum of modesty to ladies on their way to church—and to prevent creeps down below from looking up their skirts.

Cost and Hours: 30 kn, art buffs enjoy the 50-kn English book, daily April-Oct 9:00-18:00, Nov-March 9:00-17:00.

Visiting the Museum: Turn left from the entry and work your way clockwise around the cloister. The room in the far corner contains paintings from the **"Dubrovnik School,"** the Republic's circa-1500 answer to the art boom in Florence and Venice. Though the 1667 earthquake destroyed most of these paintings, about a dozen survive, and five of those are in this room. Don't miss the triptych by Nikola Božidarović with St. Blaise holding a detailed model of 16th-century Dubrovnik (left panel)—the most famous depiction of Dubrovnik's favorite saint. You'll also see reliquaries shaped like the hands and feet that they hold.

Continuing around the courtyard, duck into the next room. Here you'll see a painting by **Titian** depicting St. Blaise, Mary Magdalene, and the donor who financed this work.

At the next corner of the courtyard is the entrance to the striking **church** at the heart of this still-active monastery. Step inside.

The interior is decorated with modern stained glass, a fine 13th-century stone pulpit that survived the earthquake (reminding visitors of the intellectual approach to scripture that characterized the Dominicans), and a precious 14th-century Paolo Veneziano crucifix hanging above the high altar. Behind the altar, find the Vukovar Cross, embedded with panels painted by different artists from the Croatian school of Naive Art—offering an enticing taste of this unique and fascinating style. Perhaps the finest piece of art in the church is the *Miracle of St. Dominic,* showing the founder of the order bringing a child back to life (over the altar to the right, as you enter). It was painted in the Realist style (late 19th century) by Vlaho Bukovac.

Museum of Modern Art (Umjetnička Galerija)

While salty old Dubrovnik and modern art don't quite seem to go together, the city has a fine modern art gallery a 10-minute walk outside the Ploče Gate. You'll see a permanent collection with 20th-century Croatian art (including some paintings by local artist Vlaho Bukovac—whose home in Cavtat offers a more intimate look at his life and works), as well as changing exhibits.

Cost and Hours: 40 kn, Tue-Sun 9:00-20:00, closed Mon, put Frana Supila 23, tel. 020/426-590, www.ugdubrovnik.hr.

Near the Old Port (Stara Luka)

The picturesque Old Port, carefully nestled behind St. John's Fort, faces away from what was Dubrovnik's biggest threat, the Vene-

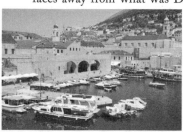

tians. At the port, you can haggle with captains selling excursions to nearby towns and islands (described in the next chapter) and watch cruise-ship passengers coming and going on their tenders. The long seaside building across the bay on the left is the Lazareti, once the medieval quarantine house. In those days, all visitors were locked in here for 40 days before entering town. (Today it hosts folk-dancing shows—described later, under "Entertainment in Dubrovnik.") A bench-lined harborside walk leads around the fort to a breakwater, providing a peaceful perch. From the breakwater, rocky beaches curl around the outside of the wall.

Maritime Museum (Pomorski Muzej)

In the 15th century, when Venice's nautical dominance was peaking, Dubrovnik emerged as another maritime power and the Mediterranean's leading shipbuilding center. The Dubrovnik-built "argosy" boat (from "Ragusa," an early name for the city) was the Cadillac of ships, even mentioned by Shakespeare. This small museum traces the history of Dubrovnik's most important industry with contracts, maps, paintings, and models—all well-described in English. The main floor takes you through the 18th century, and the easy-to-miss upstairs covers the 19th and 20th centuries. Boaters will find the museum particularly interesting.

Cost and Hours: Covered by 70-kn combo-ticket with Rector's Palace and Rupe Ethnographic Museum, 7-kn English booklet, hours flex on demand—usually March-Oct Tue-Sun 9:00-18:00, until 16:00 in Nov-Feb, closed Mon year-round, upstairs in St. John's Fort, at far/south end of Old Port, tel. 020/323-904.

Aquarium (Akvarij)

Dubrovnik's aquarium, housed in the cavernous St. John's Fort, is an old-school place, with 31 tanks on one floor. A visit here allows you a close look at the local marine life and provides a cool refuge from the midday heat.

Cost and Hours: 40 kn, kids-15 kn, English descriptions, daily July-Aug 9:00-21:00, progressively shorter hours off-season until 9:00-16:00 Nov-March, ground floor of St. John's Fort, enter from Old Port, tel. 020/323-978.

Between the Stradun and the Mainland

These two museums are a few steps off the main promenade toward the mainland.

▲Synagogue Museum (Sinagoga-Muzej)

When the Jews were forced out of Spain in 1492, a steady stream of them passed through here en route to today's Turkey. Finding Dubrovnik to be a flourishing and relatively tolerant city, many stayed. Žudioska ulica ("Jewish Street"), just inside the Ploče Gate, became the ghetto in 1546. It was walled at one end and had a gate (which would be locked at night) at the other end. Today, the same street is home to the second-oldest continuously functioning synagogue in Europe (after Prague's), which contains Croatia's only Jewish museum. The top floor houses the synagogue itself. Notice the lattice windows that separated the women from the men (in accordance with Orthodox Jewish tradition). Below that, a small museum with good English descriptions gives meaning to the various Torahs (including a 14th-century one from Spain) and other items—such as the written orders *(naredba)* from Nazi-era Yugoslavia, stating that Jews were to identify their shops as Jewish-owned and wear armbands. (The Ustaše—the Nazi puppet government in Croatia—interned and executed not only Jews and Roma/Gypsies, but also Serbs and other people they considered undesirable.) Of Croatia's 24,000 Jews, only 4,000 survived the Holocaust. Today Croatia has about 2,000 Jews, including a dozen Jewish families who call Dubrovnik home.

Cost and Hours: 25 kn, 10-kn English booklet; May-mid-Nov daily 10:00-20:00; mid-Nov-April Mon-Fri 10:00-13:00, closed Sat-Sun; Žudioska ulica 5, tel. 020/321-204.

▲War Photo Limited

If the tragic story of wartime Dubrovnik has you in a pensive mood, drop by this gallery with images of warfare from around the world. The brainchild of Kiwi-turned-Croatian photojournalist Wade Goddard, this thought-provoking museum attempts to show the ugly reality of war through raw, often disturbing photographs taken in the field. You'll find well-displayed exhibits on two floors; a small permanent exhibit (on the top floor) captures the wars in the former Yugoslavia through photography and video footage. Each summer, the gallery also houses various temporary exhibits. Note that the focus is not solely on Dubrovnik, but on war anywhere and everywhere.

Cost and Hours: 40 kn; June-Sept daily 10:00-22:00; May and Oct Tue-Sun 10:00-16:00, closed Mon; closed Nov-April; Antuninska 6, tel. 020/322-166, www.warphotoltd.com.

Between the Stradun and the Sea

▲Serbian Orthodox Church and Icon Museum
(Srpska Pravoslavna Crkva i Muzej Ikona)

Round out your look at Dubrovnik's major faiths (Catholic, Jewish, and Orthodox) with a visit to this house of worship—one of the most convenient places in Croatia to learn about Orthodox Christianity. Remember that people from the former Yugoslavia who follow the Orthodox faith are, by definition, ethnic Serbs. With all the hard feelings about the recent war, this church serves as an important reminder that all Serbs aren't bloodthirsty killers.

Dubrovnik never had a very large Serb population (an Orthodox church wasn't even allowed inside the town walls until the mid-19th century). During the recent war, most Serbs fled, created new lives for themselves elsewhere, and saw little reason to return. But some old-timers remain, and Dubrovnik's dwindling, aging Orthodox population is still served by this **church.** The candles stuck in the sand (to prevent fire outbreaks) represent prayers: The ones at knee level are for the deceased, while the ones higher up are for the living. The gentleman selling candles encourages you to buy and light one, regardless of your faith, so long as you do so with the proper intentions and reverence.

A few doors down, you'll find the **Icon Museum.** This small collection features 78 different icons (stylized paintings of saints, generally on a golden background—a common feature of Orthodox churches) from the 15th through the 19th centuries, all identified in English. In the library—crammed with old shelves holding some 12,000 books—look for the astonishingly detailed calendar, with portraits of hundreds of saints. The gallery on the ground floor, run by Michael, sells original icons and reproductions (open longer hours than museum).

Cost and Hours: Church—free but donations accepted, good 20-kn English book explains church and museum; daily May-Sept 8:00-14:00 & 16:00-21:00 or 22:00, until 19:00 in shoulder season, until 17:00 in winter; short services daily at 8:30 and 19:00, longer liturgy Sun 10:00-11:00; museum—10 kn; May-Oct Mon-Sat 9:00-13:00 or possibly later, closed Sun; Nov-April Mon-Fri 9:00-13:00, closed Sat-Sun, Od Puča 8, tel. 020/323-283.

The Serbian Orthodox Church

The emphasis of this book is on the Catholic areas of the former Yugoslavia, but don't overlook the rich diversity of faiths in this region. Dubrovnik's Serbian Orthodox church, as well as Orthodox churches in Kotor, Montenegro (see page 126), offer invaluable opportunities to learn about a faith that's often unfamiliar to American visitors.

As you explore an Orthodox church, keep in mind that these churches carry on the earliest traditions of the Christian faith. Orthodox and Catholic Christianity came from the same roots, so the oldest surviving early-Christian churches (such as the stave churches of Norway) have many of the same features as today's Orthodox churches.

Notice that there are no pews. Worshippers stand through the service, as a sign of respect (though some older parishioners sit on the seats along the walls). Women stand on the left side, men on the right (equal distance from the altar—to represent that all are equal before God). The Orthodox Church uses essentially the same Bible as Catholics, but it's written in the Cyrillic alphabet, which you'll see displayed around any Orthodox church. Following Old Testament Judeo-Christian tradition, the Bible is kept on the altar behind the iconostasis, the big screen in the middle of the room covered with curtains and icons (golden paintings of saints), which separates the material

▲Rupe Granary and Ethnographic Museum (Etnografski Muzej Rupe)

This huge, 16th-century building was Dubrovnik's biggest granary, and today houses the best folk museum I've seen in Croatia. *Rupe* means "holes"—and it's worth the price of entry just to peer down into these 15 cavernous underground grain stores, designed to maintain the perfect temperature to preserve the seeds (63 degrees Fahrenheit). When the grain had to be dried, it was moved upstairs—where today you'll find a surprisingly well-presented Ethnographic Museum, with tools, jewelry, clothing, instruments, painted eggs, and other folk artifacts from Dubrovnik's colorful history. Borrow the free English information guide at the entry. The museum hides several blocks uphill from the main promenade, toward the sea (climb up Široka—the widest side street from the Stradun—which becomes Od Domina on the way to the museum).

Cost and Hours: Covered by 70-kn combo-ticket with Rector's Palace and Maritime Museum, Wed-Mon 9:00-18:00—or until 14:00 off-season, closed Tue year-round, od Rupa 3, tel. 020/323-013.

world from the spiritual one. At certain times during the service, the curtains or doors are opened so the congregation can see the Holy Book.

Unlike the decorations in many Catholic churches, Orthodox icons are not intended to be lifelike. Packed with intricate symbolism, and cast against a shimmering golden background, they're meant to remind viewers of the metaphysical nature of Jesus and the saints rather than of their physical form, which is considered irrelevant. You'll almost never see a statue, which is thought to overemphasize the physical world...and, to Orthodox people, feels a little too close to violating the commandment, "Thou shalt not worship graven images." Orthodox services generally involve chanting (a dialogue that goes back and forth between the priest and the congregation), and the church is filled with the evocative aroma of incense.

The incense, chanting, icons, and standing up are all intended to heighten the experience of worship. While many Catholic and Protestant services tend to be more of a theoretical and rote consideration of religious issues (come on—don't tell me you've never dozed through the sermon), Orthodox services are about creating a religious experience. Each of these elements does its part to help the worshipper transcend the physical world and join in communion with the spiritual one.

Above Dubrovnik

▲▲▲Mount Srđ

After adding Dubrovnik to his holdings, Napoleon built a fortress atop the hill behind the Old Town to keep an eye on his new subjects (in 1810). During the

city's 20th-century tourism heyday, a cable car was built to effortlessly whisk visitors to the top so they could enjoy the fine views from the fortress and the giant cross nearby. Then, when war broke out in the 1990s, Mount Srđ (pronounced like "surge") became a crucial link in the defense of Dubrovnik—the only high land that locals were able to hold. The fortress was shelled and damaged, and the cross and cable car were destroyed. Minefields and unexploded ordnance left the hilltop a dangerous no-man's land. But more recently, the mountain's fortunes have reversed. The landmines have been removed, and in 2010, the cable car was rebuilt to once again connect Dubrovnik's Old Town to its mountaintop. Visitors head to the top

both for the spectacular sweeping views and to ponder the exhibits in a ragtag museum about the war.

Warning: While this area has officially been cleared of land-mines, nervous locals remind visitors that this was once a war zone. Be sure to stay on clearly defined paths and roads.

Getting There: The **cable car** is easily the best option for reaching the summit of Mount Srđ (94 kn round-trip, 50 kn one-way, kunas or credit cards only—no euros; at least 2/hour—gener-ally departing at :00 and :30 past each hour, more frequent with demand, 3-minute ride; daily from 9:00, June-Aug until 24:00, Sept until 22:00, April-May and Oct until 20:00, Feb-March and Nov until 17:00, Dec-Jan until 16:00; doesn't run in Bora wind or heavy rain, last ascent 30 minutes before closing, tel. 020/325-393, www.dubrovnikcablecar.com). The lower station is just above the Buža Gate at the top of the Old Town (from the main drag, huff all the way to the top of Boškovićeva, exit through gate, and climb up-hill one block, then look right). You may see travel agencies selling tickets elsewhere in town, but there's no advantage to buying them anywhere but here. The line you may see at the cable-car station is not to buy tickets, but to actually ride up. For tips on avoiding a long wait, see below.

If you have a **car,** you can drive up. From the high road above the Old Town, watch for the turnoff to *Bosanka,* which leads you to that village, then up to the fortress and cross—follow signs for *Srđ* (it's twisty but not far—figure a 20-minute drive from the Old Town area). If you're coming south from the Old Town, once you reach the main road above, you'll have to turn left and backtrack a bit to reach the *Bosanka* turnoff. For **hikers,** a switchback trail (used to supply the fortress during the siege) connects the Old Town to the mountaintop—but it's very steep and provides minimal shade. (If you're in great shape and it's not too hot, you could ride the cable car up, then hike down.)

Crowd-Beating Tips: The cable car has a limited capacity, and lines can get long when several cruise ships are in town. It tends to be most crowded in the morning, shortly after the cruises arrive (peaking around 11:00). If you come during this peak time, you may have to wait your turn while watching several cable cars fill and ascend. But as the day goes on, the lines tend to get shorter. I'd aim to visit later in the day—par-ticularly if you can do it at sunset.

Mountaintop: From the top cable-car station, head up the stairs to the panoramic terrace. The bird's-eye **view** is truly spectacular, looking straight down to the street plan of Dubrovnik's Old Town. From this

lofty perch, you can see north to the Dalmatian islands (the Elaphite archipelago, Mljet, Korčula, and beyond); south to Montenegro; and east into Bosnia-Herzegovina. Gazing upon those looming mountains that define the border with Bosnia-Herzegovina—which, centuries ago, was also the frontier of the huge and powerful Ottoman Empire—you can appreciate how impressive it was that stubborn little Dubrovnik managed to remain independent for so much of its history.

The **cross** was always an important symbol in this very Catholic town. After it was destroyed, a temporary wooden one was erected to encourage the townspeople who were waiting out the siege below. During a visit in 2003, Pope John Paul II blessed the rubble from the old cross; those fragments are now being used in the foundations of the city's newest churches. Nearby stands a huge red, white, and blue flagpole—the colors of the Croatian flag.

To reach the museum in the old fortress, walk behind the cable-car station along the rocky red soil.

Fort and Museum: The Napoleonic-era Fort Imperial (Trđava Imperijal) houses the **Dubrovnik During the Homeland War (1991-1995) Museum** (30 kn, various books for sale, same hours as cable car). As you enter, temporary exhibits are on the right, and the permanent exhibit is to the left. Photos, documents, and artifacts tell the story (with English descriptions) of the overarching war with Yugoslavia and how the people defended this fortress. The descriptions are too dense and tactical for casual visitors, but you'll see lots of photos and some actual items used in the fighting: primitive, rusty rifles (some dating from World War II) that the Croatians used for their improvised defense, and piles of spent mortar shells and other projectiles that Yugoslav forces hurled at the fortress and the city. Look for the wire-guided Russian rockets. After being launched at their target, the rockets would burrow into a wall, waiting to be detonated once their operators saw the opportunity for maximum destruction. The tattered Croatian flag seems soaked in local patriotism. A video screen shows breathless international news reports from the front line during the bombing. You'll also learn how a squadron of armed supply ships became besieged Dubrovnik's only tether to the outside world.

While the devastation of Dubrovnik was disturbing, this museum could do a far better job of fostering at least an illusion of impartiality. Instead, descriptions rant one-sidedly against "Serbian and Montenegrin aggression" and the "Serbian imperialist war,"

and the exhibits self-righteously depict Croats exclusively as victims (which was essentially true here in Dubrovnik, but ignores Croat atrocities elsewhere). All of this serves only to trivialize and distract from the human tragedy of this war.

After seeing the exhibit, climb up a few flights of stairs to the **rooftop** for the view. The giant communications tower overhead flew the Croatian flag during the war, to inspire the besieged residents below. You might see some charred trees around here—these were claimed not by the war, but more recently, by forest fires. (Fear of landmines and other explosives prevented locals from fighting the wildfires as aggressively as they might otherwise, making these fires more dangerous than ever.)

Eating: Boasting undoubtedly the best view in Dubrovnik, **Restaurant/Snack Bar Panorama** has reasonable prices and drop-dead, astonishing views over the rooftops of the Old Town and to the most beautiful parts of three different countries. While there's glassed-in seating inside, in good weather I'd exit the building to find the outdoor terrace—the Old Town floats just under your nose (25-35-kn drinks, 55-75-kn cocktails, 80-90-kn pastas, 100-160-kn main dishes, open same hours as cable car).

Activities in Dubrovnik

Swimming and Sunbathing

If the weather's good and you've had enough of museums, spend a sunny afternoon at the beach. There are no sandy beaches on the mainland near Dubrovnik, but there are lots of suitable pebbly options, plus several concrete perches.

The easiest and most atmospheric place to take a dip is right off the **Old Town.** From the Old Port and its breakwater, uneven steps clinging to the outside of the wall lead to a series of great sunbathing and swimming coves (and even a showerhead sticking out of the town wall). Another delightful rocky beach hangs onto the outside of the Old Town's wall (at the bar called Cold Drinks "Buža" I).

A more convenient public beach is **Banje,** just outside the Ploče Gate, east of Old Town. While this is dominated by the EastWest nightclub, by day it's a public beach with an inviting swath of sand and pebbles, ideal for sunbathing and wading with a spectacular backdrop of Dubrovnik's Old Town. To reach the beach, leave the Old Town through the Ploče Gate, walk about five minutes gradually uphill on the main road, then watch for the two staircases marked *EastWest* and climb

down. (While the stairs nearer the Old Town passes through the EastWest café/bar, it is public access.) The café/bar itself is slick and swanky (in keeping with its nightclub's exclusive vibe), serving pricey food and drink. You can also rent a very expensive sun bed (100-200 kn, depending on level of luxury), but it's much more affordable to bring your own towel and find a comfy patch of sand. Pay showers are nearby.

My favorite hidden beach—**St. Jakob**—takes a lot longer to reach, but if you're up for the hike, it's worth it to escape the

crowds. Figure about a 25-minute walk (each way) from the Old Town. Go through the Ploče Gate at the east end of the Old Town, and walk along the street called Frana Supila as it climbs uphill above the waterfront. At Hotel Argentina, take the right (downhill) fork and keep going on Vlaha Bukovca. Eventually you'll reach the small church of St. Jakob. You'll see the beach—in a cozy protected cove—far below. Curl around behind the church and keep an eye out for stairs going down on the right. Unfortunately, these stairs are effectively unmarked, so it might take some trial and error to find the right ones. (If you reach the rusted-white gateway of the old communist-era open-air theater, you've gone too far.) Hike down the very steep stairs to the gentle cove, which has rentable chairs and a small restaurant for drinks (and a WC). Enjoy the pebbly beach and faraway views of Dubrovnik's Old Town.

Other, even more distant beaches are worth considering. If you're staying at—or visiting—the resorty zone of **Lapad Bay,** you'll find a fine beach there (near Hotel Kompas).

Locals prefer to swim on **Lokrum Island,** because there are (relatively) fewer tourists there. While there are no sandy or even pebbly beaches, there are several rocky ones, with ladders to lower yourself gingerly into the water. As the rocks here can be particularly jagged, you'll want to wear good water shoes, and beware of uneven footing (both underwater, and on your way to the ladders).

Finally, for the best sandy beach in this part of Croatia, you'll have to take a boat to the island of Lopud, then hike (or ride a golf cart) across the spine of the island to the gorgeous **Šunj Beach.** Making an all-day trek out here (by public ferry) is worth visiting only if you're desperate for a long, lingering day at the beach. If you're cruising the Elaphite Islands, you'll likely stop on Lopud for two or three hours—enough time for a quick dip at Šunj.

Sea Kayaking

Paddling a sleek kayak around the outside of Dubrovnik's imposing walls is a memorable experience. Several outfits in town offer
half-day tours (most options 250-350 kn); popular itineraries include loops along the city walls, to secluded beaches, and around
Lokrum Island; many include a break for snorkeling, and some
are timed to catch the sunset while bobbing just offshore from
the city walls. As this scene is continually evolving, look for fliers
locally.

Shopping in Dubrovnik

Most souvenirs sold in Dubrovnik—from lavender sachets to plas-
ter models of the Old Town—are pretty tacky. Whatever you buy,
prices are much higher along the
Stradun than on the side streets.

A classy alternative to the
knickknacks is a type of local jewelry called *Konavoske puce* ("Konavle
buttons"). Sold as earrings, pendants,
and rings, these distinctive and fash-
ionable filigree-style pieces consist
of a sphere with several small posts.
Though they're sold around town, it's
least expensive to buy them on Od Puča street, which runs parallel
to the Stradun two blocks toward the sea (near the Serbian Orthodox Church). The high concentration of jewelers along this lane
keeps prices reasonable. You'll find the "buttons" in various sizes,
in both silver (affordable) and gold (pricey).

You'll also see lots of jewelry made from red coral, which can
only be legally gathered in small amounts from two small islands
in northern Dalmatia. If you see a particularly large chunk of coral,
it's likely imported. To know what you're getting, shop at an actual
jeweler instead of a souvenir shop.

Gift-Shop Chains: Several pleasant gift shops in Dubrovnik
(with additional branches throughout Dalmatia) hawk fun, if
sometimes made-in-China, items. Look for these chains, which
are a bit classier than the many no-name shops around town: **Aqua**
sells pleasant nautical-themed gifts, blue-and-white-striped sail-
or shirts, and other gear. **Bonbonnière Kraš** is Croatia's leading
chocolatier, selling a wide array of tasty candies. **Uje** has artisan
olive oils and other boutiquey edibles.

Entertainment in Dubrovnik

Musical Events

Dubrovnik annually hosts a full schedule of events for its Summer Festival (July 10-Aug 25, www.dubrovnik-festival.hr), which is quickly followed by its Late Summer Festival. But the town also works hard to offer traditional music outside of festival time.

Spirited **Linđo folk-music** concerts are performed for tourists twice weekly (in good weather, likely at the Jadran summer cinema or possibly at the newly renovated Lazareti—old quarantine building—just outside the Old Town's Ploče Gate; rainy-day location is Sloboda movie theater below the Bell Tower; 100 kn, usually at 21:30, www.lindjo.hr).

The **Dubrovnik Symphony Orchestra** performs crowd-pleasing classics twice weekly in summer (and once weekly through winter)—usually at the Rector's Palace in good weather, or the Dominican Monastery in bad weather (100-250 kn, typically at 21:00, www.dso.hr).

Since Dubrovnik is trying to become a year-round destination, the city also offers tourist-oriented musical events most nights throughout the winter (often at a hotel). For the latest on any of these festivals and concerts, check the events listings in the *Best in Dubrovnik* brochure, or ask the TI.

Also consider the folk dancing and market each Sunday morning at Čilipi, a small town near the airport. Dubrovnik-based companies offer excursions that include transportation there and back.

Nightlife

Dubrovnik's Old Town is one big, romantic parade of relaxed and happy people out strolling. The main drag is brightly lit and packed

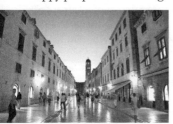

with shops, cafés, and bars, all open late. This is a fun scene. And if you walk away from the crowds or out on the port, you'll be alone with the magic of the Pearl of the Adriatic. Everything feels—and is—very safe after dark.

If you're looking for a memorable bar after dark, consider these:

▲▲▲Drinks with a View

Cold Drinks "Buža" offers, without a doubt, the most scenic spot for a drink. Perched on a cliff above the sea, clinging like a barnacle to the outside of the city walls, this is a peaceful, shaded getaway from the bustle of the Old Town...the perfect place to watch cruise ships disappear into the horizon. *Buža* means "hole in the wall"—and that's exactly what you'll have to go through

to get to this place. There are actually two different Bužas, with separate owners. My favorite is Buža II (which is actually the older and bigger of the pair). Filled with mellow tourists and bartenders pouring wine from tiny screw-top bottles into plastic cups, Buža II comes with castaway views and Frank Sinatra ambience. This is supposedly where Bill Gates hangs out when he visits Dubrovnik. When the seats fill up—as often happens around sunset—you can order a drink at the bar and walk down the stairs to enjoy it "on the rocks"...literally (26-45-kn drinks, summer daily 9:00-into the wee hours, closed mid-Nov-Jan). Buža I, with a different owner, is more casual, plays hip rather than romantic music, and has concrete stairs leading down to a beach on the rocks below. While lacking a bit of Buža II's panache—and its shade—Buža I is often a bit less crowded, making it a viable alternative (18-45-kn drinks).

Getting There: Both Bužas are high above the bustle of the main drag, along the seaward wall. To reach them from the cathedral area, hike up the grand staircase to St. Ignatius' Church, then go left to find the lane that runs along the inside of the wall. To find the classic Buža II, head right along the lane and look for the *Cold Drinks* sign pointing to a literal hole in the wall. For the hipper Buža I, go left along the same lane, and locate the hole in the wall with the *No Toples No Nudist* graffiti.

Wine Bar

D'Vino Wine Bar, just a few steps off the main drag, has a relaxed atmosphere and a knowledgeable but unpretentious approach—making it the handiest place in Dalmatia to sample and learn about Croatian wines. Run by gregarious Aussie-Croat Sasha and his capable staff (including Anita), this cozy bar sells more than 60 wines by the glass and lots more by the bottle. The emphasis is on Croatian wines by small-production wineries, but they also have a few international vintages. Each wine is well-described on the menu, and the staff is happy to guide you through your options—just tell them what you like. Sit in the tight interior or linger at the sidewalk tables (20-80-kn glasses—most around 25-35 kn, 50-kn wine flights; light food—70-kn 2-person cheese plate, 90-kn antipasti plate; daily 10:30-late, Palmotićeva 4a, tel. 020/321-130, www. dvino.net). Sasha takes wine-lovers on all-day wine tours to the Pelješac Peninsula; also ask about the organized tastings and other events in his adjacent tasting room.

Cocktails and People-Watching

The no-name square tucked behind cathedral is jammed with tables from a half-dozen different cafés, which fill with tourists and
locals each evening. Live jazz is provided nightly by **Jazz Caffè
Troubadour,** but as their drink prices are outlandish (80-100-kn
cocktails), most people prefer to sit at a nearby place where you can
hear the music nearly as well.

Nonenina, a few steps from the cathedral on Pred Dvorom,
is an outdoor lounge with big, overstuffed chairs at a fine vantage
point for people-watching. They brag that they serve 180 different
types of cocktails (60-80 kn, also 35-45-kn beers, daily 9:00-2:00
in the morning, shorter hours off-season, across from Rector's Palace).

The Gaffe Irish Pub, with a nice pubby interior and a small
courtyard, is a rollicking spot to drain a pint and watch some rugby
(Miha Pracata 4, mobile 098-196-2149, see full listing under "Eating in Dubrovnik," later).

Nightclubs

Dubrovnik has a variety of nightclubs. The streets branching off
from the Stradun are lined with several options with drinks and
pumping music, including **Sky Bar** (toward the water on Marojice
Kaboge) and **Africa** (toward the mountain at Vetranićeva 3). Just
follow the beat.

More places are near or just beyond the Ploče Gate at the
east end of town. Head under the Bell Tower, then up the street
past the Dominican Monastery. You'll pass the hole-in-the-
wall entrance (right) for the snobby, upscale **360°** cocktail bar
(www.360dubrovnik.com). Then, after crossing the bridge, look
(on the left) for the entrance to **Revelin**—a dance club that fills
one of the city wall's fortress towers (www.revelinclub-dubrovnik.
com). Then head out and up the street until you reach Banje Beach,
half of which is occupied by the **EastWest** dance club (www.ew-
dubrovnik.com). Note that some of these bars and clubs are more
exclusive and may charge admission on weekends.

Movies

The Old Town has a pair of movie theaters showing American
blockbusters (usually in English with Croatian subtitles, unless the
film's animated or for kids). The **Sloboda** cinema, right under the
Bell Tower on Luža Square, has comfortable seating and a high-
school auditorium vibe—nothing special. But in good weather,
head for the fun outdoor **Jadran** cinema, where you can lick ice
cream (B.Y.O.) while you watch a movie with a Dubrovnik-moun-
taintop backdrop. This is a cheap, casual, and very Croatian scene,
where people smoke and chat, and the neighbors sit in their win-

Sleep Code

(5 kn = about $1, €1 = about $1.30, country code: 385, area code: 020)

S = Single, **D** = Double/Twin, **T** = Triple, **Q** = Quad, **b** = bathroom. The modest tourist tax (about 7 kn per person, per night) is not included in these rates. Hotels generally accept credit cards and include breakfast in their rates, while most *sobe* accept only cash and don't offer breakfast. While rates are listed in euros, you'll pay in kunas. Everyone listed here speaks English.

Rates: If I've listed two sets of rates for an accommodation, I've noted when the second rate applies (generally off-season, Oct-May); if I've listed three sets of rates, separated by slashes, the first is for peak season (July-Aug), the second is for shoulder season (May-June and Sept-Oct), and the third is for off-season (Nov-April). The dates for seasonal rates vary by hotel, and prices can change without notice; verify the hotel's current rates online or by email. For the best prices, always book direct.

Price Ranges: To help you sort easily through these listings, I've divided the accommodations into three categories based on the price for a double room with bath in peak season:

  $$$ **Higher Priced**—Most rooms €95 or more.
    $$ **Moderately Priced**—Most rooms between €55-95.
     $ **Lower Priced**—Most rooms €55 or less.

dowsills to watch the movie (most nights in summer only, shows begin shortly after sundown; in the Old Town near the Pile Gate).

Sleeping in Dubrovnik

You basically have two options in Dubrovnik: a centrally located room in a private home *(soba);* or a resort hotel on a distant beach, a bus ride away from the Old Town. Since Dubrovnik hotels are generally a poor value, I highly recommend giving the *sobe* a careful look.

Be warned that the Old Town is home to many popular discos. My listings are quieter than the norm, but if you're finding a place on your own, you may discover you have a late-night soundtrack—particularly if you're staying near the Stradun.

No matter where you stay, prices are much higher mid-June through mid-September, and highest in July and August. Reserve ahead for these peak times. Most accommodations prefer to list their rates in euros (and I've followed suit), but you'll pay in kunas.

Sobe (Private Rooms): A Dubrovnik Specialty

In Dubrovnik, you'll almost always do better with a *soba* than with a hotel. All of my favorite *sobe* are run by friendly English-speaking Croatians and are inside or within easy walking distance of the Old Town. There's a range of places, from simple and cheap rooms where you'll share a bathroom, to downright fancy places with private facilities, air-conditioning, kitchenettes, and satellite TV, where you can be as anonymous as you like. Most *sobe* don't include breakfast, so I've listed some suggestions later, under "Eating in Dubrovnik."

To search from home, you can use the regular booking sites (such as TripAdvisor.com or Booking.com)—but if you want to book one of the places I've listed here, **please book direct** (by sending them an email), which saves both you and your host money. There's no point booking through a third party, which only adds a middleman to the process. Another good place to search is www.dubrovnikapartmentsource.com, run by an American couple and offering a range of carefully selected, well-described accommodations.

In the Old Town, Above the Stradun Promenade

These are some of my favorite accommodations in Dubrovnik. All are located at the top of town, high above the Stradun, and all are good values. The first four are within a few steps of each other, along a little block dubbed by some "Rickova ulica." If you don't mind the very steep hike up, you'll find this to be a wonderful enclave of hospitality. When one of these places is full, they work together to find space for you. The last two listings are a few blocks over, and nearly as nice (and equally steep). Because all of these hosts live off-site, be sure to let them know when you'll arrive so they can let you in.

$$ Villa Ragusa, offers my favorite rooms for the price in the Old Town. Pero and Valerija Carević have renovated a 600-year-old house at the top of town that was damaged during the war. The five

comfortable, modern rooms come with atmospheric old wooden beams, antique furniture, and thoughtful touches. There are three doubles with bathrooms (including a top-floor room with breathtaking Old Town views for no extra charge—request when you reserve) and two singles that share a bathroom (S-€40/€35/€25, Db-€80/€70/€50, €8 breakfast can be eaten here or more scenically at nearby Stradun café, cash only, air-con, lots of stairs with no elevator, free Wi-Fi, Žudioska ulica 15, mobile 098-765-634, www.villaragusadubrovnik.

DUBROVNIK

Old Town Hotels & Restaurants

To **14**

BJELOKOSICA

To Ferry Terminal,
Main Bus Station,
Cruise Ship Port,
Boninovo Bay &
Lapad Hotels

BRANITELJA

IZMEĐU VRTA

M. BLAŽIĆA

DUBROVNIKA

17   **34**

B DEPARTING
BUS

P

PILE

i   **B** ARRIVING
BUS

BUS TICKET
OFFICE

SV. ĐURĐA

PILE
GATE

WALL
TICKET
OFFICE

BIG
FOUNTAIN

31

BOKAR
FORTRESS

FORT OF
ST. LAWRENCE

MINČETA
TOWER

PUT IZA GRADA

MINČETE

FRANCISCAN
MONASTERY
MUSEUM

ST.
SAVIOR

GARGOYLE

A   STRADUN

GARIŠTE

ZLAT.

OD SIG.

19

MEDOVIĆA

16

29

30

ZA ROKOM

OD DOMINA

OD RUPA

RUPE
MUSEUM

CUBRAN.

BORĐ.

ŠIROKA

SERBIAN
ORTHODOX
CHURCH

JOSIPA

BOŽIDAREVIĆA

PUČA

27

OD KAŠTELA

28

STROSS-

A d r i a t i c   S e a

CITY

13

WALLS

OD

PALMOTIĆEVA

ANTUN-

STROSS-
MHA

N

100 Meters

100 Yards

Accommodations

1. Villa Ragusa & Apts. Paviša
2. Apartments Martecchini
3. Raič Apartments
4. Apartments Kovač
5. Plaza Apartments
6. Minerva Apartments
7. Fresh Sheets B&B
8. Apartments Amoret (4)
9. Old Town Garden Cottage
   & Studio
10. Karmen Apartments
11. Apartments Placa
12. Renata Zijadić Rooms
13. Fresh Sheets Hostel
14. To Benussi Rooms
15. Villa Adriatica
16. Hotel Stari Grad
17. Hilton Imperial Dubrovnik
18. To Viktorija Apartments,
    Hotel Excelsior &
    Grand Villa Argentina

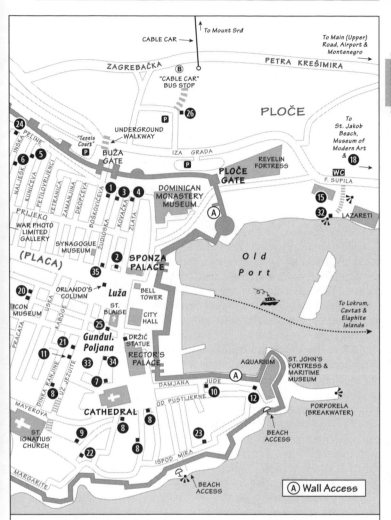

Eateries

- ⑲ Nishta Restaurant
- ⑳ Dalmatino & The Gaffe Irish Pub
- ㉑ Konoba Kamenice
- ㉒ Kopun Restaurant
- ㉓ Azur Restaurant
- ㉔ Lady Pi-Pi
- ㉕ Oliva Pizzeria
- ㉖ Tabasco Pizzeria
- ㉗ Spaghetteria Toni
- ㉘ Taj Mahal Restaurant
- ㉙ Buffet Škola
- ㉚ Dolce Vita Ice Cream
- ㉛ Orhan Restaurant
- ㉜ Komarda Restaurant
- ㉝ Produce Market
- ㉞ Konzum Groceries (2)
- ㉟ Dubrava Bistro

com, villa.ragusa@du.t-com.hr). Pero offers his guests airport transfers for a reasonable €30, and can drive you on an all-day excursion (such as to Montenegro or Mostar) for €250—if you can split this cost with other guests, it's a good value (same price for up to 6 people).

$$$ Apartments Paviša, next door to Villa Ragusa and run by Pero and Davorka Paviša, has three good, older-feeling rooms at the top of the Old Town (Db-€100/€70-80/€50, book direct by email for these prices, no breakfast, cash only, air-con, lots of stairs, free Wi-Fi, Žudioska ulica 19, mobile 098-427-399 or 098-175-2342, www.apartmentspavisa.com, pero.pavisa@gmail.com). They have two more rooms in the **Viktorija** neighborhood, about a 20-minute mostly uphill walk east of the Old Town. While it's a long-but-scenic walk into town, the views from these apartments are spectacular (same prices as in-town rooms, Frana Supila 59, bus stop nearby). Pero and Davorka also manage **Apartments Martecchini,** three units a bit closer to the main drag in the Old Town (small apartment-€100/€70-80/€50, bigger apartment-€120/€80-90/€60, biggest apartment-€130/€90-100/€60, prices depend on size and views, book direct by email for these prices, no breakfast, cash only, air-con, free Wi-Fi, www.apartmentsmartecchini.com).

$$ Ivana and Anita Raič are sisters renting three apartments with kitchenettes and modern, stylish flourishes (Db-€90/€70-80/€50, no breakfast, cash only, air-con, free Wi-Fi, Žudioska ulica 16, Ivana's mobile 098-996-0858, Anita's mobile 099-592-1568, www.apartments-raic.com, ivanaraic@gmail.com).

$$$ Apartments Kovač, a lesser value but decent, has two simple, older apartments just inside the upper wall (Db-€100/€90/€70, extra person-€10, no breakfast, cash only, air-con, free Wi-Fi, Peline 1, mobile 098-975-4284, www.apartmentskovac-dubrovnik.com, info@apartmentskovac-dubrovnik.com, Ana and Zvonko).

$$ Plaza Apartments, run by Lidija and Maro Matić, rents three clean, well-appointed, modern apartments on a plant-filled lane—the steepest and most appealing stretch of stairs leading up from the Stradun. Lidija's sweet personality is reflected in the cheerful rooms, which are a fine value if you don't mind the hike (Db-€90/€80/€70, big two-story seaview apartment-€110/€85/€75, cheaper Nov-April, these prices for Rick Steves readers, no breakfast, cash only, air-con, free Wi-Fi, all apartments have kitchenettes and laundry machines, climb the stairs past Dolce Vita gelato shop to Nalješkovićeva 22, tel. 020/321-493, mobile 091-517-7048, www.dubrovnik-online.com/apartment_plaza, lidydu@yahoo.com).

$$ Minerva Apartments has two cozy ground-floor units near the top of a similar lane, in the home of Dubravka Vidosavljević-Vučić (Db-€80/€75/€65, cheaper Nov-April, cash only, no break-

fast, air-con, free Wi-Fi, laundry machine, Antuninska 14, mobile 091-252-9677, duvivu@gmail.com).

In the Old Town, near the Cathedral and St. John's Fort

The following places are south of the Stradun, mostly clustering around the cathedral and St. John's Fort, at the end of the Old Port. To find the Karmen and Zijadić apartments from the cathedral, walk toward the big fort tower along the inside of the wall (follow signs for *akvarji*); for the Old Town Garden Cottage and Studio, climb up the grand staircase to the Jesuit St. Ignatius Church.

$$$ Fresh Sheets B&B, well-run by Canadian-Croatian couple Jon and Sanja, rents six bright, stylish, modern rooms in an ideally located building—next door to the cathedral and squeezed between two of Dubrovnik's most happening squares. Three of the rooms have shared bathrooms, and all have views over interesting squares and landmarks in the heart of the Old Town. While pricey, the hospitality, well-appointed rooms, and great location can make it worthwhile (D-€138-168, Db-€148-198, family suite-€308-338, price depends on season, for best prices book direct by email, air-con, free Wi-Fi, Bunićeva Poljana 6, tel. 091-896-7509, www.freshsheetsbedandbreakfast.com, beds@igotfresh.com).

$$$ Apartments Amoret, run by Branka Dabrović and her husband Ivica, are in all the guidebooks. The spendy but comfortable apartments, with furnishings that are a step up from the norm, are in four different buildings: two over Amoret Restaurant in front of the cathedral (at Restičeva 2); nine more sharing an inviting terrace on a quiet, untouristy lane a few blocks east (at Dinka Ranjine 5); and four more nearby (at Ilije Sarake 4 and Gradičeva 1). All four classes of apartments are comparably good; in every case, the furnishings are a tasteful mix of traditional and modern. Since Branka and Ivica don't live on-site, arrange a meeting time and place when you reserve ("regular" apartments-€100/€90/€80; "standard" apartments-€120/€110/€100; "superb" apartments-€140/€130/€110; "royal" apartments for up to 4-€160/€140/€120, extra person-€20; cheaper Nov-April, 30 percent more for 1-night stays, 20 percent more for 2-night stays, 10 percent more for 3-night stays, no breakfast, cash only, air-con, free Wi-Fi, mobile 091-530-4910, tel. 020/324-005, www.dubrovnik-amoret.com, amoret-dubrovnik@hotmail.com).

$$ Old Town Garden Cottage and Studio, conscientiously run by Roberto and his mother Marija, is unique and a top value. Hiding off of the big square in front of the Jesuit St. Ignatius Church is a very rare private garden—a peaceful oasis smack-dab in

the heart of the bustling city. Here you'll find two options: A cozy freestanding cottage that sleeps up to four (Db-€90/€80/€70, extra bed-€10); and an elegant, bright, spacious, artistically appointed studio apartment (€10 more). Each comes with its own outdoor space, where you're welcome to sit and relax, and even order food from the neighboring restaurant (the recommended Kopun)...very cool, particularly in a city with virtually no green space (€20 more for 1-night stay, cash only, air-con, kitchenette, free Wi-Fi, mobile 091-541-6637, bobdel70@yahoo.com). Robert and Marija also plan to renovate a roomy two-bedroom apartment (sans private garden)—ask them for details.

$$$ Karmen Apartments are well-run by a Brit named Marc and his Croatian wife Silva, who offer four welcoming apartments just inside the big fort. While a bit pricey, the apartments are big, well-equipped, and homey-feeling, each with a bathroom and kitchen. The decor is eclectic but tasteful, drawing from Marc and Silva's extensive art collection; the stairwell has a virtual mini-museum of historic Dubrovnik maps and documents (smaller apartment-€95/€75/€55, mid-sized apartment-€145/€110/€85, bigger apartment-€175/€120/€100, 5 percent discount for Rick Steves readers who book direct via email, usually 3-night minimum, no breakfast, cash only, air-con, free Wi-Fi, near the aquarium at Bandureva 1, tel. 020/323-433, mobile 098-619-282, www.karmendu.com, marc.van-bloemen@du.t-com.hr).

$$$ Apartments Placa (PLAH-tsah; not to be confused with Plaza Apartments, described earlier) is run by Tonči (TOHN-chee). He rents three apartments with some antique furnishings and some modern, overlooking the market square in the heart of the Old Town. You might get some early-morning noise from the market set-up, but the double-paned windows help, and the location is wonderfully central. Since Tonči lives elsewhere, clearly communicate your arrival time (Db-€100/€90/€80, cheaper Nov-April, no breakfast, cash only, no extra charge for 1- or 2-night stays, several flights of stairs, air-con, free Wi-Fi, Gundulićeva poljana 5, mobile 091-721-9202, www.dubrovnik-online.com/apartments_placa, tonci.korculanin@du.t-com.hr).

$$ Renata Zijadić, a friendly mom who speaks good English, offers three well-located rooms with slanting floors. One modern, sleek apartment enjoys grand views over the Old Port (€130/€100); a smaller, older, simpler double features an ornate old cabinet and no views (Db-€65/€55); and a top-floor apartment comes with low ceilings and fine vistas (€95/€85; second price is for June and Sept, cheaper Oct-May, no extra charge for 1- or 2-night stays, no breakfast, cash only, air-con, free Wi-Fi; follow signs for wall access and walk up the steps marked *ulica Stajeva* going over the

street to find Stajeva 1; tel. 020/323-623, www.dubrovnik-online. com/house_renata, renatadubrovnik@yahoo.com).

$ Fresh Sheets, a bright, stylish, and appealingly funky hostel run by fun-loving Jon and Sanja (who also run the recommended Fresh Sheets B&B), is your best inexpensive option in the Old Town. The 18 bunks (two 6-bed dorms, one 4-bed dorm, and a double room) sit above a tight but enjoyable common area. Located at the very top of Dubrovnik just inside the City Walls, it's a steep hike up from the main drag, but worth it if you enjoy youthful backpacker bonding (€22-36/bunk in a dorm, €28-38/person in a private room, likely closed Nov-March, free breakfast, free guest computer and Wi-Fi, lockers, kitchenette, Svetog Šimuna 15, mobile 091-799-2086, www.freshsheetshostel.com, beds@igotfresh. com).

Outside Pile Gate, Just West of the Old Town

While the area in front of the Pile Gate is a congested tourist hub, one of my favorite Dubrovnik lodgings sits high on the hill above the chaos, offering a warm welcome to travelers hardy enough to make the hike.

$$$ Jadranka and Milan Benussi rent two apartments in a quiet, traffic-free neighborhood. Their delightful stony-chic home, complete with a leafy terrace, is a steep 10-minute hike above the Old Town—close enough to be convenient, but far enough to take you away from the bustle and into a calm residential zone. Jadranka speaks good English, enjoys visiting with her guests, and gives her place a modern Croatian class unusual for a *soba*. This is one of your most comfortable home bases in Dubrovnik, if you don't mind the walk (small apartment-€110/€105/€100, big apartment with balcony-€120/€115/€110, cheaper Nov-April, 30 percent extra for 1-night stays, no breakfast, cash only, air-con, kitchenettes, free Wi-Fi, Miha Klaića 10, tel. 020/429-339, mobile 098-928-1300, www.dubrovnik-benussi.com, jadranka@dubrovnik-benussi.com). To find the Benussis, go to the big Hilton Hotel just outside the Pile Gate (across from the TI). Walk up the little stepped lane called Marijana Blažića at the upper-left corner of the Hilton cul-de-sac. When that lane dead-ends, go left up ulica Don Iva Bjelokosića (more steps) until you see a little church on the left. The Benussis' house is just before this church.

Beyond the Ploče Gate, East of the Old Town

To reach these options, you'll go through the Ploče Gate and walk along the road stretching east from the Old Town (with fine views back on the Old Port). This area is shared by giant waterfront luxu-

DUBROVNIK

ry hotels and residential areas, so it has a bit less character than the Old Town listings (which I prefer).

$$$ Apartments Paviša has two fine apartments in the Viktorija neighborhood about a 20-minute walk or short bus ride from town.

$$$ Villa Adriatica is overpriced, but has one of the finest views in Dubrovnik. Its four old-fashioned rooms sit above a travel agency and a family home just outside the Ploče Gate, a few steps from the Old Town. The rooms are antique-furnished, but have modern bathrooms, TVs, and air-conditioning. While impersonal and a lesser value than my other listings, it could be worth it just for the huge, shared terrace with priceless Old Port views, plus a common living room and kitchen furnished with museum-piece antiques. Teo manages the rooms; ask for him at the Perla Adriatic travel agency, just outside the Ploče Gate (Db-€110-120/€100-110/€80-90, cheaper Nov-April, price depends on size and view, no breakfast, cash only, air-con, free Wi-Fi in some areas, Frana Supila 4, mobile 098-334-500, tel. 020/411-962, www.villa-adriatica.net, booking@villa-adriatica.net, Tomšić family).

Hotels

If you must stay in a hotel, you have only a few good options. There are just two hotels inside the City Walls—and one of them charges $500 a night (Pucić Palace, www.thepucicpalace.com). Any big, resort-style hotel within walking distance of the Old Town will run you at least €200. These inflated prices drive most visitors to Boninovo Bay or the Lapad Peninsula, a bus ride west of the Old Town. In the mass-tourism tradition, many European visitors choose to take the half-board option at their hotel (i.e., dinner in the hotel restaurant). This can be convenient and a good value, but the Old Town is a much more atmospheric place to dine.

In and near the Old Town

$$$ Hotel Stari Grad knows it's the only real hotel option inside the Old Town—and charges accordingly. It has eight extremely stylish rooms a half-block off the Old Town's main drag. The rooftop terrace enjoys an amazing view over orange tiles. This place books up fast, so reserve early (Sb-€220/€160/€120, Db-€290/€230/€168, no extra charge for 1- or 2-night stays, includes breakfast, air-con, lots of stairs with no elevator, free Wi-Fi, Od Sigurate 4, tel. 020/322-244, www.hotelstarigrad.com, info@hotelstarigrad.com).

$$$ Hilton Imperial Dubrovnik, sitting regally just outside the Pile Gate, is the closest big hotel to the Old Town. This grand 19th-century building was recently overhauled to create 147 plush rooms. If you want predictable Hilton comfort at outlandish prices

a short walk from the Old Town, this is the place (Db-€250-300, less off-season, €60 extra for sea view, €70 extra for balcony but no view, €130 extra for balcony and view, most rates include breakfast, air-con, elevator, free Wi-Fi in lobby, pay Wi-Fi in rooms, parking-€27/night, Marijana Blažića 2, tel. 020/320-320,www.hilton. com, sales.dubrovnik@hilton.com).

$$$ Adriatic Luxury Hotels is a chain with several plush hotels near Dubrovnik. Location-wise, the most enticing are **Hotel Excelsior** (Frana Supila 12) and **Grand Villa Argentina** (Frana Supila 14)—which are a scenic 10-minute walk outside the Ploče Gate, east of the Old Town—as well as the Hotel Bellevue (described in the next section). For top-of-the-top luxury lodgings without regard for the price tag, browse their options at www.adriaticluxuryhotels.com (figure a peak-season rack rate of Db-€500-600—but you'll rarely pay that much).

Near Boninovo Bay

Boninovo Bay (boh-NEE-noh-voh) is your best bet for an affordable and well-located hotel. Above this bay are Dubrovnik's only three-star hotels within walking distance of the Old Town (not to mention the city's only official youth hostel). These places offer slightly better prices and closer proximity to the Old Town than the farther-out Lapad Bay resorts. They're on or near the water, but don't have views of the Old Town (which is around the bend). Boninovo Bay is an uphill 20-minute walk or five-minute bus ride from the Old Town (straight up Branitelja Dubrovnika). Once you're comfortable with the buses, the location is great: Any bus that leaves the Pile Gate stops first at Boninovo Bay. You'll see the bay on your left as you climb the hill, then get off at the stop after the traffic light (or stay on bus #4, which stops even closer to the hotels). To reach the hotels from the Boninovo bus stop, go up Pera Čingrije (the busy road running along the top of the cliff overlooking the sea). There's a super little bakery, Pekarnica Klas, on the right (across the street from Hotel Bellevue).

$$$ Hotel Bellevue has a striking location, with its back against the cliff rising up from Boninovo Bay and an elevator plunging directly to its own pebbly beach. Its 91 top-notch rooms—all but two with sea views, many with balconies—offer upscale woodgrain elegance (standard Db-generally €250/€220, less Nov-April, very flexible rates, €50 more for balcony, air-con, elevator, free guest computer and Wi-Fi, Pera Čingrije 7, tel. 020/330-000, www.hotel-bellevue.hr, welcome@hotel-bellevue.hr).

$$$ Hotel R, a homey enclave with just 10 rooms, feels friendlier and less greedy than all the big resort hotels. Well-run by the Rešetar family, it's a decent small-hotel value (Sb-€90/€75/€60, Db-€140/€115/€90, closed Nov-Easter, 10 percent more for balco-

ny, half-board-€13, air-con, free Wi-Fi, just beyond the big Hotel Lero at Iva Vojnovića 16, tel. 020/333-200, www.hotel-r.hr, help-desk@hotel-r.hr).

$$$ Hotel Lero, 250 yards up the street from the bus stop, has 155 recently renovated rooms and a fine outdoor pool. Choose between so-so sea views with some road noise, or quieter back rooms (soft rates, but generally Sb-€110/€85, Db-€140/€106, cheaper mid-Oct-April; in busy times, you may be quoted more than these rates—try asking for a better deal; "executive" rooms with balcony not worth the extra €30/person, air-con, elevator, pay guest computer, free Wi-Fi, half-board-€10, wellness and fitness center, Iva Vojnovića 14, tel. 020/341-333, www.hotel-lero.hr, sales@hotel-lero.hr).

$ Dubrovnik's official **Youth Hostel** is quiet, modern, and well-run by proud manager Laura. It's institutional, with 82 beds in 19 fresh, woody dorms and few extra hostel amenities (bunk in 4- to 6-bed dorm-€16-21 depending on season, €1.50 more for nonmembers, includes sheets, includes breakfast, air-con in restaurant and halls but not in rooms, free guest computer and Wi-Fi; reception open daily May-Oct 7:00-4:00 in the morning, Nov-April 8:00-14:00 & 18:00-20:00; 2:00 a.m. curfew in summer, none in winter; up the steps at ulica bana Jelačića 15-17 to ulica Vinka Sagrestana 3, tel. 020/423-241, www.hfhs.hr, dubrovnik@hfhs.hr). From the Boninovo bus stop, go down Pera Čingrije toward Hotel Bellevue, but take the first right uphill onto ulica bana Jelačića and look for signs up to the hostel on your left, on ulica Vinka Sagrestana. Several houses nearby rent rooms to those who prefer a double...and pick off would-be hostelers as they approach.

Eating in Dubrovnik

Dubrovnik disappoints diners with high prices, surly service, and mediocre quality. With the constant influx of deep-pocketed tourists corrupting greedy restaurateurs, places here tend to go downhill faster than a game of marbles on the *Titanic*. Promising new restaurants open all the time, but most quickly fade, and what's great one year can be miserable the next. Therefore, lower your expectations, take my suggestions with a grain of salt, and ask around locally for what's good this month. Don't bother looking for a "local" favorite anywhere near the Old Town—people who live here eat out at restaurants in the 'burbs. The good news is that it's atmospheric. Anywhere you dine, breezy

outdoor seating is a no-brainer, and scrawny, adorable kittens beg for table scraps. In general, seafood restaurants are good only at seafood; if you want pasta, go to a pasta place.

In the Old Town

Nishta ("Nothing"), featuring a short menu of delicious vegetarian-fusion cuisine with Asian flair, offers a welcome change of pace from the Dalmatian seafood-pasta-pizza rut. Busy Swiss owner/chef Gildas cooks, while his wife Ruža and their staff cheerfully serve a steady stream of return diners. This tiny place—which has been a reliable and affordable crowd-pleaser for years—has just a few cramped indoor and outdoor tables. Even if you're not a vegetarian, it's worth a visit; reserve the day ahead in peak season (35-45-kn starters, 65-85-kn main courses, Mon-Sat 11:30-22:00, closed Sun and Jan-Feb, on the restaurant-clogged Prijeko street—near the Pile Gate end of the street, tel. 020/322-088).

Dalmatino offers some of the best traditional Dalmatian cooking in the city, combined with a few modern twists. This is quality food and attentive service at prices that won't blow your budget. South African-Croatian owner Robert prides himself on cooking each dish to order; while this may take a few minutes longer, you can taste the results. While there are only a few outdoor tables tucked along the alley, there's a spacious, classy-but-not-stuffy dining room (50-160-kn pastas, 80-160-kn main dishes, daily 11:00-23:00, Miha Pracata 6, tel. 020/323-070, http://dalmatino-dubrovnik.com). Don't confuse Dalmatino's tables with its neighbors'.

On the Market Square: The square called Gundulićeva poljana, tucked two short blocks from the Stradun, is filled with outdoor tables. **Konoba Kamenice,** a no-frills fish restaurant, is a local institution offering inexpensive, fresh, and good meals on a charming market square, as central as can be in the Old Town. On the limited menu, the seafood dishes are excellent (try their octopus salad, even if you don't think you like octopus), while the few non-seafood dishes are uninspired. Some of the waitstaff are notorious for their playfully brusque service, but loyal patrons happily put up with it. Arrive early, or you'll have to wait (45-75-kn main courses, daily 8:00-23:00, until 22:00 off-season, Gundulićeva poljana 8, tel. 020/323-682).

Kopun, with picturesque seating on the big square in front of the Jesuit St. Ignatius Church, serves up regional specialties from Dubrovnik and elsewhere in Croatia—all well-explained in the menu. Several dishes make use of the restaurant's namesake, *kopun*—a rooster that's castrated young and plumps up. While a bit pricey and new to the scene, this place is off to a promising start (60-130-kn pastas and starters, 80-160-kn main courses, daily

11:00-23:00, Poljana Ruđera Boškovića 7, tel. 020/323-969, www. restaurantkopun.com).

Azur, tucked high inside the City Walls (near the two Buža cocktail bars), offers relief to travelers needing a break from the typical Croatian menu. The sort-of-Asian-fusion menu might not fly in big cosmopolitan cities, but here on the Croatian coast, appreciative international diners cling to it like a sesame-oil life preserver (45-75-kn starters and snacks, 90-150-kn main dishes, daily 11:00-24:00, Pobijana 10, tel. 020/324-806).

Lady Pi-Pi, named for a comical, anatomically correct, and slightly off-putting statue out front, sits high above town just inside the wall. The food, prepared on an open grill, is just an excuse to sit out on their vine-covered terrace, with several tables overlooking the rooftops of Dubrovnik. Come early or be prepared to line up (70-75-kn pastas, 65-150-kn main dishes, daily May-Sept 9:00-24:00, closed Oct-April and in bad weather, Peline b.b., tel. 020/321-288).

Pizza: Dubrovnik seems to have a pizzeria on every corner. Little separates the various options—just look for a menu and outdoor seating option that appeals to you. **Oliva Pizzeria,** just behind St. Blaise's Church, puts out consistently good food (40-70-kn pizzas, Lučarica 5, daily 10:00-24:00, tel. 020/324-594; don't mistake this for their sister restaurant next door, Oliva Gourmet, with a pricier non-pizza menu). Around the side is a handy take-out window for a bite on the go. Close to the Old Town, but just far away to be frequented mostly by locals, **Tabasco Pizzeria** is tucked at the corner of the parking lot beneath the cable-car station. Unpretentious and affordable, this is the place to come if the pizza is more important than the setting—though the outdoor terrace does have views of the City Walls...over a sea of parked cars (40-50-kn pizzas, 70-85-kn "jumbo" pizzas, daily 9:00-23:00, Hvarska 48A, tel. 020/429-595).

Pasta: **Spaghetteria Toni** is popular with natives and tourists. While nothing fancy, it offers good pastas at reasonable prices. Choose between the cozy 10-table interior or the long alley filled with outdoor tables (50-95-kn pastas, 55-70-kn salads, daily in summer 11:00-23:00, closed Sun in winter, closed Jan, Nikole Božidarevića 14, tel. 020/323-134).

Bosnian Cuisine: For a break from Croatian fare, try the grilled meats and other tasty Bosnian dishes at the misnamed **Taj Mahal.** Though the service can be lacking, the menu offers an enticing taste of the Turkish-flavored land to the east. Choose between the tight interior, which feels like a Bosnian tea house, or tables out on the alley (50-65-kn salads, 60-145-kn main courses, daily 10:00-24:00, Nikole Gučetića 2, tel. 020/323-221).

Sandwiches: **Buffet Škola** is a rare bit of pre-glitz Dubrovnik

just a few steps off the Stradun, serving take-away or sit-down sandwiches on homemade bread. Squeeze into the hole-in-the-wall interior, or sit at one of the outdoor tables (25-30 kn, 60-80-kn ham and cheese boards, daily 8:00-22:00 or 23:00, Antuninska 1, tel. 020/321-096).

Ice Cream: Dubrovnik has lots of great *sladoled*, but locals swear by the stuff at **Dolce Vita.** In addition to good ice cream, they have tasty crêpes (daily 9:00-24:00, a half-block off the Stradun at Nalješkovićeva 1A, tel. 020/321-666).

The Old Town's "Restaurant Row," Prijeko Street: The street called Prijeko, a block toward the mainland from the Stradun promenade, is lined with outdoor, tourist-oriented eateries—each one with a huckster out front trying to lure in diners. (Many of them aggressively try to snare passersby down on the Stradun, as well.) Don't be sucked into this vortex of bad food at outlandish prices. The only place worth seeking out here is Nishta (described earlier); the rest are virtually guaranteed to disappoint. Still, it can be fun to take a stroll along here—the atmosphere is lively, and the sales pitches are entertainingly desperate.

Just Outside the Old Town, with a View

Orhan Restaurant, overlooking the tranquil cove at the Pile neighborhood outside the Old Town, feels just beyond the tourist crush. It features disinterested service and unremarkable food, but great views on a large terrace (reserve a seat here in advance). Watch the people walk the City Walls across the cove. This is a handy spot for a scenic breakfast (70-115-kn pastas, 95-160-kn main courses, daily 8:00-23:00, cash only, Od Tabakarije 1, tel. 020/414-183, www.restaurant-orhan.com).

Komarda serves up forgettable food on a memorably romantic terrace, with views of Dubrovnik's walls and Old Port. Tables are scattered around a tranquil garden just above the sea and a concrete beach. As there's no point eating here unless you have a good view, consider dropping by early in the day to pick out and reserve the table of your choice for dinner (75-90-kn pastas, 90-150-kn main courses, daily 7:00-2:00 in the morning, reservations essential in summer, mobile 098-428-239, http://komarda.hr). To find it, exit the Old Town through the Ploče Gate (east). After walking through the final fortification, you'll reach a block of travel agencies. Once you pass these, look for the stairs down to Komarda, on the right.

Picnic Tips

Dubrovnik's lack of great restaurant options makes it a perfect place to picnic. You can shop for fresh fruits and veggies at the open-air produce market (each morning near the cathedral, on the

square called Gundulićeva Poljana). Supplement your picnic with grub from the cheap **Konzum grocery store** (one location on the market square near the produce-vendors: Mon-Sat 7:00-20:00, Sun 7:00-13:00; another near the bus stop just outside Pile Gate: Mon-Sat 7:00-20:00, Sun 8:00-13:00). Good picnic spots include the shaded benches overlooking the Old Port; the Porporela breakwater (beyond the Old Port and fort—comes with a swimming area, sunny no-shade benches, and views of Lokrum Island); and the green, welcoming park in what was the moat just under the Pile Gate entry to the Old Town.

Breakfast

If you're sleeping in a *soba*, you'll likely be on your own for breakfast. Fortunately, you have plenty of cafés and pastry shops to choose from, and your host probably has a favorite he or she can recommend. In the Old Town, **Dubrava Bistro**—which locals call "Snack Bar"—has great views and fine outdoor seating at the most colorful end of the Stradun. While the ham resembles Spam and the continental breakfast is paltry, you can't beat the real estate. Locals who hang out here—catching up with their friends as they stroll by—call this their low-tech version of "Facebook" (basic 38-46-kn egg dishes, 23-kn caffè lattes; you'll pay 25 percent less if you sit inside—but then there's no point eating here; daily 8:00-24:00, Placa 6, tel. 020/321-229). For better food in a less atmospheric setting, **The Gaffe Irish Pub** has a good menu of breakfast options (36-45 kn, served daily 9:00-11:00, Miha Pracata 4, tel. 020/640-152). In the Pile neighborhood, I like **Restaurant Orhan,** right on the cove (described earlier; 50 kn for omelet or continental breakfast, served daily 8:00-11:00). Some of the other restaurants listed in this section (including **Konoba Kamenice**) also serve breakfast. Not many places serve before 9:00 or 10:00; if you'll be departing early, stock up on groceries the night before.

Dubrovnik Connections

Note that the boats listed here leave from Dubrovnik's Port Gruž, a bus ride away from the Old Town (described earlier, under "Arrival in Dubrovnik—By Car Ferry or Catamaran"). Be aware that eventual redevelopment of the port area will likely move the Jadrolinija ferries and *Nona Ana* catamaran departure point out to the far end of the port, under the big bridge. If I've listed a range of prices, the specific fare depends on the season.

From Dubrovnik by Big Jadrolinija Car Ferry: From June to September only, the big boats leave Dubrovnik twice weekly in the morning and go to **Sobra** on Mljet Island (1.25 hours, plus a

1.25-hour bus ride to the national park), **Korčula** (4.5 hours), **Stari Grad** on Hvar Island (8.75 hours), **Split** (11 hours), and **Rijeka** (21 hours including overnight from Split to Rijeka). These ferries do not run October through May (confirm schedules at www.jadrolinija.hr).

From Dubrovnik by Speedy *Nona Ana* **Catamaran:** This handy service connects Dubrovnik to popular islands to the north (Mljet, Korčula, and Lastovo). This schedule is subject to change from year to year, so carefully confirm the details before planning your trip. In the summer (June-Sept), the boat departs Dubrovnik each morning and heads for **Sobra** (1 hours) and **Polače** (1.5 hours) on Mljet Island. In the peak months of July and August, it sometimes continues on to **Korčula** (4/week, 2.25 hours) and **Lastovo Island** (2/week, 3.5 hours). In the winter (Oct-May), the boat goes only to Sobra and Polače on Mljet—not all the way to Korčula or Lastovo. The catamaran leaves from Dubrovnik's Port Gruž. Tickets—which can sell out, especially in peak season—are sold at the kiosk next to the boat. The ticket window opens one hour before departure, but in peak season, it's smart to show up 1.5 hours ahead to be sure you get on the boat. Confirm schedules—and get advice about how early to show up to get tickets—at the Dubrovnik TI, or check www.gv-line.hr.

By Bus to: Split (at least hourly, typically at the top of the hour, less off-season, 3.5-5 hours), **Korčula** (summer: 2/day at 9:00 and 15:00; off-season: Mon-Sat 1/day at 15:00, Sun 2/day at 15:00 and 18:00; 3.5 hours; also consider the shuttle-bus service described next), **Rijeka** (4/day, 12.5-13 hours), **Zagreb** (10/day including some overnight options, 10 hours), **Kotor** in Montenegro (3/day in summer, 2/day in winter, 2.5 hours), **Mostar** (3/day, 4-5 hours), **Sarajevo** (4/day in summer, 2/day in winter, 5-6.5 hours; includes a night bus in summer only at 22:30), **Pula** and **Rovinj** (1/day overnight departing at 15:30, 15 hours to Pula, 16 hours to Rovinj). As usual, schedules are subject to change—confirm locally before making the trip to the bus station. For bus information, check www.libertasdubrovnik.com or call 060-305-070 (a pricey toll line, but worth it).

By Shuttle Bus to Korčula: Korčula-based Korkyra Info Travel Agency runs a handy door-to-door shuttle service from your Dubrovnik accommodations to Korčula; reserve ahead (typically departs at 14:00 and at 17:00, daily May-Sept, by request only off-season, may stop briefly in Ston if you want, 2 hours, 150 kn one-way, mobile 091-571-4355, www.korkyra.info, info@korkyra.info). Korkyra Info can also arrange for a private transfer, including stops (such as wine-tastings and a quick stop at Ston; €140 for up to 8 people).

By Plane: To quickly connect remote Dubrovnik with the

rest of your trip, consider a cheap flight. For information on Dubrovnik's airport, see "Arrival in Dubrovnik—By Plane," earlier.

Can I Get to Greece from Dubrovnik? Your best bet is to
fly (though there are no direct flights, aside from the occasional
charter flight from Dubrovnik to Athens—you'll generally have to
transfer elsewhere in Europe). Even though Croatia and Greece are
nearly neighbors, no direct boats connect them, and the overland
connection is extremely long and rugged.

What About Italy? Flying is the easiest option, though there
are only a few direct flights (on Croatia Airlines to Rome or Venice; or on easyJet to Rome or Milan). You can take a direct night
boat from Dubrovnik to Bari, or head to Split for more boat connections. The overland connection is overly long (figure 5 hours to
Split, then 5 hours to Zagreb, then 7 hours to Venice).

NEAR DUBROVNIK

Excursions from Dubrovnik's Old Port • Cavtat • Trsteno Arboretum • Pelješac Peninsula • Mljet National Park

The more time you spend here, the clearer it becomes: Dubrovnik isn't just a town, it's an entire region. Stretching up and down the glimmering Dalmatian Coast from Dubrovnik are a variety of worthwhile getaways. Just offshore from the city's Old Town—and accessible via scenic boat trip from its historic port—are enticing islands and villages, where time stands still for lazy vacationers: the playground islet of Lokrum and the archipelago of the Elaphite Islands. The serene resort town of Cavtat, just south of Dubrovnik, has some of the best art treasures of this part of Dalmatia (including a gorgeous mausoleum designed by Ivan Meštrović). To the north is a lush arboretum called Trsteno, with a playful fountain, a 600-year-old aqueduct, a villa, a chapel...and, of course, plants galore. Poking into the Adriatic is the vineyard-covered Pelješac Peninsula, anchored by the mighty little town of Ston. And out at sea is the sparsely populated island called Mljet, a third of which is carefully protected as one of Croatia's most appealing national parks, where you can hike, bike, boat, and swim to your heart's content. Best of all, there's no better place to "come home to" than Dubrovnik—after a busy day exploring the coastline, strolling the Stradun to unwind is particularly sweet.

Planning Your Time

Give yourself at least a full day and two nights to experience Dubrovnik itself. But if you can spare the time, set up in Dubrovnik for several nights and use your extra days for some of these excursions. (This also gives you the luxury of keeping an eye on the weather reports and saving the most weather-dependent activities for the sunniest days.) Use a map to strategically line up these at-

Dubrovnik Day Trips at a Glance

The international excursions to Bosnia-Herzegovina and Montenegro—which are worth considering for overnight stops—are covered in their own chapters.

In Bosnia-Herzegovina

▲▲▲**Mostar** The side-trip with the highest degree of cultural hairiness—but, for many, also the greatest reward—lies to the east, in Bosnia-Herzegovina. With its iconic Old Bridge, intriguing glimpse of European Muslim lifestyles, and still-vivid examples of war damage, Mostar is unforget-

table. Allow a full day or more (best reached by bus or car).

Međugorje Devout Catholics may want to consider a trip to this pilgrimage site in Bosnia-Herzegovina, with a holy hill that some believe is visited regularly by an apparition of the Virgin Mary. Allow a full day or more (best reached by car or bus).

In Montenegro

▲▲**The Bay of Kotor** For rugged coastal scenery that arguably rivals anything in Croatia, head south of the border to Montenegro. The Bay of Kotor is a dramatic, fjord-like inlet crowned by the historic town of Kotor, with twisty Old World lanes, one of Europe's best town walls, and oodles of atmosphere. Allow a full day or more (best reached by car or bus).

The Montenegrin Interior A visit to Montenegro's scruffy but historic former capital, Cetinje, comes with a twisty drive up a moun-

tain road and across a desolate, forgotten-feeling plateau. Allow a full day or more (best reached by car).

Budva Riviera Montenegro's best stretch of sandy beaches isn't worth a special trip, but it's a fun excuse for a drive if you've got extra time to kill. The highlight is the famous resort peninsula of Sveti Stefan. Allow a full day or more (best reached by car).

On the Mainland near Dubrovnik

▲**Cavtat** A charming resort/
beach town, unassuming Cavtat
holds a pair of wonderful and
very local art experiences: an
elaborate mausoleum designed
by the sculptor Ivan Meštrović,
and the house and museum of
Cavtat-born modern painter
Vlaho Bukovac. Allow a few
hours (best reached by boat or bus).

▲**Pelješac Peninsula** This long, narrow, scenic spit of land—
between the main coastal road and Korčula Island—is a favorite
of wine lovers, who can joyride through its vineyards and sample
its product. Allow a half-day to a full day (best reached by car).

▲**Trsteno Arboretum** Plant lovers will enjoy this surprisingly engaging botanical garden just outside Dubrovnik, punctuated by
a classical-style fountain and aqueduct. Allow a half-day (best
reached by bus or car).

Ston A small town with giant fortifications, Ston (on the Pelješac
Peninsula) is worth a short stop to scramble up its extensive walls.
Allow an hour (best reached by car or bus).

Off the Coast of Dubrovnik

▲**Mljet National Park** While this largely undeveloped island is
time-consuming to reach from Dubrovnik, Mljet offers an opportunity to romp on an island without all those tacky tourist towns.
This is for serious nature lovers eager to get away from civilization. Allow a full day (best reached by boat).

Lokrum Island The most convenient excursion from Dubrovnik,
this little island—just a short hop offshore from the Old Port—is a
good chance to get away from (some of) the tourists. Allow a few
hours (best reached by boat).

Elaphite Islands This inviting archipelago offers a variety of island
experiences without straying too far from Dubrovnik. With more
time, Korčula (for a small town) or Mljet (for a back-to-nature
experience) are better, but the "Elafiti" are more convenient.
Allow a half-day to a full day (best reached by boat).

tractions—for example, you can easily do Trsteno, Ston, and the Pelješac Peninsula on a drive between Dubrovnik and Korčula, while Cavtat pairs nicely with a trip to the airport or Montenegro.

I've listed these day trips in order of ease from Dubrovnik—the farther down the list, the more difficult to reach (Montenegro and Mostar, the most time-consuming, are covered in their own chapters). Choose the trips that sound best to you, and ask locals and other travelers for their impressions...or for new leads.

Getting There

Cavtat and the Elaphite Islands are easy to reach by private **excursion boat** from Dubrovnik's Old Port; Cavtat also works by bus. A **city-run boat** links the Old Port to nearby Lokrum. **Public ferries** connect Dubrovnik's Port Gruž to the Elaphite Islands (the

Near Dubrovnik

HERZEGOVINA

Nevesinje

Gacko

Bileća

Bilećko Lake

Trebinje

Nikšić

MONTENEGRO

Dubrovnik

Lokrum

Cavtat

Ćilipi

Debeli Brijeg

Perast

Kotor

Podgorica

KONAVLE

Herceg Novi

Cetinje

CROATIA

Bay of Kotor

Konfin

Budva

Budva Riviera

Skadarsko Lake

Sveti Stefan

25 Kilometers

25 Miles

most appealing is Lopud). The other destinations are farther afield, best reached by **boat** (Mljet) or by **car** or **bus** (Montenegro, Mostar, Trsteno, Pelješac Peninsula).

I've listed public transportation options for each, but consider **renting a car** for the day. Or you can splurge for your own **private driver**; to make it more affordable, rally other travelers to accompany you and split the cost.

Alternatively, a variety of travel agencies in Dubrovnik offer **guided excursions** (by bus and/or boat) to nearby destinations. Popular itineraries include everything mentioned in this chapter, plus Korčula and others (figure €30-100/person, depending on

the itinerary). While these excursions can be a convenient way to see otherwise difficult-to-reach destinations, the quality can be hit-or-miss. The two dominant agencies—Atlas and Elite—are efficient mass-tourism machines, which means things work well, but you'll be jammed into buses and boats until every seat is filled. The guides typically do their spiel (mostly a memorized script) in several languages. Smaller outfits offer a more casual experience with more personal attention, but lack the polish of the big players. Unfortunately, since this scene is constantly evolving, it's difficult to recommend one company in particular. Look around for flyers and ask locals for their best tips—but be aware that many smaller agencies simply sell seats on the big Atlas and Elite trips.

Excursions from Dubrovnik's Old Port

At Dubrovnik's salty Old Port, captains set up tiny booths to hawk touristy boat trips. It's fun to chat with them, page through their sun-faded photo albums, and see if they can sell you on a short cruise. In addition to the islands noted below, you can also take a boat from the Old Port to **Cavtat** (described later).

Panorama Cruise

The basic option is a 45-minute "panorama cruise" out into the water and back again (75 kn, departures about every hour). You'll loop around the city walls—which offer a unique view on Dubrovnik's stout defenses—and do a circuit around Lokrum Island as well. Understandably, these cruises are most popular at or shortly before sunset.

Several companies offer these cruises, using a variety of vessels—modern, old-fashioned, glass-bottomed, you name it. You could just hop on whichever one is departing next, but I enjoy the **Sv. Ivan,** a cargo boat dating from 1878. Prowling its decks and leaning back against rope railings just feels right in this seafaring town. They also offer a 20 percent discount to readers of this book (that is, you'd pay 60 kn for a 45-minute panorama cruise; look for their desk among the many sales kiosks at the Old Port, mobile 099-441-2054, www.dubrovnik-panoramacruise.com).

Lokrum Island

This island, just offshore from the Old Town, provides a handy escape from the city. When the Old Town just gets too jam-packed with tourists, locals hop a boat out here for some peace and quiet.

They call it the "Island of Love," because it offers many secluded spots where courting couples can get away. The main attractions here are hiking (on shaded paths that curl up, over, and around the thickly wooded island) and bathing (on jagged, rocky beaches—many of which are designated nude beaches).

NEAR DUBROVNIK

Getting There: Lokrum is reachable only by an official city-run boat, which departs twice hourly from the end of the pier in Dubrovnik's Old Port (60 kn round-trip, 15-minute crossing, runs April-Oct 9:00-18:00, mid-June-Aug until 20:00, none Nov-March).

Visiting the Island: From the Lokrum boat dock, walk up to the pink building—the visitors center—to pick up a map of the island for 21 kn. Continuing up, you'll reach a fork: To head across the narrow middle of the island, continue straight ahead, where you'll find a monastery-turned-Habsburg-palace, a small botanical garden, uneven rocks that lead to ladders where you can ease yourself into the sea, and a small lake (fed by an underwater canal from the sea) called the "Dead Sea" (Mrtvo More) that's suitable for swimming. Or you can hook left and curl around the cove to the island's most popular beach, on the Bay of Portoč, that's famous for its nude sunbathing. If you'd like to (carefully) subject skin that's never seen the sun to those burning rays, follow the *FKK* signs from the boat dock for about five minutes to the slabs of waterfront rock, where naturists feel right at home. Continuing past this beach, you can work your way up and over to the other side of the island (on very rocky trails).

For an even more serious hike, head right from the boat dock for the two-hour hike that goes all the way around the island, and consider a detour to its highest point (at 315 feet above sea level), capped by Fort Royal, an old Austro-Hungarian military fortification.

You'll find a few cafés scattered around the island, mostly along the main path from the boat dock to the monastery complex.

Elaphite Islands (Elafiti)

This 13-island archipelago, just north of Dubrovnik, is popular among day-trippers because it allows you to hit three different islands in a single day: Koločep, Lopud, and Šipan. These "Deer Islands" (supposedly named for their shape—though I don't see it)

are a bit overhyped and can't hold a candle to some of the more distant Dalmatian islands, such as Korčula and Hvar. Skip them unless you've got time to kill, need a break from Dubrovnik's crowds, and want a lazy day cruising Dalmatia. Along the way, you'll discover fishing ports, shady forests, inviting beaches, and forgotten escape mansions of old Dubrovnik aristocracy. The two smaller islands (Koločep and Lopud) are traffic-free, making them a restful backwater getaway. While there's little to actually see on each island, each church, beach, and walking path is well-signed, making it easy to just wander. Bring decent footwear for hiking uneven trails, and pack along swimwear if you like. While time is short on land, each island has some sort of beach relatively near the boat dock; on a hot day, you could just wear your swimsuit on the boat and make a point to take a dip at each stop.

Getting There: The easiest way to cruise the Elafiti is to buy an excursion at Dubrovnik's Old Port, which usually includes a "fish picnic" cooked up by the cap-tain as you cruise (about 250 kn with lunch, several boats depart daily around 10:30-11:00, return around 15:45-19:30; so they can be sure to buy enough food, companies prefer you to reserve and pay a 50-kn de-posit the day before). For a bigger and more memorable ship—and a more

corporate experience—you can book an excursion through Atlas to go on their *Karaka*, a modern replica of the traditional cargo ships once built here in Dubrovnik (www.atlas-croatia.com). Regard-less of which company you go with, you generally spend about two to three hours on Lopud and about an hour each on Koločep and Šipan, with about 2.5 hours on the boat. To get to the Elaphite Is-lands without a tour (on a cheap ferry), you'll sail from Dubrovnik's less convenient Port Gruž.

I've described the islands below from nearest to farthest from Dubrovnik; various excursions may visit the islands in a different order than this.

Koločep

The nearest island to Dubrovnik, and the sleepiest, Koločep's har-bor arcs away from its boat dock. Walking around it, you'll quickly reach a small main square with al fresco cafés spilling out onto the seawall; beyond that is a sandy beach in front of a hotel, with rentable chairs. Near the boat dock, well-signed steps lead up into the hills, passing several small churches as well as Koločep's little museum of ecclesiastical art (the only museum I saw on the Elafi-ti). On a short visit, you'll barely have time to stroll the harbor; if your excursion leaves you here a bit longer, consider a low-impact

hike over the spine of the island to the village on the opposite side, Gornje Čelo (about 1.5 miles away). You'll climb up stairs past an old guard tower, pass a pink stucco church near a cemetery, then follow the narrow path between high stone walls and past olive groves. You'll wind down to a little port town with an inviting beach; looping around to Placet takes you to a wall of dramatic cliffs. *Donje Čelo* signs lead you back to your boat.

▲Lopud

The main attraction of the Elaphite Islands, Lopud feels like a humbler Cavtat without all the great art. But Lopud's trump card is its fine beaches, including one of the nicest beaches in the area (a long hike or short golf-cart ride away). Lopud feels a bit bigger, more vital, and more inviting than the other two islands. Most excursions give it far more time than Koločep or Šipan; it's also accessible by public ferry, and may be worth considering for an all-day beach getaway.

Your boat docks near the stout Franciscan monastery, which pokes out into the sea, dominating the townscape. From there, a picturesque promenade winds past several beaches (sand, then pebbles, then sand) and the entrance to a lush garden, before stretching all the way to a luxury hotel. Near the boat dock, you'll find a **TI** (July-Aug Mon, Wed, and Fri-Sun 8:00-20:00, Tue and Thu 8:00-13:00 & 18:00-20:00; May-June and Sept-mid-Oct Sat-Thu 8:00-13:00 & 17:00-19:00, closed Fri; closed mid-Oct-April; Obala Iva Kuljevana 12, tel. 020/759-086).

For beach bums, the main attraction on Lopud is at the other end of the island: **Šunj Beach.** This gorgeous, shallow, sandy

beach—hemmed in on both sides by forested cliffs—is squeezed between beach bars and ritzy yachts and sailboats that drop anchor to take a dip. The almost entirely sandy floor and gentle incline makes this beach ideal for waders and families. The catch is that it takes a bit of effort to reach: It's a moderately strenuous 1.5-mile walk over the scraggly spine of the island. Making things easier, locals zip arriving tourists over to the beach on golf carts (20 kn/person each way). While you might see the carts waiting near the promenade, more likely you'll have to walk partway to reach them: Follow the promenade as far as the abandoned Grand Hotel, then head inland (on a drab, poorly maintained concrete trail), following signs for *Šunj Beach.* Soon you'll see the golf carts. From here, if you prefer, you can continue to hike the rest of the way. It's not worth attempting to visit Šunj if your excursion has only a brief stopover on Lopud—anything less than

two hours, and you're probably better off sticking with the beaches in town.

Šipan

By far the biggest island (at just over six square miles), and the northernmost, Šipan has two different port towns. Your ship will most likely use the one facing Lopud, called Suđurađ (named for the local patron saint, George—remember, that đ symbol is pronounced like a hard "j"—soo-juarj). Suđurađ's harbor is watched over by the fortified, castle-like 16th-century villa of a local aristocrat. A beach beckons just across the bay from the boat dock. Next to the harbor, the small Church of

St. George—with a large covered porch—has a vivid fresco over the altar of George slaying the dragon while being watched over by two other locally revered saints, Blaise (Dubrovnik's protector) and Nicholas (the patron saint of sailors).

If you need an excuse for a short hike, head from the harbor straight up the street away from the water, following signs for the Church of Sv. Duh (Holy Spirit). After passing through a humble residential zone, you'll arrive at a stout, fortress-like church, with raw-stone walls. If it's open, poke inside to see the rough-and-tumble interior (desperate for a renovation). The stairs to the right of the altar lead up to the rooftop, where you can see the large, fertile valley that sits in the middle of this island. If you're tempted to ring the bell, resist—locals ring it only when a member of the local community dies.

Cavtat

This sleepy little resort town—just 12 miles to the south, near the Montenegrin border—offers a milder alternative to bustling Dubrovnik. With its strategic location sheltered inside a nearly 360-degree bay, this settlement was thriving long before there was a Dubrovnik. The Greeks called it Epidaurus, while the Romans called it Epidaurum—but these days, it's Cavtat (TSAV-taht). The town is best known as a handy spot to find a room when Dubrovnik's booked up, and a fun excuse to take a cruise from Dubrovnik's Old Port. Even those suffering from beach-resort fatigue will enjoy a side-trip to Cavtat, if they appreciate local art. The restaurant- and people-lined promenade is inviting, but the town's best features are its two gems of Croatian art: a breathtaking hill-

top mausoleum by the great Croatian sculptor Ivan Meštrović, and the former home-turned-museum of the Cavtat-born, early 20th-century painter Vlaho Bukovac.

Getting to Cavtat

Boats to Cavtat leave about hourly from Dubrovnik's Old Port (80 kn round-trip, 50 kn one-way, about 45 minutes each way, hourly return boats from Cavtat). The boat deposits you right along Cavtat's main seafront promenade. Note that a round-trip ticket is cheaper, but you'll have to return with the same company (rather than on whichever boat is leaving next).

You can also reach Cavtat by public **bus** #10, which leaves from Dubrovnik's main bus station and also stops at the "cable car" bus stop above the Old Town (1-2/hour, 30-40 minutes, 20 kn). The bus brings you to Cavtat's parking lot (described next). Because of Dubrovnik's one-way street system, the returning bus can't use the cable car stop. Coming back from Cavtat, hop off at the bus stop that's along the main road high above the Old Town—about a 5- to 10-minute walk down into town.

For variety, consider going to Cavtat by boat (buy a one-way ticket), then returning by bus.

Drivers find Cavtat an easy detour when heading to points south, including Montenegro or the airport; the town is well-signed off the main road. The big parking lot is at the back of Cavtat's peninsula, just around the corner from the main part of town and seafront promenade: Just walk past the TI, hook right at the busy street, and head for the waterfront.

Orientation to Cavtat

Cavtat is set within an idyllic, horseshoe-shaped harbor hemmed in by a pair of peninsulas. Tucked around the back side of the peninsula is the parking lot, left-luggage office *(garderoba),* and **TI** (July-Aug daily 8:00-21:00; Sept and June daily 8:00-20:00; May and Oct Mon-Sat 8:00-19:00, Sun 8:00-14:00; Nov-April Mon-Fri 8:00-15:00, closed Sat-Sun; Zidine 6, tel. 020/479-025, www.tzcavtat-konavle.hr). Cavtat is basically a one-street town, but that street is a fine pedestrian promenade running along the harbor, with a few narrow lanes winding steeply up into the hill. Capping the hill above town is a cemetery with the Meštrović mausoleum.

Sights in Cavtat

Waterfront Wander

Strolling along Cavtat's waterfront, you'll be immersed in a wrap-around bay and surrounded by Europeans vacationing well. At

the near end of the promenade, notice the big water polo court roped off in the bay; Cavtat and Dubrovnik are the birthing ground for many of the core players of the Croatian national water-polo team. Across the street is **St. Nicholas Church,** with a humble, dull interior (though hanging high in the altar area are Vlaho Bukovac's paintings of the four evangelists). Next door is the skippable **Baltazar Bogišić Collection,** a museum with a library and other items that once belonged to a wealthy lawyer. About halfway along the drag, one of the narrow lanes leading up the hill (appropriately named Bukovčeva) takes you to the fine **Vlaho Bukovac House** (described next). At the end of the main waterfront area is the **Church of Our Lady of the Snows,** commemorating a freak—and seemingly miraculous—mid-summer snowstorm in ancient Roman times, believed to have been a sign sent by the Virgin Mary. Inside, above the altar, is a Vlaho Bukovac painting (from 1909) of Mary and the Baby Jesus watching over Cavtat. Climbing the steep steps up to the right of the church leads you up to Ivan Meštrović's **Račić Mausoleum** (described later). With more time, consider continuing your walk around the peninsula to its pointy tip for distant views of Dubrovnik's Old Town. This is one of the favorite spots in this area for watching the sunset. (If you continue all the way around the point, in about 20 minutes you'll wind up back at the parking lot at the start of town.)

▲Vlaho Bukovac House (Kuća Bukovac)

One of the joys of traveling is getting the opportunity to learn about locally beloved artists who are little known outside their homelands. Cavtat proudly introduces you to native son Vlaho Bukovac (1855-1922), who grew up in this very house and went on to become the most important Croatian painter of the modern period. Bukovac moved to New York City with his uncle at age 11, beginning a life of great adventure. After a brief career as a sailor (traveling to Peru and San Francisco), he trained as an artist in Paris, then in Zagreb. For his last 20 years, Bukovac spent his summers in Prague and his winters here in Cavtat. Touring the collection (with good English explanations), you'll get to know Bukovac's life and his works. Bukovac's paintings are mostly realistic (in accordance with his formal Salon training in Paris), but

shimmer with a hint of Post-Impressionism; his later works echo the slinky Art Nouveau Slavic pride of the Czech painter Alfons Mucha, who was Bukovac's contemporary. The ground floor displays photos of his early life; upstairs you'll find old furniture, early

sketches, and portraits of Bukovac and his family (the painting of his children's disembodied heads hanging on the wall is macabre but strangely tender). The top floor houses one big atelier room filled with canvases from various periods, allowing you to survey his impressive artistic development with a sweep of the head. Throughout the house are murals painted by Bukovac in his early days, offering a glimpse of a burgeoning artist who would go on to make Cavtat very proud.

Cost and Hours: 20 kn, good 40-kn guidebook; May-Oct Tue-Sat 9:00-13:00 & 16:00-20:00, Sun 16:00-20:00, closed Mon; Nov-April Tue-Sat 9:00-13:00 & 14:00-17:00, Sun 14:00-17:00, closed Mon; Bukovčeva 5, tel. 020/478-646, www.kuca-bukovac.hr.

▲▲Račić Family Mausoleum (Mauzolej Obitelji Račić)

This harmonious masterwork of Croatia's greatest artist is the gem of Cavtat, and worth ▲▲▲ to fans of Ivan Meštrović's powerful sculptures.

Cost and Hours: 10 kn, Mon-Sat 10:00-17:00, closed Sun and mid-Oct-mid-April. If she's not too busy, helpful Nena will show you around.

Getting There: Capping the hill above town, it's a steep 10-minute walk from the Cavtat waterfront. From the Church of Our Lady of Snows at the far end of the waterfront, climb up the stairs (following *mauzolej* signs).

Visiting the Mausoleum: Over the course of one tragic year, all four members of the wealthy Račić family—father, mother, son, daughter—died of the Spanish flu. From 1920-1922, in accordance with their will, Ivan Meštrović was commissioned to craft their final resting place. He used the opportunity to create a cohesive meditation on Christian faith and death, made entirely of brilliant white stone from the island of Brač. As you enter, take a moment to appreciate how the interior ponders birth, life, and death. The four inner walls of the octagonal hall hold the

tombs of the departed; above each tomb, an angel lovingly carries their souls up to heaven—spiriting them into a cupola studded with angel heads. The floor has symbols for the four evangelists: Matthew (angel), Mark (lion), Luke (bull), and John (eagle). The chapel to the left holds a crucifix; to the right, an altar to St. Rok (the patron saint of illness, to whom the chapel is dedicated—the dog licking the wound in his leg is his symbol). Straight ahead is an altar with Mary holding the Baby Jesus above a relief of the Lamb of God, and below that, Jesus' body being taken down from the cross. Flanking this altar, notice the bases of the twisting candelabras: alternating angels look down to honor the dead. The chapel rewards those who linger over the details, such as the bronze doors, with four saints, Glagolitic in-scriptions, and the 12 Apostles. The saints chosen for this door preach both ecumenism and Yugoslav unity: Cyril and Methodius

(the Byzantine missionaries who first brought Christianity to this region), along with a Catholic bishop (Bishop Gregory of Nin) and an Orthodox saint (St. Sava). Taken together, the mausoleum is an astonishing display of talent, especially considering it was Meštrović's first architectural work.

Nearby: The mausoleum sits in the middle of a tranquil cem-etery that's still used for the funerals of Cavtat residents (a plot costs €20,000). As you exit the mausoleum, head straight out and a bit to the right to find two communal graves for the poor—with smaller markers lined up along a large plinth. Also in this cemetery is the grave of the artist Vlaho Bukovac.

Near Cavtat

A village near Cavtat, **Čilipi,** hosts a Sunday-morning folk fes-tival through the summer (Easter-Oct, starting at 9:00). There's a special Mass at the church, an open-air market, and—starting at 11:15—a costumed folk-dancing show (tel. 020/771-007, www.cilipifolklor.hr).

Trsteno Arboretum

Take a stroll through the shaded, relaxing botanical garden in Trsteno (worth ▲), just up the coast from Dubrovnik. Non-garden-

ers may find it a bit dull, but Trsteno is a horticulturalist's heaven. Spread over 63 acres on a bluff overlooking the sea, this arboretum features hundreds of different Mediterranean, Asian, and American plants (each one labeled in six languages, including English). The whole complex is laced with easy footpaths and sprinkled with fun attractions—a column-studded Renaissance Garden, a desolate villa, a little chapel, an old mill and olive-oil press, and a seaview pavilion.

As you wander, the world melts away and you're alone with the sounds of nature: wind, water, birds, and frogs. The garden's centerpiece is the whimsical 18th-century Neptune Fountain, featuring the god of the sea flanked by water-spouting nymphs and fishes as he holds court over a goldfish-stocked, lily-padded pond. Circling around behind the fountain, you'll discover that it's fed by an impressive 230-foot-long aqueduct that was built in the 15th century.

Cost and Hours: 40 kn, daily May-Oct 8:00-19:00, Nov-April 8:00-16:00, tel. 020/751-019.

Nearby: On the waterfront below the arboretum, next to the little village harbor, you'll see the shell of a once-grand 18th-

century palace, which was damaged during the siege of Dubrovnik and is now abandoned. It's still owned by the government, but investors are lining up for a chance to buy this prime real estate—possibly the most desirable ruin in Croatia.

Getting There: Trsteno is best reached by car, particularly if you're taking your time driving to Dubrovnik from the north (the main coastal road goes through the town of Trsteno, right past the well-marked arboretum). You also have two bus options from Dubrovnik (around 20 kn, 20-30 minutes). Any long-distance northbound bus can drop you in Trsteno—ask about the next bus at the main station. Alternatively, the slower local buses #12 and #15 also reach Trsteno. Coming

back from Trsteno to Dubrovnik is trickier: Wait at the bus stop with the glass canopy by the park entrance and wave down any Dubrovnik-bound bus that passes (at least hourly).

Pelješac Peninsula

North of Trsteno, the skinny, 55-mile-long Pelješac (PEHL-yeh-shahts) Peninsula—practically an honorary island—splits off from the Croatian coastline as if about to drift away to Italy. (The far tip of Pelješac comes within a stone's throw of Korčula island.) This sparsely populated peninsula, famous for its rugged terrain—and the grapes that thrive here—is worth a detour for wine lovers. But its heavily fortified town of Ston, just a short side-trip from the main coastal road, merits a stretch-your-legs visit for anyone. Notice that if you're connecting from Korčula to anywhere else in Croatia by car, you'll probably be taking the ferry to the Pelješac Peninsula anyway; consider slowing down to sample a few wines, to scramble up the walls at Ston, or to have a meal at Mali Ston.

Getting There: Buses between Dubrovnik and Korčula traverse the Pelješac Peninsula, but drivers have the option of stopping where they like (such as at Ston or a winery). Some public buses also stop at Ston.

Ston

The town of Ston, at the base of the peninsula, is the gateway to Pelješac. This "Great Wall of Croatia" town is famous for the im-

pressive wall that climbs up the mountain behind it (about a half-mile encloses the town itself, while another three miles clamber up the hillsides). The unassuming town was heavily fortified (starting in 1333) for two reasons: to defend its strategic location, where mountains and bays create a bottleneck along the road from Dubrovnik to Pelješac, near the Republic of Dubrovnik's northern boundary; and to protect its impressive salt pans, which still produce the mineral. Filling a low-lying plain that sprawls in front of Ston's doorstep, these pans provided Dubrovnik with much of its wealth, back in the days when salt was worth more than its weight in gold. The pans would be flooded with saltwater, then sealed and left to evaporate—leaving the salt easy to harvest.

Today, the sleepy town—with more than its share of outdoor cafés and restaurants—is notable only for the chance to scramble

A Bridge Too Far?

If you're driving along the coast between Split and Dubrovnik, you may be surprised when you have to stop and show your passport to enter another country—Bosnia-Herzegovina, around the resort town of Neum. How is it that Bosnia wound up with its very own five-and-a-half-mile stretch of the Dalmatian Coast? During the heyday of the Republic of Dubrovnik, the city's leaders granted this land to the Ottoman Empire to provide a buffer between Dubrovnik's holdings and the Republic of Venice, to the north. (They knew the Venetians would never enter the territory of the Ottomans—their feared enemy—in order to invade Dubrovnik.) Later, as the borders of Europe were being redrawn in modern times, Bosnia retained possession of this strip of land as a sort of inheritance from their former rulers.

For years, coastal Bosnians and their Croatian neighbors have coexisted, albeit tensely at times. Prices for hotel rooms, groceries, and other staples are slightly cheaper in Neum, whose rest stops lure tourist buses with low prices and generous kickbacks for bus drivers. Visitors are inconvenienced by having to go through a passport checkpoint as they enter Bosnia and again, just a few minutes later, as they exit Bosnia. From a practical standpoint, this is rarely an issue. But on busy days, there can be lines, and it's always smart to have your passport and rental car's "green card" (proof of insurance) ready.

Croatians are irritated with the red tape, and—even more—by the way Neum merchants undersell the Croatian alternatives nearby. As Croatia extends its expressway southward, the most logical approach would be a route through Bosnia to Dubrovnik. But some Croatian politicians have been looking for a way to avoid Neum altogether. One solution is to build a 1.5-mile-long bridge from just north of Neum to the Peljesac Peninsula, then re-join the coastal road back in Croatia, just south of Neum—effectively bypassing Bosnian territory. Environmentalists worry about the impact the bridge will have on the ecosystem around Mali Ston. But, because of the proposed bridge's popularity with a certain segment of the voting population, work actually began on this project prior to a recent election (notice that one mountaintop on Peljesac has already been cleared). After the election—and with the global economic crisis—plans were put on hold. It remains to be seen whether this very expensive project will ever come to fruition...and if it does, whether the bridge will be completed before Croatia and Bosnia both join the EU's Schengen Agreement and open their borders anyway.

up its massive **fortifications** (park your car in the big lot, then cross the street into town and look right; the entrance to the walls is in the big tower). These walls have been undergoing an extensive restoration, and the long, skinny strip running over the ridge to the town of Mali Ston (described next) is already complete. For a short wall experience, you can just do a circle around the stout lower walls (about 20-30 minutes); for a more serious hike, you can climb all the way up and over to Mali Ston (figure 45-60 minutes). Be warned that the walls—with all that glistening limestone reflecting heat—are much hotter than at ground level, and there's virtually no shade (30 kn to enter walls regardless of how far you walk, 5-kn info booklet, daily April-Oct 8:00-19:00, Nov-March generally 9:00-15:00).

Other than the walls, there's not much to do in Ston. The town's deserted feel is a result of a devastating 1996 earthquake, from which Ston is still rebuilding. But there are several inviting cafés for a lazy drink. If you want a meal, skip Ston's mediocre offerings and head over to Mali Ston instead.

Eating near Ston, in Mali Ston: From Ston, the walls scamper over a ridge to its little sister, the bayside village of Mali Ston ("Small Ston"). Surrounded by a similar, but smaller, fortified wall, Mali Ston is known for its many mussel and oyster farms, and for its good restaurants. A local favorite is **Kapetanova Kuća,** a memorable place with a fine location on Mali Ston's waterfront. Celebrity chef Lidija Kralj prides herself on her unpretentious but delicious food, made with fresh produce from the restaurant's own garden. For dessert, her bizarre *makaruli* —macaroni cake—is tastier than it sounds (10-kn cover charge, 75-100-kn pastas, 100-130-kn seafood and meat dishes, daily 9:00-23:00, tel. 020/754-264).

Pelješac Wine Country

Farther along, the sparsely developed Pelješac Peninsula is blanketed with vineyards. Wine is a big draw here, and several vintners open their doors for passing visitors to sample their products. While it's a bit distant from Dubrovnik (about a two-hour drive to the heart of the wine-producing area), it's a worthwhile pilgrimage for wine lovers and an easy stop-off for those driving from Korčula.

Tours of Pelješac: To really do the peninsula justice, consider hiring a guide to take you for a spin around Pelješac. **Sasha Lušić,** who runs the D'Vino Wine Bar in Dubrovnik, is a gregarious Aussie-Croat guide. He prides himself on taking you to a wide variety of vintners, who represent the best of what's happening here. Sasha's tours can go late into the evening (also offers cheaper half-day

tours to areas closer to Dubrovnik, www.dvino.net, sasha@dvino.net). Other Dubrovnik-based drivers also do good wine tours (which also include several other worthwhile, scenic stops), including **Petar Vlašić**.

◊ Self-Guided Driving Tour: I've arranged this tour in the order you'll come from the tip of Pelješac (Orebić, just across the channel from Korčula). If you're doing it from Dubrovnik, begin by driving all the way to the village of Potomje (you can skip the section between there and Orebić) and visit the wineries on your way back (since it's a long, skinny peninsula, you'll have to backtrack anyway). I've included a detour to some of Croatia's finest (and largely undiscovered) vineyards, and saved the best wines for last.

If you're crossing from Korčula Island, you'll begin the tour in **Orebić**. It's basically one main road from here back to Ston (where you'll meet up with the main coastal road to Dubrovnik or Split), so you can't really get lost—though we will make an off-the-beaten-path vineyard detour.

Follow the main road (toward Dubrovnik and Split) up, up, up for about 15 minutes to a dramatic **viewpoint** (there's a pullout on the right with benches—watch for the giant wine bottle) looking back toward Korčula. The jagged cliffs to your left are the Pelješac Peninsula (where we're about to drive), and the island poking out to the left is Mljet National Park. Straight ahead is Korčula, and behind that, Lastovo. On a clear day, you can almost see to Italy. This also gives you a good view of the two best wine-growing regions of Pelješac: Below you and to the right, you can see some vineyards in the **Postup** region; to the left (not quite visible from here) are the vineyards of **Dingač**. Both areas are steeply angled, so they catch a maximum amount of sun, which creates very sweet grapes that produce high-alcohol, very dark (actually called "black" in Croatian) wine with strong legs (or, as Croatians call them, "tears"). The rugged, rocky limestone provides natural irrigation (since water can flow freely through it), and the high winds here keep off bugs and other pests. It all adds up to extremely healthy vines; because disease is rare, pesticides are not needed.

Continuing along the road, you'll crest the hill and pass the turnoff for Trpanj (where ferries connect to the mainland); soon after, watch on the left for **Peninsula Wine Bar**. Operated by two local vintners, Boris and Baldo, this is a good place to learn about and try wine from a variety of different producers (unlike the wineries later on this trip, which typically sell only their own wines). They usually have about 30 wines available. You can sample wine by the taste (usually free, maybe 5-25 kn for premium wines, 30-40-kn tasting flights listed on the chalkboard), by the glass (12-60 kn each—most around 20-30 kn), and by the bottle (40-250 kn).

They also offer tastings of local olive oil and grappa (April-mid-Oct daily 9:00-23:00, closed mid-Oct-March, tel. 020/742-503, www. peninsula.hr).

After the wine bar, you'll drop down into a **plateau** surrounded by cliffs. The vines you'll see in this so-called "continental" area are the same kind of grapes as in Postup and Dingač, but they receive less sun and are less sweet. These *plavac mali* ("little blue") grapes are a distant relative of California zinfandel and Italian *primitivo*. Notice that many of the vines appear to be almost wild; these are older vineyards, which aren't irrigated, so they must let the vines grow this way to help them survive the hot summer months. This method maximizes yield but reduces quality. Newer vineyards are irrigated and use guide wires, and generally look more manicured.

Soon you'll arrive in the village of **Potomje,** which is at the center of this important wine-growing area. Several wineries clus-

ter here, including some that are open for tastings and tours. Three are particularly accessible to visitors and offer a helpful introduction to Pelješac wines: Madirazza, Matuško, and Violić. While the first two can be quite touristy (with big bus tours passing through occasionally), Violić is an appealingly Back Door experience, and worth saving for last. All three are staffed by friendly English-speakers who are eager to introduce you to their wines; while the tastings are free, they're hoping you'll buy a bottle or two. (If you want a more elaborate tasting with food pairings or for a small group, call ahead.) All three are open long hours daily (around 8:00-20:00, close earlier in shoulder season, generally closed Nov-March—but call ahead and they may be able to open for you, cash only).

The reds are the real draw here; I'd skip the whites. The wines, which are quite fruity, come in various types. In general, bottles marked with the type of grape *(plavac mali)* are lower-quality, from the vines here in the valley. The ones marked with the specific region (Dingač and Postup) come from the sunny slopes and are of better quality, fuller-bodied, and more expensive; they go well with red meat and dark chocolate. Winery staff enjoy explaining (often with the help of photos) that the climate and growing conditions are entirely different in the valley than in the extremely steep and sun-drenched Dingač area, just over the mountain and facing the sea; it's far easier to harvest the valley grapes than the Dingač grapes, which makes Dingač much higher-priced...but worth paying extra for. All three wineries also have various brandies to try (including *travarica*, an herb-infused brandy).

First, near the far end of town, look for the big, pink building of the **Madirazza** winery. Notice the roses that line the vineyards—like a canary in a coal mine, these are more quickly affected by disease than the vines, offering an early-warning system in the event of an unwanted infestation. Madirazza's oaky, fairly acidic wines cost 40-90 kn per bottle (reserve bottles for 130-240 kn, mobile 098-212-163, www.dingac.hr, Mina).

Across the main road from Madirazza's parking lot is a smaller road (marked with *Matuško* and *Tunel Dingač* signs) leading to the **Matuško** winery. With smoother wines than Madirazza's, this place also has a sprawling network of atmospheric cellars where tour groups sip wines between aging barrels (20-110-kn bottles, most 20-90 kn, reserve bottles for 150-700 kn, free tastings upstairs, good place for a WC stop, tel. 020/742-393, mobile 098-428-676 www.matusko-vina.hr).

Backtrack to the road that leads to the tunnel. As you face the entrance to the tunnel, turn left, following *Boris Violić* signs to the unassuming **Violić** family home and winery. Offering a good contrast to the polished and almost "corporate"-feeling wineries described earlier, Boris Violić-Matuško and his wife Marine invite passing visitors to enjoy some home-style hospitality. In addition to sampling their wines (four reds and two whites, 30-150-kn bottles), consider buying some brandy, olive oil, or their delicious grandma-made treats (Potomje 6, tel. 020/742-082, mobile 091-525-3731).

If you want more wine before leaving this valley, consider paying a visit to the well-regarded **Miličić,** also in Potomje (back on the main road, past Madirazza).

When you're ready to move on, look for the **tunnel** through the mountain marked *Tunel Dingač,* with the picture of a donkey. Before this tunnel was dug, beasts of burden trod surefootedly up and over this mountain to carry the grapes from Dingač, on the far side, to this village. The donkey remains a symbol of this wine-growing region. In the 1970s, this tunnel was built to make everyone's lives easier. Take advantage of it by driving through the mountain and into another world.

Popping out at the sea, you're in the heart of the **Dingač** vine-

yards. Turn left (toward *Borak*) and drive on the one-lane road above all those vines, with a green and jagged waterline that looks almost Celtic. (Drive carefully: While it's a paved road, it's narrow, with a very steep shoulder.) Croatia's best reds are lovingly raised right here, bathed in

ample sunshine as they struggle against a very rocky soil. Locals explain that these grapes are bathed in sunlight from every angle—not just the sun above, but the reflection of those rays from both the sea and the white soil. Dingač never freezes (unlike the valley), and rainfall runs off immediately through its porous limestone soil, making these plants very disease-resistant. By the time they are harvested, Dingač grapes are withered by the sun—halfway to raisins, packed with sugar, and ideal for producing top-quality wines. At the fork, continue down to the right, toward *Dingač/Borak;* at the next fork, when the Borak road turns sharply down and to the right, keep going straight onto the smaller road.

As you drive, keep enjoying dramatic views of Mljet Island. When you enter an area of trees, look across the harbor to see

a building perched on a cliff over the water—that's our next stop. Soon you'll come to the village of Trstenik; at the T-intersection, make a sharp right turn, then turn left to pass along its little waterfront. At the far end of town, on the way up the hill, turn into the parking lot for the **Grgić** winery. Perhaps the best-known and best-regarded Croatian vintner, Mike Grgić's facility is less appealing than the others we've visited, and you have to pay for the tasting (30 kn)...but the quality of the wine compensates. This place is surprisingly humble (and might, at first glance, not even seem open to the public), emphasizing substance over flashy style. Keeping things simple, Grgić does a white wine (*pošip*, with grapes grown on Korčula but produced here, 135 kn per bottle) and a red wine (210 kn per bottle); breaking with convention, he names his red simply *plavac mali* partly to help promote this largely unknown and underappreciated grape (grown here in Trstenik and in Dingač). He also sells wines from his California winery, Grgich Hills, at or below their California prices (200-440 kn; daily 9:00-17:00, tel. 020/748-090).

Exiting the winery, turn right (uphill) and twist up to the main road, where you'll turn right, toward Ston. Cresting the hill, you'll see the other side of the peninsula and the channel separating it from the mainland—as if to emphasize the narrowness of this spit of land. From here, you'll continue straight along all the way to Ston. You may be tempted by the *vino* signs in **Janjina,** but these are aimed mainly at Croatians buying table wine in bulk—100 liters at a time.

Leaving Janjina, keep following signs for *Ston* and *Dubrovnik.*

You'll twist down and follow the **Bay of Ston,** which is famous for its shellfish production. Here where the Neretva River (which runs under Mostar's Old Bridge) empties into the sea, conditions are perfect for cultivating mussels, oysters, and clams. (You'll spot many such farms out in the bay—look for the areas roped off with buoys.) The road climbs up once more, passing the aptly named Bella Vista viewpoint café (which overlooks the dock for the ferry to the national park on Mljet Island), before continuing into the walled town of **Ston.**

Leaving Ston, turn right (toward Dubrovnik) once you hit the main road; from here, it's about an hour back into town. En route, watch out for the speed traps at the towns of Doli and Orešac.

Mljet National Park

Carefully protected against modern development, the island hideaway of Mljet National Park offers a unique back-to-nature escape. With ample opportunities for hiking, swimming, biking, and boating—and without a nightclub, tacky T-shirt, or concrete "beach" pad in sight—Mljet (muhl-YAYT) is a potential highlight for active, outdoorsy travelers.

Though Mljet Island is one of Dalmatia's largest, it has fewer than 1,500 residents. Nearly three-quarters of the island is covered in forest, leaving it remarkably untamed. Aside from its beautiful national park, Mljet has inspired some of the most memorable tales of the Croatian coast—the poet Homer, his protagonist Ulysses, and the Apostle Paul all spent time here...or so the locals love to boast.

Many Croatians swoon over Mljet. Take this with a grain of salt. They appreciate it primarily for its relative lack of people. One local told me, "Mljet is basically Hvar or Korčula with no towns." For foreign visitors, the park, while enjoyable, is a bit overrated. Still, if a peaceful, uncrowded island sounds like your kind of scene, make the trip.

Planning Your Time

Thanks to a handy catamaran connection, Mljet works perfectly as a full-day side-trip from Dubrovnik (only possible in summer). But because of inconvenient boat schedules to other destinations, it's challenging to splice it into a one-way itinerary (say, between Korčula and Dubrovnik). So if you want to visit Mljet, either do it as a day trip on your own from Dubrovnik, or buy a package day-trip excursion from Korčula, Hvar, or Split. For details, see "Mljet Connections," at the end of this chapter.

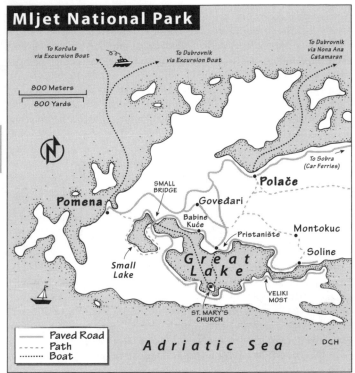

Mljet National Park

To Korčula via Excursion Boat

To Dubrovnik via Excursion Boat

To Dubrovnik via Nona Ana Catamaran

800 Meters
800 Yards

NEAR DUBROVNIK

To Sobra (Car Ferries)

SMALL BRIDGE

Polače

Pomena

Govedari

Babine Kuće

Pristanište

Montokuc

Soline

Small Lake

G r e a t
L a k e

VELIKI MOST

ST. MARY'S CHURCH

Paved Road
Path
Boat

A d r i a t i c   S e a

DCH

No matter how you arrive, one day is plenty for Mljet. I've suggested a day-trip plan under "Sights on Mljet."

Be warned that everything's very seasonal and weather-dependent, so visiting outside of peak season (June-Sept) may come with some frustration.

Orientation to Mljet

The island of Mljet is long (23 miles) and skinny (less than two miles wide). The national park occupies the western third of the island. You're likely to reach Mljet via one of three port towns. **Polače** (POH-lah-cheh) and **Pomena** (POH-meh-nah) are handy entry points into the national park, while **Sobra** (SOH-brah) is much less convenient (a 1.25-hour bus trip across the island from the park). The *Nona Ana* catamaran from Dubrovnik puts in at Polače and Sobra; most excursions use Pomena; and the car ferries (the big Jadrolinija Korčula-Dubrovnik car ferry, plus smaller ferries to the mainland) use Sobra.

Polače and Pomena flank the heart of the national park, a pair of saltwater "lakes" called simply **Great Lake** (Veliko Jezero)

and **Small Lake** (Malo Jezero). The two bodies of water meet at a cute little bridge, appropriately named **Small Bridge** (Mali Most), where you can rent kayaks and bikes and catch a boat out to the little **island** in the Great Lake. A 15-minute walk around the Great Lake from the Small Bridge brings you to **Pristanište** (meaning, roughly, "transit hub"), where you can also catch a boat to the island or a shuttle bus to Polače. The nearby cliff-climbing town of **Goveđari** is home to many of the people who work at the park, but is not interesting to tourists.

Everything's well-signed, and there are enough landmarks that it's difficult to get really lost. Even so, I bought the detailed park map (at the entry kiosk) and was glad I had it.

Tourist Information

The **TI** is in Polače, just across from where the *Nona Ana* catamaran from Dubrovnik docks (tel. 020/744-186). The island's lone hotel, the **Hotel Odisej** in Pomena, acts as a second tourist information point. The hotel is a hub of services for visitors (whether you stay there or not): bike, scooter, car, and boat rentals; scuba diving lessons; walking tours around the island; cruises to some of the island's caves; and even help finding private accommodations. For more on the hotel, see "Sleeping and Eating on Mljet," later.

The general-information website for the island (which covers the towns, Hotel Odisej, *sobe* and apartments, and more) is www.mljet. hr; for information on the national park, visit www.np-mljet.hr.

Arrival in Mljet

At Polače: Arriving on the *Nona Ana* catamaran from Dubrovnik, exit the boat to the right, walk a few steps, and look for the TI on your left. A few minutes' walk up the coast (near the Roman ruins) is a kiosk where you can buy your park entry ticket and catch a minibus to the Pristanište transit hub at the Great Lake (runs hourly, scheduled to coincide with boat arrival). From Pristanište, you can take a boat out to the island in the Great Lake (about hourly), or walk around the lake toward the Small Bridge, Small Lake, and on to Pomena.

At Pomena: If you arrive at Pomena, you're most likely on a package excursion, in which case your park entry ticket is included and you'll probably stick with your guide for a while. But in case you're on your own, exit the boat to the left (passing Hotel Odisej) and buy your park entry ticket at the kiosk. A few steps up the road beyond the kiosk, you'll see a shortcut to the right that takes you up and down some steps on your way to the Small Lake; once at the lake, bear left and continue to the Small Bridge, where you can catch the boat to the island in the Great Lake or rent a bike or kayak.

Note that there's no official bus between Polače and Pomena,

but Hotel Odisej operates a shuttle to coincide with the Dubrovnik catamaran. Several informal minibus-taxis can also take you for a fee.

At Sobra: If you come on a car ferry, you're in for a long haul over to Polače and Pomena—about a 1.25-hour bus trip on twisty roads. Avoid arriving via Sobra unless you're desperate.

Sights on Mljet

▲Mljet National Park
All of the following attractions are inside the park.

Cost and Hours: The steep 90-kn entry fee (100 kn in July-Aug) includes the shuttle bus from Polače to the Great Lake and a boat ride to the lake's island. The park is open daily May-mid-Oct 7:00-19:00, shorter hours in shoulder season, closed Nov-Feb; park information tel. 020/744-041.

Day-Trip Plan: If you're doing the trip on your own from Dubrovnik, try this itinerary: From Polače, take the minibus to Pristanište, where you can catch the boat to the island in the Great Lake. Take the boat back to Mali Most (Small Bridge), where you can rent a bike for a ride along the shore of the Great Lake. If you're heating up, take a dip in the Small Lake at the beach near the Small Bridge. When you're ready for a bit of civilization, walk into Pomena and relax by the seaside, then take the hotel's shuttle bus or a minibus-taxi back to Polače to catch the catamaran back home to Dubrovnik. With more energy, skip Pomena and hike up to Montokuc (you can hike down to Polače on the other side).

The Lakes
The "Great Lake" and "Small Lake" are technically saltwater bays—fed by the sea and affected by ocean currents (as you'll clearly see if you're at the little channel by the Small Bridge at the right time of day). Scientists love these lakes, which contain various shellfish species unique to Mljet.

The Island
The main activity in the park is taking a boat out to the Great Lake's little island-in-an-island (boats depart about hourly from the Small Bridge and from Pristanište). The tiny island's main landmark is St. Mary's Church (Sv. Marija) and the attached monastery, left behind by Benedictine monks who lived on Mljet starting in the 12th century. Though the monastery complex has been modified over the ages, fragments of the original Romanesque structure still survive. You can hike the easy trail up to the top of the island, passing remains of fortifications and old chapels, and look for the island's only permanent residents: a handful of goats, donkeys, and chickens. You'll have about an hour to explore, but it only takes half that to see everything—then relax with an overpriced drink at the restaurant by the boat dock.

The Tales of Mljet

For a mostly undeveloped island, Mljet has had a surprisingly busy history. Home to Illyrians, Greeks, Romans, Slavs, Venetians, Habsburgs, Yugoslavs, and now Croatians, the island has hosted some interesting visitors (or supposed visitors) that it loves to brag about.

Around the eighth century B.C., the Greek epic poet Homer possibly spent time here. He was so inspired by Mljet that he used it as the setting for one of the adventures of his hero Ulysses (a.k.a. Odysseus). This is the island where Ulysses fell in love with a beautiful nymph named Calypso and shacked up with her in a cave for seven years. Today there's a much-vaunted "Ulysses' Cave" (Odisejeva Spilja), a 40-minute hike below the island's main town, Babino Polje (at the far end of the island—skip it unless you're a Ulysses groupie).

Flash forward nearly a millennium, when a real-life traveler found his way to Mljet. According to the Bible (Acts 28), the Apostle Paul was shipwrecked on an island called "Melita"—likely this one—for three months. While on the island, Paul was bitten by a deadly snake, which he threw into a fire. The natives were amazed that he wasn't affected by the poison, and he proceeded to cure their ailments. This event was long believed to have happened on the similarly named isle of Malta, in the Mediterranean Sea. But more recently, many historians began to believe that Paul was on Mljet. The most convincing argument: Malta never had poisonous snakes. Incidentally, Mljet no longer does, either—the Habsburgs imported an army of Indian mongooses to rid the island of problematic serpents. Because of this historical footnote, people from Mljet are nicknamed "mongooses" by other Croatians.

The heroics continue with today's "mongooses." There have been more than 100 fires on the island in the last 20 years (most caused by lightning, some by careless visitors), but only three have spread and caused significant destruction. That's because the people of Mljet—well aware of the fragility of the island that provides their income—are also a crack volunteer firefighting force, ready to spring into action and save their home at the first wisp of smoke.

Biking

The Great Lake is surrounded by a paved, mostly level road that's good for an hour or two of pedaling (unfortunately, you can't go all the way around because the path is broken by the channel connecting the lakes to the sea). The unpaved path around the Small Lake is rough and rocky, making biking there more difficult. The handiest place to rent a bike for a quick ride around the Great Lake is right at the lake itself, by the Small Bridge. Other bike rental points are scattered around the island, including in both Polače and

Pomena. But those towns are separated from the lakes—and from each other—by steep hills, making cycling from either town to the lakes a headache for casual bikers.

Swimming

Options are everywhere, most temptingly at the Great Lake and Small Lake. Even though it's fed by seawater, the Small Lake is always about seven degrees Fahrenheit warmer than the sea. The beach by the Small Bridge is particularly handy (but there are no showers or WCs).

Boating

You can rent kayaks at the Small Bridge. Motorized boats—except for the occasional local resident's dinghy—aren't allowed on the island's lakes.

Hiking to Montokuc

The most rewarding hike takes you up to the national park's highest point, Montokuc. At 830 feet above sea level, this is a serious hike up a steep hill—skip it unless you're in good shape, and be sure to bring water (allow at least one hour round-trip at a steady pace). The trail runs between Polače, at the north end of the island, and the village of Soline, beyond the far end of the Great Lake (past the old, broken bridge called Veliki Most). If you're doing this or any other hike, the park map is essential (sold at park entry kiosks and other merchants).

Sleeping and Eating on Mljet

(€1 = about $1.30, country code: 385, area code: 020)

$$$ Hotel Odisej, the only hotel on the island, has more charm than most renovated communist hotels. Sitting right on the waterfront, with 157 rooms, it's a predictably comfortable home base (Db-€200 in peak season, but rates flex with demand; closed mid-Oct-mid-April, air-con, elevator, tel. 020/362-111, www.hotelodisej.hr, info@hotelodisej.hr).

$-$$ Sobe *and Apartments:* Mljet has a wide range of private accommodations, with a few in each town or village. If you arrive without a room, the TI in Polače or Hotel Odisej in Pomena can help you find something. If you're looking in advance, check out the island website, www.mljet.hr. I'd choose a place in the population centers of Polače or Pomena (for their easy access to the park) or in the cute Great Lake-front village of Babine Kuće (near the Small Bridge). To really get away from it all, little end-of-the-road Soline (near the channel connecting the Great Lake to the sea) is rustic and remote, and has several options.

For **eating,** many good restaurants are scattered around the island. There isn't one that's particularly worth seeking out—just eat when it fits your itinerary (or bring a picnic).

Mljet Connections

To Dubrovnik and Korčula by Catamaran: The speedy, made-for-day-trippers catamaran called *Nona Ana* runs daily in each direction between Dubrovnik and Mljet. In the summer (June-Sept), it goes every morning from **Dubrovnik** to **Sobra,** then on to **Polače** (the best stop for the national park, 1.5 hours). In the peak months of July and August, it sometimes continues to **Korčula** town (45 minutes beyond Polače, 4/week) and **Lastovo Island** (2 hours beyond Polače, 2/week). In the afternoon, it returns to Dubrovnik via the same route, bringing tired but happy side-trippers back to the city. It's less handy in the winter (Oct-May), when it departs Dubrovnik in the afternoon and goes only as far as Sobra and Polače. Confirm the schedule at www.gv-line.hr, and double-check your plans with the Dubrovnik TI. To be sure you get a ticket in peak season, show up early (ideally 1.5 hours before the boat leaves).

Even though this boat works perfectly in summer for day-tripping from Dubrovnik to Mljet National Park, it doesn't work as well for connecting to Korčula, because it just goes there on some mornings and is handy only if you're heading north after spending the night on Mljet.

Between Mljet and Other Destinations: All other destinations (including Hvar, Split, and day-tripping from Korčula) are more conveniently connected to Mljet by **excursion** than by public transit. The approximately €50 price tag for an all-day excursion seems high, but remember that it includes the 90-kn (€12) park admission fee and saves you the hassle of getting to the island on your own. Otherwise, you can reach Mljet only by the **car ferry** that stops at Sobra (2/week in peak season going between Dubrovnik and Korčula, plus other connections from the mainland).

MONTENEGRO

Crna Gora

MONTENEGRO

The Bay of Kotor • Kotor • The Montenegrin Interior •
The Budva Riviera

If Dubrovnik is the grand finale of a Croatian vacation, then Montenegro is the encore. One of Europe's youngest nations awaits you just south of the border, with dramatic scenery, friendly locals proud of their unique land, and a rough-around-the-edges appeal. If you're looking for the "next Croatia," this is it.

Crossing the border, you know you've left sleek and tidy Croatia for a place that's gritty, raw, and a bit exotic. While Croatia's showpiece Dalmatian Coast avoided the drab, boxy dullness of the Yugoslav era, less affluent Montenegro wasn't so lucky. Between the dramatic cliffs and time-passed villages, you'll drive past grimy, broken-down apartment blocks and some truly unfortunate concrete architecture. Montenegro is also a noticeably poorer country than its northern neighbor, with all that entails.

Historically, Montenegro has been even more of a crossroads of cultures than Croatia or Slovenia. In some ways, there are two Montenegros: the remote, rugged, rustic mountaintop kingdom that feels culturally close to Serbia; and this chapter's focus, the sun-drenched coastline of staggeringly strategic importance that has attracted a steady stream of rulers over the millennia. At one point or another, just about every group you can imagine—from the usual suspects (Venetians, Austrians) to oddball one-offs (Bulgarian kingdoms, Napoleon's Ljubljana-based Illyrian Provinces, Russian czars)—has planted its flag here. In spite of their schizophrenic lineage, or maybe because of it, Montenegrins have forged a unique cultural identity that defies many of the preconceived notions of the Balkans. Are they like Serbs or Croats? Do they use the Cyrillic or the Roman alphabet? Do they worship

the Roman Catholic God or the Eastern Orthodox one? Yes, all of the above.

Since gaining independence in 2006, the Montenegrin coast has become a powerful magnet for a very specific breed of traveler: millionaires from Russia (and, to a lesser extent, Saudi Arabia), who have chosen to turn this impressionable, fledgling country—with its gorgeous coastline—into their very own Riviera. The Tivat airport is jammed with charter flights from Moscow, signs along the coast advertise Russian-language radio stations, and an extravagant luxury yacht marina is being built near Tivat (Porto Montenegro, www.portomontenegro.com). And so Montenegro finds itself in an awkward position: trying to cultivate an image as a high-roller luxury paradise, while struggling to upgrade what is—in places—a nearly Third World infrastructure. Glittering new €500-a-night boutique hotels are built, then suffer power and water outages. It sometimes feels as if Montenegro is skipping right past an important middle step in its tourist development (that of an on-the-rise, moderately priced destination). I guess what I'm saying is...lower your expectations, and don't expect a fancy facade and high prices to come with predictable quality.

Still, nothing can mar the natural beauty of Montenegro's mountains, bays, and forests. For a look at the untamed Adriatic,

a spin on the winding road around Montenegro's steep and secluded Bay of Kotor is a must. The area's main town, also called Kotor, has been protected from centuries of would-be invaders by its position at the deepest point of the fjord—and by its imposing town wall, which scrambles in a zigzag line up the mountain behind it. Wander the enjoyably seedy streets of Kotor, drop into some Orthodox churches, and sip a coffee at an al fresco café.

With more time, romantics can corkscrew up into the mountains to sample the Balkans' best smoked ham at Njeguši and visit the remote original capital of the country at Cetinje, beach bums will head for the Budva Riviera, and celebrity-seekers can daydream about past glories at the striking hotel-peninsula of Sveti Stefan.

Getting to Montenegro

This chapter is designed for day-tripping to Montenegro from Dubrovnik; all of the sights are within about a three-hour drive of Dubrovnik, and within about an hour of each other.

Montenegro Almanac

Official Name: After being part of "Yugoslavia," then "Serbia and Montenegro," it's now the Republic of Montenegro (Republika Crna Gora)—which means "Black Mountain." It might have gotten its name from sailors who saw darkly forested cliffs as they approached, or it may have been named for a mythical mountain in the country's interior.

Snapshot History: Long overshadowed by its Croatian and Serbian neighbors, Montenegro finally achieved independence on June 3, 2006, in a landmark vote to secede from Serbia—its influential and sometimes overbearing "big brother."

Population: Montenegro is home to 662,000 people. Of these, the vast majority are Eastern Orthodox Christians (45 percent Montenegrins, 29 percent Serbs), with minority groups of Muslims (including Bosniaks and Albanians, about 13 percent total) and Catholics (1 percent).

Area: 5,415 square miles (slightly smaller than Connecticut).

Red Tape: Americans and Canadians need only a passport (no visa required) to enter Montenegro.

Geography: Montenegro is characterized by a rugged, rocky terrain that rises straight up from the Adriatic and almost immediately becomes a steep mountain range. The country has 182 miles of coastline, about a third of which constitutes the Bay of Kotor. The only real city is the dreary capital in the interior, Podgorica (144,000 people). Each of Yugoslavia's six republics had a town called Titograd, and Podgorica was Montenegro's.

Economy: Upon declaring independence in 2006, Montenegro's economy was weak. But the privatization of its economy

By Car: Driving is the best option, giving you maximum flexibility for sightseeing—but be aware of possible border delays (see "Helpful Hints," later). I've narrated a handy self-guided driving tour of the Bay of Kotor, and another for the most accessible slice of the Montenegrin interior. Even if you don't have a rental car during your Dubrovnik visit, consider renting one just for the day to visit Montenegro. Perhaps most satisfying—but expensive—is to hire your own Dubrovnik-based driver to bring you here. While this is pricey (€250 for the day), you can try to team up with other travelers to share the cost.

By Bus: Bus service between Dubrovnik and Montenegro is workable but infrequent (2-3/day each way between Dubrovnik and Kotor town, 2.5 hours). In theory, you can try to day-trip from Dubrovnik to Kotor, but bus schedules won't leave you with enough time to merit the long trip: The first morning bus departs Dubrovnik at 10:30, arriving in Kotor around 13:00 (later if there are delays); the return bus to Dubrovnik departs Kotor at 15:55.

(including its dominant industry, aluminum) and the aggressive development of its tourist trade (such as soliciting foreign investment—mostly Russian—to build new luxury hotels) have turned things around. In fact, in 2008, Montenegro had the most foreign investment, per capita, of any country in Europe. But it's still a poor place: Montenegro's unemployment rate hovers around 19 percent, and its per capita GDP is just $18,000.

Currency: Though it's not a member of the European Union, Montenegro uses the euro as its currency: €1 = about $1.30.

Language and Alphabet: The official language is Montenegrin, which is nearly identical to Serbian but predominantly uses "our" Roman alphabet (rather than Cyrillic). Still, you'll see plenty of Cyrillic here—targeting the country's large Serb minority as well as Russian tourists and investors.

Telephones: Montenegro's country code is 382. When calling from another country, first dial the international access code (00 from Europe, 011 from the US), then 382, then the area code (minus the initial zero), then the number. Note that Montenegro recently changed its area codes. If you see the former code for the Bay of Kotor area, 082, you'll have to replace it with the new one: 032.

Flag: It's a red field surrounded by a gold fringe. In the middle is the national seal: a golden, two-headed Byzantine eagle topped with a single crown, holding a scepter in one hand and a ball in the other (symbolizing the balance between church and state). The eagle's body is covered by a shield depicting a lion with one paw raised (representing the resurrected Christ).

And, of course, if you ride the bus, you can't stop to explore the sights along the way. As the schedule is always in flux, it's important to confirm times carefully at the Dubrovnik TI or bus station.

It's also possible to take a bus directly from Montenegro to **Mostar** in Bosnia-Herzegovina. The daily bus via Trebinje (run by Globtour in Mostar) departs Budva at 14:15 and Kotor at 15:00, arriving in Mostar at 20:00. The return bus from Mostar departs at 7:00, and arrives at Kotor at 12:30 and Budva at 13:30. There is also a daily bus connection via Dubrovnik.

By Excursion: As a last resort, consider taking a package excursion that follows basically the same route covered in this chapter (sold by various travel agencies in Dubrovnik).

Planning Your Time

Assuming you have your own car, for a straightforward one-day plan, drive to Kotor and back (figure about eight hours, includ-

ing driving time and sightseeing stops). To extend your time, you can add as much Montenegro as you like. Get an early start (to avoid lines at the border, I'd leave Dubrovnik as early as 7:30 in the morning). It takes about two hours to drive from Dubrovnik to Kotor (add about 1.5 hours if you stop in Perast for the boat trip out to the island). Kotor is worth two or three hours. From Kotor, you can return directly to Dubrovnik (about 1.5 hours if you use the ferry shortcut); or drive another hour up to Njeguši and Cetinje in the Montenegrin interior, or a half-hour to the Budva Riviera (from either place, figure about 2.5-3 hours back to Dubrovnik). To cram everything into one extremely long day, you can do Dubrovnik-Kotor-Cetinje-Budva Riviera-Dubrovnik. If you're taking the bayside road home (not the ferry shortcut) and don't mind getting to Dubrovnik late, consider stopping for dinner at the recommended Konoba Ćatovića Mlini or Stari Mlini restaurants.

Helpful Hints

Border Delays: The main Croatian-Montenegrin border is at **Debeli Brijeg.** When it's not busy, this border is relatively straightforward—just stop and show your passport (and potentially your rental car's proof of insurance, called a "green card"). However, Montenegro is an increasingly popular side-trip destination for Dubrovnik vacationers, and—since Croatia joined the EU in 2013—this border is now also the border of the European Union, which has tightened things up a bit. You'll most likely encounter long waits (of an hour or more) on Saturdays and Sundays in August, and to a lesser degree in July and early September. To avoid these long backups, you have two options: Get an early start (locals suggest reaching the border by 8:00—leaving Dubrovnik around 7:30 or 7:45 to beat the tour buses), or use a different crossing.

A secondary crossing, called **Konfin,** rarely has a line (because big buses are not allowed). While this can save you time on a busy day, it's a bit less straightforward (with a few turn-offs rather than a straight shot on the main road) and takes a few more miles. I've narrated a scenic route ("Konfin Border Detour") in my self-guided driving tour, later.

Afternoon Delays: The Debeli Brijeg border crossing can also be severely delayed coming back to Dubrovnik in the afternoon. (Lines are worst in summer around 16:00 or 17:00—when a long chain of excursion buses all head back at the same time.) If this happens, bail out and use the secondary (and much less crowded) Konfin border crossing.

Local Guide: While many Dubrovnik-based drivers/guides can

bring you to Montenegro, if you really want the Montenegrin perspective, consider hiring a local guide here. I spent a great day learning about this area from **Stefan Đukanović,** a young, energetic, knowledgeable guide who speaks good English and has an infectious enthusiasm for his homeland. Hiring Stefan is a great value. The catch is that he can't come and get you in Dubrovnik, so it works best if you drive yourself to Montenegro and pick him up when you get there. Stefan is also an excellent choice if you're arriving in Kotor by cruise ship (guiding only: €60/half-day, €80/day, extra for driver if going outside of Kotor; sample shore excursions: half-day tour of Kotor and Perast, including driving-€200, full-day drive around Montenegro including Kotor/Njeguši/Cetinje/Budva Rivera-€300, these prices for up to 6 people; mobile 069-297-221 or 069-369-994, www.miroandsons.com, djukan@t-com. me).

The Bay of Kotor

With dramatic cliffs rising out of the glimmering Adriatic, ancient towns packed with history and thrilling vistas, an undeveloped ruggedness unlike anything in Croatia, and a twisty road to tie it all together, the Bay of Kotor represents the best of Montenegro. To top it off, it's easy to reach by car from Dubrovnik.

Self-Guided Driving Tour

▲▲Bay of Kotor Day Trip (from Dubrovnik)

The Bay of Kotor (Boka Kotorska—literally the "Mouth of Kotor"; sometimes called "Boka Bay") is Montenegro's most enjoyable and convenient attraction for those based in Dubrovnik. This self-guided tour narrates the drive from the Croatian border to the town of Kotor, in the Bay of Kotor's deepest corner.

The Montenegrin border is about 30-45 minutes south of Dubrovnik (don't forget your passport). Simply follow the main coastal road south (signs to *Ćilipi*), past Cavtat and the airport.

From Dubrovnik to the Border

As you leave Dubrovnik, the jagged cliffs on your left eventually give way to a pastoral countryside called **Konavle** (literally "canal," recalling how the Romans built aqueducts through this area to supply their settlement at today's Cavtat). This farming region—effectively Dubrovnik's hinterland—was badly damaged during the recent war, when the Yugoslav People's Army invaded from the

Cruising into Kotor

With cruise-ship crowds reaching capacity in nearby Dubrovnik, the Montenegrin town of Kotor has emerged as a hugely popular port of call on Mediterranean cruises. Major American lines (including Royal Caribbean, Celebrity, Holland America, Carnival, Oceania, Seabourn, and Silversea) and European ones (Costa, MSC, and some German lines) have started to call here; in 2014, an estimated 350,000 passengers are expected to come to Kotor on cruise ships. If you're one of them, here are some pointers.

Arrival in Kotor by Cruise Ship: Kotor is one of the easiest Mediterranean ports to arrive in. Ships either dock at or tender to the long pier that juts out directly in front of the Old Town. All passengers are funneled out of the same port gate, with the Old Town straight ahead. As you leave the port gate, look left to find an **ATM** in a freestanding orange kiosk (though the main square of the Old Town, less than a five-minute walk away, also has ATMs); and look right to see an official **taxi** stand. (Unscrupulous taxis have been known to camp out near here to commandeer cruise passengers; be sure to use one at an official stand, and with a taxi logo and phone number on the side of the car.)

Exiting the port gate, continue straight ahead with the water on your right. Watch for the crosswalk (on your left, marked with brown *Kotor* sign) over the busy harborfront road, which you can use to get to the square in front of the Old Town, the TI, and the start of my self-guided walk.

south, forcing villagers to flee to safety in Dubrovnik. But today it's bouncing back, and is home to many appealing *konoba*s (taverns) serving traditional local food.

Soon after the turn-off for the Bosnian border, on the right, you'll pass **Kupari,** with one of the few buildings that's still damaged from the wars of the 1990s. Originally Tito's villa, the building later became a vacation home for Yugoslav military officers. Now it's a ruin, awaiting investors.

From Kupari, you'll curl around the picturesque **Bay of Cavtat,** where some of the world's richest people tie up their yachts. Partway along the bay, after the village of Plat, you'll pass (on the left) an electrical plant, which harnesses the power of an underground river to generate more than enough clean energy for the entire city.

After the pleasant resort town of **Cavtat,** then the airport, you have the option of turning off (on the right, toward *Molnat*) to take advantage of the less crowded border crossing at Konfin (described next). Otherwise, just cruise along the main road until you reach the primary Debeli Brijeg border crossing. (If there's

Amenities: Free **Wi-Fi** is available near the TI kiosk. The two **pharmacies** in the Old Town are open long hours daily (for locations, see the map on page 121).

Sightseeing Options: The **Old Town of Kotor** itself is the obvious place to spend your day—though seeing everything, including my self-guided orientation walk and all of the museums—won't take you more than a couple of hours. Add a couple more hours if you're up for the stiff hike to the fortress above town (and maybe another hour or so, just to recover). With more time, you may want to venture farther afield. The easiest choice is **Perast,** where you can explore a charming seaside village and ride a small boat out to one of the islands in the middle of the fjord (for details, see page 114); allow about four hours total for the round-trip to Perast and the island. Public buses connect Kotor town to Perast, or you can spring for a taxi (legitimate cabbies charge €20-25 one-way or €40-50 round-trip, including waiting time; negotiate a fixed price up front). For either of these trips—or to reach other, more distant Montenegrin destinations explained in this chapter—consider hiring a **local guide;** I recommend Stefan Đukanović, listed on page 105.

Sail-in and Sail-away: Cruisers visiting Kotor are treated to a spectacular sail-in and sail-away, through the fjordlike bay and the narrow Verige Strait. If the weather's good and you enjoy dramatic scenery, this is not a day to sleep in or nap during the sail-away.

MONTENEGRO

a line-up when you arrive, it's easy to backtrack to the alternate crossing: Just after the town of Gruda, follow signs for *Pločice*, then *Vitaljina*, then *Herceg Novi*, joining up with the route described next.)

Optional Konfin Border Detour

If you suspect that there will be long lines at the primary border crossing, consider this scenic and uncongested detour via the secondary one (at Konfin). Soon after passing the airport, take the turn-off on the right for *Molunat*. You'll pass through a tranquil, nearly Tuscan landscape of pointy cypresses, vineyards, olive groves, and fig trees. Just before the village of Radovčići, on the right, watch for **Kojan Koral,** a horse farm that hosts "celebrity" equines when they come here to perform in the HBO show *Game of Thrones* (which is filmed locally). They offer horseback rides and ATV safaris (www.kojankoral.hr).

Farther along, you'll enjoy fine views (on the right) down on the dramatic, elongated peninsula of **Molunat**. Notice that the H-shaped peninsula forms two protected bays. The larger one, facing

MONTENEGRO

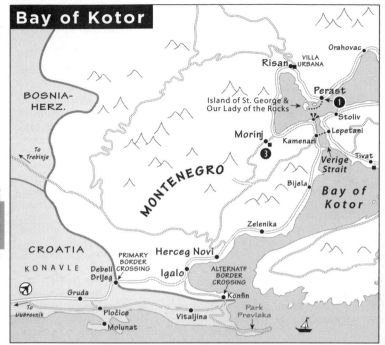

Bay of Kotor

Orahovac

BOSNIA-HERZ.

Risan • VILLA URBANA

Perast ①

Island of St. George & Our Lady of the Rocks

• Stoliv

Morinj • ③

Kamenari

Lepetani

→To Trebinje

MONTENEGRO

Verige Strait

Tivat

Bijela

Bay of Kotor

CROATIA

Zelenika

KONAVLE

PRIMARY BORDER CROSSING

Herceg Novi

Debeli Drijeg

Igalo

ALTERNATE BORDER CROSSING

✈

Gruda

Konfin

←To Dubrovnik

Pločice

Vitaljina

Park Prevlaka

Molunat

north (toward Dubrovnik), is used to harbor ships in winter, while the smaller, south-facing one is better in summer.

When the road reaches a T-intersection, turn left for *Dubrovnik* and *Park Prevlaka*, then follow signs right for *Đurinići*, then right again for *Vitaljina*. As you continue on this road—through the villages of Đurinići, Višnjići, and Vitaljina—high on the mountains to your left is the point locals call **Tromeđe** ("Three Borders"), where Croatia, Bosnia-Herzegovina, and Montenegro all converge.

Continue straight along this road all the way to the border, following signs for *Herceg Novi* and *GP Konfin*. You'll pass a turnoff on the right for **Park Prevlaka,** an old Austro-Hungarian and Yugoslav army fortress that has recently been converted into a park; you can see it at the tip of the peninsula poking out on your right— the southernmost point in Croatia.

Before long, you'll arrive at the Croatian border post, and then the Montenegrin one. After entering Montenegro, you'll curve along the small bay into Igalo, where you can pick up the self-guided driving tour.

• *From either border, you can make it to Kotor in about an hour without stopping, but with all the diversions en route you should plan for much more time. Coming back, you can trim a good half-hour off the drive by*

MONTENEGRO

Legend:
1. Conte Hotel/Restaurant & Admiral Hotel/Restaurant
2. Restoran Stari Mlini
3. Konoba Ćatovića Mlini & Tramontana
4. Restoran Konak

crossing the fjord at its narrowest point, using the Lepetani–Kamenari ferry. Navigating on this tour is really simple: It's basically the same road, with no turn-offs, from Dubrovnik to Kotor. First, you'll approach the coast at the town called...

Igalo

Driving through Igalo, keep an eye out (on the right) for a big concrete hotel called **Institut Dr. Simo Milošević** (no relation to war-criminal Slobodan). This internationally regarded spa is one of the world's premier treatment facilities for arthritis and nerve disorders. Especially popular among Scandinavians, it's capable of hosting more than 1,000 patients at once. Yugoslav President-for-Life Tito had a villa nearby and took treatments here.

• *A couple of miles beyond Igalo, you enter the biggest city you'll see today...*

Herceg Novi

The drab economic and industrial capital of the Bay of Kotor, Herceg Novi (with 25,000 people) is hardly the prettiest introduction to this otherwise striking landscape. Herceg Novi flourished during the Habsburg boom of the late 19th century, when a railroad

The History of Kotor

With evidence of prehistoric settlements dating back to 2500 B.C., the Bay of Kotor has been a prized location for millennia. Its unique bottleneck shape makes the Bay of Kotor the single best natural harbor between Greece and Venice. Predictably, this scenic and strategic strip has attracted more than its share of overlords across the centuries—so many, in fact, that it's difficult to keep track.

One of the earliest known civilizations in Kotor (third century B.C.) was that of the Illyrians, whose Queen Teuta held court here until her lands were conquered by the Romans. Later, when the Roman Empire split (fourth century A.D.), Montenegro straddled the cultural fault line between West (Roman Catholic) and East (Orthodox Christian). As Rome crumbled in the sixth and seventh centuries, the Slavs moved in. Initially rejecting Roman culture, many later converted to Christianity (some Orthodox, some Catholic).

By the 10th century, Montenegro's Slavs had organized into a sovereign state, affiliated with but partially independent from the Byzantine (Eastern Roman) Empire. Thanks to its protected location, medieval Kotor became a major city of the salt trade.

The Bay of Kotor further flourished in the 14th century, under the Serbian emperor Dušan the Mighty. Notorious for his aggressive law enforcement—chopping off the hand of a thief, slicing off the nose of a liar—Dušan made the Bay of Kotor a particularly safe place to do business. One of his strategies was making the nobility responsible for safe passage. If a visiting merchant was robbed, the nobleman who controlled that land would be ruthlessly punished. Soon 2,000-horse caravans could pass without a worry along this fjord. During storms, ships would routinely seek

line connected it to Dubrovnik, Sarajevo, and Vienna. Back then, Austrians vacationed here—but more recent development has been decidedly less elegant than the Habsburgs'. While there is a walled Old Town core to Herceg Novi, it's not worth stopping to see; skip the turnoff for the town center, carrying on along the main road toward Budva.

Passing above Herceg Novi's Old Town, keep an eye out on the right for the town's stout 15th-century **fortress,** which was built by the Ottomans—who controlled this area, but never made it deeper into the bay.

Also in Herceg Novi, watch for tropical trees. Locals pride themselves on their particularly mild climate, kept warm year-round thanks to the mitigating effects of the water from the adjacent fjord. Supposedly, "it never drops below 50 degrees Fahrenheit." This town even has some banana trees (not visible from the road)—and even though the trees are just decorative (the fruit they

protection in this secluded bay.

But the Serbian Empire went into steep decline after Dušan. As the Ottomans threatened to invade in the 15th century, Kotor's traders turned to Venice for help. The Venetian Republic would control this bay for the next 450 years, and it was never taken by enemies. In fact, Montenegro managed to evade Ottoman rule entirely...unlike its neighbors Albania, Kosovo, Serbia, and Bosnia-Herzegovina. (Meanwhile, neighboring Croats enjoy pointing out that, while the Bay of Kotor was nominally part of Venice, much of the territory was privately owned by a Croat family.)

In the late 19th century, when Venice fell to Napoleon, the Bay of Kotor came briefly under the control of France, then Russia, then Austria. Feudal traditions fell by the wayside, industry arrived, and the area's old-fashioned economy went into a sharp decline. As trading wealth dried up, the Bay of Kotor entered a period of architectural stagnation. But thanks to this dark spell in Montenegrin history, today's visitors can enjoy some wonderfully preserved time-warp towns.

When Montenegro became part of Yugoslavia following World War I, the Serbs (who felt a cultural affinity with the Montenegrins that wasn't always reciprocated) laid claim to the Montenegrin coast as their own little patch of seafront. Serbs flooded into Montenegro, altering the demographics and making it, in effect, an outpost of the Republic of Serbia. This helped Montenegro avoid the initial violence of the breakup of Yugoslavia, but put them in an awkward position when it came time for them to request secession a few years later. For the rest of the story, see the "Montenegro: Birth of a Nation" sidebar, later.

MONTENEGRO

produce is too small to eat), they're a local symbol. So is the mimosa flower, which blooms all winter long, and is the inspiration for the town's annual Mimosa Festival—held each February, when much of Europe (including most of Montenegro) is under a blanket of snow.

Other than its banana trees and mimosas, Herceg Novi is basically a mess. (Don't worry—the drive gets much prettier later on.) Why so much ugliness compared to Croatia? For one thing, Tito viewed Croatia's Dalmatian Coast as a gold mine of hard Western currency—so he was inclined to keep it Old World-charming. And Croatia remained in the cultural and political orbit of Zagreb, which was motivated to take good care of its historic towns. But Belgrade, which exerted more influence on Montenegro, didn't offer it the same degree of TLC. And because Montenegro has traditionally been poorer than Croatia, its officials are more susceptible to bribery and corruption. ("Would a few thousand dinar

convince you to ignore my new hotel's code violations?") From an architectural point of view, it's a sad irony that gorgeous Dubrovnik was devastated by bombs and the gritty cities of Montenegro survived the war essentially unscathed. To this day, locals aren't crazy about the Serbs who flock here in summer for as-cheap-as-possible beach holidays. Instead, Montenegrins are encouraging the construction of top-end resort hotels to lure high rollers from around the world (such as James Bond, who played poker in the 2006 movie version of *Casino Royale* in "Montenegro"—though it was actually filmed in the Czech Republic). But even this new development is poorly regulated, threatening to turn Montenegro into a charmless, concrete Costa del Sol-style vacation zone. Enjoy the Bay of Kotor's pristine areas (which we'll enter soon) while you still can.

• *As you go through Herceg Novi, at the roundabout, follow signs for* Budva, Kotor, *and* Trajekt/Ferry.

After the tunnel, you'll pass through **Zelenika,** *once the end of the line for the Habsburg rail line from Vienna, which first brought tourism to this area.*

You'll carry on through a few more dreary towns. Entertain yourself by gazing across the strait on your right to look for caves burrowed into the cliff face at sea level. These provided shelter for Yugoslav warships. Also along this cliff, you'll see naval barracks. In **Bijela,** *you'll pass a big industrial shipyard on your right; in addition to the rusty, hardworking ships you'll likely see here, this place also services luxury yachts—another example of Montenegro's odd juxtaposition of gritty industry and nouveau wealth.*

Eventually, you'll emerge into a more rustic setting. This fjordside road is lined with fishing villages, some now developed as resorts (including a few with severe communist-era touches). Each waterfront house seems to have its own little boat dock sticking out into the glassy water. You'll pass through the town of **Kamenari,** *which has a handy ferry that you could use to shave time off your return trip to Dubrovnik (described at the end of this drive). Two minutes after leaving Kamenari (just after the* Kostanjica *sign), watch for a convenient gravel pull-out on the right (likely packed with tour buses, by the small white lighthouse). Pull over to check out the narrowest point of the fjord, the...*

Verige Strait

This tight bottleneck at the mouth of the bay is the secret to the Bay of Kotor's success: Any would-be invaders had to pass through here to reach the port towns inside the bay. It's narrow enough to carefully monitor (not even a quarter-mile wide), but deep enough to allow even today's large megaships through (more than 130 feet deep). Because this extremely narrow strait is relatively easy to

defend, whoever controlled the inside of the fjord was allowed to thrive virtually unchecked.

Centuries before Christ, even before the flourishing of Roman culture, the Bay of Kotor was home to the Illyrians—the mysterious ancestors of today's Albanians. In the third century B.C., Illyrian Queen Teuta spanned this strait with an ingenious shipwrecking mechanism to more effectively collect taxes. To this day, many sunken ships litter the bottom of this bay. (Teuta was a little too clever for her own good—her shrewdness and success attracted the attention of the on-the-rise Romans, who seized most of her holdings.)

In later times, chains were stretched across the bay here to control the entrance (the name "Verige" comes from a Slavic word for "chain"). Later still, the Venetians came up with an even more elaborate plan: Place cannons on either side of the strait, with a clear shot at any entering ships. Looking across the wide part of the bay, notice the town of Perast (by the two islands). Perast—where we'll be stopping soon—was also equipped with cannons that could easily reach across the bay. Thanks to this extensive defense network, Ottomans or any other potential invaders were unlikely to penetrate the bay, either by sea or by land.

• *Continue driving around the fjord. You'll pass through the village of...*

Morinj

This town is known for two starkly different reasons: First, it's the home of a recommended restaurant with fine food in a gorgeous setting (Konoba Ćatovića Mlini); another, more casual eatery sits nearby. And second, it was the site of a concentration camp for Croat prisoners captured during the 1991-1992 siege of Dubrovnik. Some 300 civilians from in and near Dubrovnik were forcibly brought here, where they lived in horrifying conditions. After the war, six of the guards from this camp were convicted of war crimes.

• *After going through Morinj and some other small villages, you'll pass through the larger resort town of...*

Risan

Back in Greek times, when the Bay of Kotor was known as *"Sinus Rhizonicus,"* Risan was the leading town of the bay. Later, during the Illyrian Queen Teuta's brief three-year reign, Risan was her capital. Today the town is still home to the scant remains of Teuta's castle (on the hilltop just before town), but it's mostly notable for its giant communist eyesore hotel—named, appropriately enough, Hotel Teuta.

Historians may want to turn off to the left (at the brown *Roman Mosaics* sign) in the town center for a quick look at a few partly

intact mosaic floors of the second-century A.D. Roman **Villa Urbana** (€2, daily 8:00-20:00). You'll enter through a small modern building to access the large, covered footprint of the villa. Between the knee-high stone walls are mosaics of checkerboards, stylized marine life (including calamari), and—most significant—a small mosaic of reclining Hypnos, the god of dreams.

• *Continue on to Perast. As you approach the town, take the right fork (marked with brown sign) directly down into Perast; or you can first take the left fork to pass above town for sweeping views over the bay, then backtrack down into the town center.*

Perast

This second-most appealing town on the fjord (after Kotor) is considered the "Pearl of Venetian Baroque." It's worth taking some time to wander and explore its buildings and enjoy its relaxed small-town feel (minus the bustle of bigger Kotor). During the summer, you're required to pay to park near the entrance of town, and then walk or ride the free shuttle bus into the town center; at other times, you may be allowed to drive

along the waterfront road and park for free in front of the church.

Remember that Perast, with its cannons aimed at the Verige Strait across the bay, was an essential link in the Bay of Kotor's fortifications. In exchange for this important duty, Venice rewarded Perast with privileged tax-free status, and the town became extremely wealthy. Ornate mansions proliferated here during its 17th- and 18th-century heyday. But after Venice fell to Napoleon, and the Bay of Kotor's economy changed, Perast's singular defensive role disappeared. With no industry, no hinterland, and no natural resources, Perast stagnated—leaving it a virtual open-air museum of Venetian architecture.

Go to the tallest steeple in town, overlooking a long and narrow harborfront square. Perast is centered on its too-big (and incomplete) church, **St. Nicholas**—dedicated to the patron saint of fishermen. It was originally designed to extend out into the sea (the old church, still standing, was to be torn down). But Napoleon's troops came marching in before the builders got that far, so the plans were scuttled—and this massive partial-church was instead simply grafted on to the existing, modest church.

Go inside (free, treasury-€1, sporadic hours, generally April-Nov daily 9:00-18:00, July-Aug until 19:00, closed during Mass, closed Dec-March except by request—ask locals around the church if someone can let you in). Beyond the small sanctuary, you'll find

a treasury with relics and icons. Look for the priceless crucifix from the school of the 18th-century Venetian artist Giovanni Battista Tiepolo (#1, in the display case in the center of the room), with Jesus on one side, and Mary and the saints on the other. Beyond the treasury is what was to be the main apse (altar area) of the unfinished massive church (notice it's at a right angle to the actual, in-use altar of the existing smaller church). The rough, unadorned brick walls make it clear that they didn't get very far. Check out the model of the ambitious but never-built church. The Baroque main altar is by Bernini's student Francesco Cabianca, who lived in this area and was always trying to earn money to pay off his gambling debts. The small room at the end displays old vestments.

If you have the time and energy, pay €1 to climb the **church tower** for the view.

Perast's only other "sight" is its **Town Museum,** which fills a grand old hall with paintings, furniture, navy uniforms, model ships, pistols, portraits of VIPs (very important Perastians), medals, traditional musical instruments, and other historic bric-a-brac. It's pretty dull but has nice sea views (€2.50, July-Aug Mon-Sat 9:00-21:00, Sun 9:00-14:00, progressively shorter hours off-season, closed Sun Nov-April; along the water near the start of town, in the ornate building with the arcade and balcony; tel. 032/373-519).

Eating in Perast: For an enjoyable drink or meal, consider the upscale **Conte** restaurant, filling a pier on the bay in the middle of town (€8-13 pastas, €12-20 main dishes). On the far side of the square is another, well-shaded pier restaurant, **Admiral** (€9-13 pastas, €9-20 main dishes). Both are open daily and attached to recommended hotels.

• *Before leaving Perast, take a close look at the two islands just offshore (and consider paying a visit).*

St. George (Sv. Đorđe) and Our Lady of the Rocks (Gospa od Škrpjela)

These twin islands—one natural, the other man-made—come with a fascinating story.

The **Island of St. George** (the smaller, rocky island with trees and a monastery—closed to tourists), named for the protector of Christianity, was once part of the fortification of the Bay of Kotor. Near this natural island was a small underwater reef with a small

Montenegro: Birth of a Nation

Montenegro, like Croatia and Slovenia, was one of the six republics that constituted the former Yugoslavia. When these republics began splitting away in the early 1990s, Montenegro—always allied closely with Serbia, and small enough to slip under the radar—decided to remain in the union. When the dust had settled, four of the six Yugoslav republics had seceded (Croatia, Slovenia, Bosnia-Herzegovina, and Macedonia), while only two remained united as "Yugoslavia": Serbia and Montenegro.

At first, Montenegrin Prime Minister Milo Đukanović was on friendly terms with Serbia's Slobodan Milošević. But in the late 1990s, as Milošević's political stock plummeted, Montenegro began to inch away from Serbia. Eager to keep its access to the coast (and the many Serbs who lived there), Serbia made concessions that allowed Montenegro to gradually assert its independence. In 1996, Montenegro boldly adopted the German mark as its official currency to avoid the inflating Yugoslav dinar.

By 2003, the country of Yugoslavia was no more, and the loose union was renamed "Serbia and Montenegro." Thus began a three-year transition period that allowed Montenegro to test the waters of real independence. During this time, Serbia and Montenegro were united only in defense—legislation, taxation, currency, and most governmental functions were separate. And it was agreed that after three years, Montenegro would be allowed to hold a referendum for full independence.

That fateful vote took place on May 21, 2006. In general, ethnic Montenegrins tended to favor independence, while ethnic Serbs wanted to stay united with Serbia. To secede, Montenegro needed 55 percent of the vote. By the slimmest of margins—half a percent, or just 2,300 votes—the pro-independence faction won. On June 3, 2006, Montenegro officially declared independence. (To save face, two days later, Serbia also "declared independence" from Montenegro.)

Today's Montenegrins are excited to have their own little country and enthusiastic about eventually joining the European Union. Serbia's greatest concern was that in losing Montenegro, it would also lose its lone outlet to the sea—both for shipping and for holiday-making. The Serbs also feared that Montenegrin independence might inspire similar actions in the Serbian province of Kosovo (which did, in fact, declare independence from Serbia less than two years later).

But for many people in both countries, independence is an epilogue rather than a climax. Shortly after the referendum, I asked a Montenegrin when the countries would officially separate. He chuckled and said, "Three years ago."

section poking above the surface. According to legend, two fishermen noticed a strange light emanating from the reef in the early-morning fog. Rowing out to the island, they discovered an icon of Our Lady. They attempted to bring it ashore, but it kept washing back out again to the same spot. Taking this celestial hint, local seamen returning home from a journey began dropping rocks into the bay in this same place. The tradition caught on, more and more villagers dropped in rocks of their own, and eventually more than a hundred old ships and other vessels were loaded with stones and intentionally sunk in this spot. And so, over two centuries, an entire island was formed in the middle of the bay.

Flash forward to today's **Our Lady of the Rocks** (the flat island with the dome-topped Catholic church). In the 17th century, locals built this Baroque church on this holy site and filled it with symbols of thanks for answered prayers. Step inside (free entry) to explore the collection: silver votive plaques—many of them with images of ships in storms or battles—given by appreciative sailors who survived; 1,700 silver and gold votive plaques from other grateful worshippers; 68 canvases by local Baroque painter Tripo Kokolja; and a huge collection of dried wedding bouquets given by those who had nothing else to offer (the church is a popular place for weddings). Take a close look at the main altar. That legendary icon, which refused to budge from this spot, still caps the altar today. The faithful squeeze into the very tight space behind the altar, where a hole in the back of the structure lets them reach through and touch the original reef where the icon was found.

The adjacent **museum** is an entertaining mishmash of items. The entry price includes a fun little tour by Davorka, Nataša, or

Sandra (€1, May-Oct daily 9:00-19:00, off-season opens sporadically with boat arrival—or call ahead to Davorka's mobile 069-621-322). Just inside, study the models of both islands. The artificial one—the one you're on—is shaped vaguely like a boat. The collection includes a wide range of ancient artifacts, including a glass

case displaying fragments dating—staggeringly—from 3500 B.C. (found in the hills just above Perast). There's also a small modern

MONTENEGRO

art gallery with various depictions of the two islands created by artists who came here and were inspired by this place; paintings of ships commissioned by local sailors (notice that most have a saintly image of Mary and the Baby Jesus hovering nearby); and other gifts given through the ages. Upstairs, near the gift shop counter, look for the amazing embroidery made by a local woman who toiled over it for more than 25 years. She used her own hair for the hair of the angels—which you can see fade from brown to gray as she aged (beginning at around 3 o'clock and going clockwise, you'll see the subtle change in color).

Getting There: Boats to Our Lady of the Rocks leave from in front of St. Nicholas' Church in Perast—look for the guys milling around the harborfront with boats ready to go. The going rate is €5/person round-trip, but Zoran (who has the boat with the red awning marked *Taxi Boat Perast*) says he'll charge only €4/person if you show this book.

• *When you're ready to move on, continue driving around the fjord. After the large town of Orahovac, you'll see part of the bay roped off for a mussel farm; these farms do best when located where mountain rivers spill into the bay. And a hundred or so yards later, you cross a bridge spanning the don't-blink-or-you'll-miss-it...*

Ljuta River

According to locals, this is the "shortest river in the world"—notice that the source (bubbling up from under the cliff) is just to the left of the bridge, and it meets the sea just to the right. Short as it is, it's hardly a trickle—in fact, its name means "Angry River" for its fierce flow during heavy rains. The river actually courses underground for several miles before emerging here. Like the Karst area south of Ljubljana, this is a karstic landscape—limestone that's honeycombed with underground rivers, caves, and canyons. Many other waterfalls and streams feed the Bay of Kotor with snowmelt from the surrounding mountains. Because of this steady natural flushing, locals brag that the bay's water is particularly clear and clean.

• *Immediately after the bridge, look for the turnoff (on the right) to the recommended Restoran Stari Mlini—a tranquil spot for a meal or drink. Fittingly, this "Old Mill" sits right where the river comes tumbling out—the perfect spot to harness that hydropower.*

Continuing along the fjord, as you pass through the town of Dobrota, look across the bay to the village of...

Prčanj

This town is famous as the former home of many centuries' worth of wealthy sea captains. When the Bay of Kotor was part of the Austrian Empire, Emperor Franz Josef came to Prčanj. Upon being

...eted by some 50 uniformed ship captains, he marveled that such ...ollection of seafarers had been imported for his visit...not realizing that every one of them lived nearby.

• *Keep on driving. When you see the giant moat with the town wall, and the smaller wall twisting up the hill above, you'll know you've arrived in **Kotor** (see next page).*

Before leaving Kotor, make a decision about where you want to go next. You have three basic options: Budva Riviera; the mountainous Montenegrin interior; or back to Croatia (see instructions for the third option in the next section).

Continuing past Kotor's Old Town, you'll follow the edge of the fjord. At the far end of town (and the fjord), you'll come to a roundabout. Bearing left at the roundabout takes you toward the handy tunnel to the **Budva Riviera**—or, along this same road, if you turn right after the cemetery and just before the tunnel, you'll take the extremely twisty road up, up, up into the **Montenegrin interior** (Njeguši and Cetinje).

Once you're finished in Montenegro, it'll be time to head...

Back to Croatia: Lepetani-Kamenari Ferry Shortcut

When you're ready to return to Dubrovnik, you can go back the way you came. Or, for a quicker route, consider the ferry that cuts across the narrow part of the fjord (between the towns of Lepetani and Kamenari). On the Kotor side of the bay, the boat departs from the town of Lepetani.

From Kotor, you have two options to reach the ferry: The easiest option is to leave Kotor, bear left at the roundabout at the far end of town, and take the tunnel toward Budva. Once through the tunnel, follow signs into Tivat, and continue straight through Tivat on the main road to reach Lepetani, which is a few miles beyond the end of town. Or, for a more challenging but more scenic route, simply turn right at the roundabout and continue driving on the waterfront road clockwise around the bay (through Prčanj and Stoliv) until you land in Lepetani. But be warned that this road is extremely narrow (one lane, with an Adriatic shoulder) and can be exhausting if oncoming traffic is heavy. However, it also offers grand views back across the fjord at Kotor, Perast, and other picturesque towns you came through earlier.

No matter how you approach, remember that "ferry" is *trajekt* (it's also signed for *Herceg Novi*—the big city across the bay). The boat goes continuously (in slow times, you may have to wait briefly for enough cars to show up), and the crossing takes just four minutes (it takes longer to load and unload all the cars than it does to cross). A small car and its passengers pay €4.50 each way.

On your way back to Dubrovnik after the ferry, if there are long lines at the primary border crossing, you can use the Konfin alternate crossing described earlier. After exiting Igalo, just

before the border—and just after the Hipermarket and Petrol gas station—watch for the turn-off on the left that's marked *granični prijelaz Konfin*. This takes you to the alternate crossing. From there, just can follow signs to *Dubrovnik* (on back roads at first, later merging with the main road).

Kotor

Butted up against a steep cliff, cradled by a calm sea, naturally sheltered by its deep-in-the-fjord position, and watched over by an imposing network of fortifications, the town of Kotor is as impressive as it is well-protected. Though it's enjoyed a long and illustrious history, today's Kotor is a time-capsule retreat for travelers seeking a truly unspoiled Adriatic town.

There's been a settlement in this location at least since the time of Christ. The ancient town of Catarum—named for the Roman word for "contracted" or "strangled," as the sea is at this point in the gnarled fjord—was first mentioned in the first century A.D. Like the rest of the region, Kotor's next two millennia were layered with history as it came under the control of a series of foreign powers: Illyrians, Romans, Serbs, Venetians, Russians, Napoleonic soldiers, Austrians, Tito's Yugoslavia...and now, finally, Montenegrins. Each group left its mark, and Kotor has its share of both Catholic and Orthodox churches (sometimes both at once), plus monuments and reminders of plenty of past colonizers and conquerors.

Through all those centuries, Kotor avoided destruction by warfare. But it was damaged by earthquakes—including the same 1667 quake that leveled Dubrovnik (known here as the "Great Shaking"), as well as a devastating 1979 earthquake from which the city is still cleaning up. While only 3,000 people live within the Old Town walls, greater Kotor has a population of about 12,000.

With an extremely inviting Old Town that seems custom-built for aimless strolling, Kotor is an idyllic place to while away a few hours. Though it's sometimes called a "little Dubrovnik," Kotor is more low-key, less ambitious, less historic, flatter, and much smaller than its more famous neighbor. And yet, with its own special spice that's exciting to sample, Kotor is a hard place to tear yourself away from.

Orientation to Kotor

Kotor (or Cattaro in Italian) has a compact Old Town shaped like a triangle. The two sides facing the bay are heavily fortified by a thick wall, and the third side huddles under the cliff face. A meandering

Kotor

"PARKING BENOVO"

NORTHERN GATE

Škurda River

TOWN WALLS

ST. NICHOLAS' CHURCH

ST. MARY'S

ST. LUKE'S

WC

❹

❺ WALK ENDS

St. Luke's Square

Access to Upper Town Walls

❶❸

❻

To "Parking Benovo" "Parking Urc" & Perast

Square of Arms

WC

❿

Trg od Kina

KARAMPANA WELL

MARITIME MUSEUM OF MONTENEGRO

❶

❷

WALK BEGINS

MAIN TOWN GATE

POST

❸

❷

❾

CHURCH OF OUR LADY OF HEALTH

"PARKING RIVA"

Trg od Brašna

❽

Pjaca Sv. Tripuna

CATHEDRAL OF ST. TRYPHON

CRUISE SHIP PORT

JADRANSKI PUT

❶

❶❹

Access to Upper Town Walls

Pjaca od Salate

Bay of Kotor

To Bus Station, Budva & Cetinje

❼

100 Meters

100 Yards

SOUTHERN GATE

MONTENEGRO

❶ Boutique Hotel Hippocampus
❷ Hotel Villa Duomo
❸ Hotel Vardar
❹ Hotel Cattaro
❺ Hotel Marija
❻ D&Sons Apartments
❼ Old Town Hostel
❽ La Pasteria Restaurant
❾ City Restaurant
❿ Cesarica Restaurant
⓫ Produce Market
⓬ Yo! Juices
⓭ The Old Winery
⓮ Pharmacies (2)

defensive wall climbs the mountainside directly behind and above town.

The Old Town's mazelike street plan is confusing, but it's so small and atmospheric that getting lost is more fun than frustrating. The natives virtually ignore addresses, including the names of streets and squares. Most Old Town addresses are represented simply as "Stari Grad," then a number (useless if you're trying to navigate by streets). To make matters worse, a single square can have several names—so one map labels it Trg od Katedrale (Cathedral Square), while another calls it Pjaca Sv. Tripuna (Piazza of St. Tryphon). My advice: Don't fret about street or square names. Simply navigate with a map and by asking locals for directions.

Thanks to the very manageable size of the Old Town, this is easier than it sounds.

Tourist Information

The TI is in a kiosk just outside the Old Town's main entrance gate (daily May-Oct 8:00-20:00, Nov-April 8:00-17:00, tel. 032/325-950, www.kotor.montenegro.travel/en). Pick up the free map and browse the collection of other brochures. There's a free Wi-Fi hotspot around this kiosk; look for the "TOKOTOR" network.

Arrival in Kotor

By Car: Approaching town, you'll first see Kotor's substantial wall, which overlooks a canal. You can park in one of three pay lots: "Parking Riva," along the bay immediately across from the main gate, is the closest to the Old Town but also the most expensive (€0.90/hour, to the right just after crossing the bridge by the wall); "Parking Benovo," in the lot across the canal (€0.60/hour, on the left just before the bridge by the wall—you'll be sent back here if the first lot is full); or "Parking Urc" (€0.50/hour, a bit farther out and along the water). All three are easily walkable from the Old Town entrance. Be sure you've parked legally, in one of these designated lots; while locals brazenly leave their cars anywhere they like, tourists get towed without remorse.

By Bus: The bus station is about a half-mile south of the Old Town. Arriving here, simply exit to the right and walk straight up the road—you'll run into the embankment and town wall in 10 minutes.

Sights in Kotor

Because of its tangled alleys and irregular street plan, Kotor feels bigger than it is. But after 10 minutes of wandering, you'll discover you're going in circles and realize it's actually very compact. (In fact, aimless wandering is Kotor's single best activity.) How such a cute town manages to be so delightfully lazy and traffic-free without being overrun by tourists, I'll never know (though the recent arrival of cruise ships is threatening Kotor's until-now-untrampled appeal).

As you ramble, keep an eye out for these key attractions. I've listed them roughly in the order of a counterclockwise route through town, beginning outside the main entrance gate.

▲Main Town Gate (Glavna Gradska Vrata)

The wide-open **square** fronting the bay and waterfront marina now welcomes visitors. But for centuries, its purpose was exactly the opposite. As the primary point of entry into this heavily fortified town, it was the last line of defense. Before the embankment was

built, the water came directly to this door, and there was only room for one ship to tie up at a time. If a ship got this far (through the gauntlet we saw back at the Verige Strait), it was carefully examined here again (and taxes were levied) before its passengers could disembark. This double-checkpoint was designed to foil pirates who might fly the flag of a friend to get through the strait, only to launch a surprise attack once here. By the way, pirates' primary booty wasn't silver or gold, but men—kidnapped for ransom, or, if ransom wasn't paid, as slaves to row on ships.

Check out the pinkish **gate** itself. The oldest parts of this gate date from 1555. It once featured a Venetian lion, then the double-headed eagle of the Habsburg Empire.

But today, most of the symbolism touts Tito's communism (notice the stars and the old Yugoslav national seal at the top). The big date (November 21, 1944) commemorates this area's liberation from the Nazis by Tito's homegrown Partisan Army. The Tito quote *(tuđe nećemo svoje nedamo)* means, roughly, "Don't take what's ours, and we won't take what's yours"—a typically provocative statement in these troubled Balkans.

• *Notice the **TI** in the kiosk just to the left of the gate. Then go through the gate into town. You'll emerge into the...*

Square of Arms (Trg od Oržja)

Do a quick spin-tour of the square, which is ringed with artifacts of the city's complex history. Looking to the left, you'll see a long

building lined with cafés, which was once the palace of the rector, who ruled Kotor on behalf of Venice. Princes could watch the action from their long balcony overlooking the square, which served as the town's living room. Later, the palace became the Kotor Town Hall. Beyond the long building, two other buildings poke out into the square (on either side of the lane leading out of the square). The one on the right is the Venetian arsenal, the square's namesake. The one on the left is the "French Theater," named for its purpose during the time this area was under Napoleon's control. Directly across from the gate you just came through, you'll see the town's Bell Tower, one of Kotor's symbols. The odd triangular structure at its base was once the town pillory. Wrongdoers would be chained

to this with their transgression printed on a placard hanging from their neck, open to public ridicule of the rudest kind imaginable. In the little recessed square just right of that, you'll spot the recommended, copper-roofed Hotel Vardar. Handy ATMs around this square dispense euros.

• *Walk down the long part of the square directly ahead of where you entered (toward Hotel Vardar). About 20 yards in front of the hotel, take the broad lane angling off to the right (paved with red-and-white-striped tiles), which leads past mansions of Kotor's medieval big shots. Turn left down the little lane next to the Montenegro Airlines office. After one short block, you'll hit Pjaca Sv. Tripuna (a.k.a. Trg od Katedrale), home to the...*

▲Cathedral of St. Tryphon (Katedrala Sv. Tripuna)

Even though most of today's Kotorians are Orthodox, Kotor's most significant church is Catholic. According to legend, in 809, Venetian merchants were sailing up the coast from Nicea (in today's Turkey) with the relics of St. Tryphon—a third-century martyr and today's patron saint of gardeners. A storm hit as they approached the Bay of Kotor, so they took shelter here. Every time they tried to leave, the weather worsened...so they finally got the message that St. Tryphon's remains should remain in Kotor.

Cost and Hours: €2, daily June-Sept 9:00-19:00, April-May and Oct 9:00-18:00, Nov-March 9:00-15:00, Mass on Sun at 10:00.

Visiting the Cathedral: Take in the cathedral's **exterior.** The earliest, Romanesque parts of this church, dating from the mid-12th century, are made of limestone from the Croatian island of Korčula. But the church has been rebuilt after four different earthquakes—most extensively after the 1667 quake, when it achieved its current Renaissance-Baroque blend. That earthquake, which also contributed to Dubrovnik's current appearance, destroyed three-quarters of Kotor's buildings. A fire swept the city, and all of the dead bodies attracted rats (and with them, the plague)—a particularly dark chapter in Kotor's history.

Why are the two **towers** different? There are plenty of legends, but the most likely is that restorers working after 1667 simply ran out of money before they finished the second one. Notice the Church of Our Lady of Health way up on the hill above this church—built in thanks to God by survivors of the plague (it also serves as part of the town fortifications—described later).

Within the cathedral, the **nave** of the church is marginally

interesting, with stout columns; surviving Byzantine-style frescoes under the arches—all that's left of paintings that once covered the church; and a fine 15th-century silver-and-gold altar covered by a delicate canopy.

But the best part is the **reliquary** upstairs. Find the stairs at the rear and walk up to the chapel. Behind the Baroque altar (by Bernini's student Francesco Cabianca, whose work we saw in Perast) and the screen are 48 different relics. In the center is St. Tryphon—his bones in a silver casket and his head in the golden chalice to the right. In the small room up the stairs, examine the fascinating icon of the Madonna and Child from the 15th century (it's in a freestanding wooden frame with a crucified Jesus on the other side; you may have to look around back to find it). The painting exemplifies this town's position as a bridge between Western and Eastern Christianity: The faces, more lifelike, are Western-style (Catholic) Gothic; the stiff, elongated bodies are more Eastern (Orthodox) and Byzantine-style. From here, take a slow walk around the upper gallery of the church to see its displays of paintings, vestments, and other ecclesiastical items.

• *Exit the church. Notice the recommended La Pasteria restaurant immediately across from the cathedral, with Italian- and Serb-style fare and scenic al fresco tables. On the right, the trees mark another recommended eatery, City Restaurant.*

When you're ready to continue, face the cathedral facade and exit the square to your left (down the street near City Restaurant). In a block, you'll wind up on a little square that's home to the...

Maritime Museum of Montenegro (Pomorski Muzej Crne Gore)

Like so many Adriatic towns, Kotor's livelihood is tied to the sea. This humble museum explores that important heritage. As you climb the stairway, notice the evocative maps and etchings of old Kotor. Portraits of salty swashbucklers, traditional costumes, and 98 coats of arms representing aristocratic families who have lived here (ringing the main room upstairs) are all reminders of the richness of Kotor's history. You'll see a display of rifles and swords (some with fun ornamental decorations illustrating the art of killing) and lots of model ships. The museum is housed in the Gregorina Palace, one of dozens of aristocratic mansions that dot the Old Town—yet another reminder of the historically high concentration of wealth and power in this little settlement.

Cost and Hours: €4, includes English audioguide; July-Aug Mon-Sat 9:00-20:00, Sun 9:00-13:00; mid-April-June and Sept-mid-Oct Mon-Fri 9:00-18:00, Sat-Sun 9:00-13:00; mid-Oct-mid-April Mon-Fri 9:00-15:00, Sat-Sun 9:00-13:00; on Trg Grgurina, tel. 032/304-720, www.museummaritimum.com.

MONTENEGRO

• *Facing the museum, go around the left side. After 10 yards, you'll pass a well on your left called the...*

Karampana

This well served as Kotor's only public faucet until the early 20th century. As such, it was also the top place in town for gossip, like the office water cooler. It's said that if your name was mentioned here, you knew you had arrived. Today, though the chatter is no longer raging on this square, the town's gossip magazine is called *Karampana*. While the pump still works (swing the pendulum once and keep it there), it's sometimes disconnected to prevent tourists from swinging it back and forth too aggressively.

• *Continue straight past the well into the next square...*

▲▲St. Luke's Square (Trg Svetog Luke)

There are two Serbian Orthodox churches on this pretty square, each with the typical Orthodox church features: a squat design, narrow windows, and portly domes. Little **St. Luke's Church** (Crkva Sv. Luka), in the middle of the square, dates from the 12th century. Locals debate long and hard as to whether St. Luke's was originally built as a Catholic church or an Orthodox one. (Although it "looks" Orthodox, it was constructed during the rule of Serbian King Vukan Nemanjić, when even Catholic churches were built in the Orthodox style.) Regardless of its origin, during the Venetian era, the church did double duty as a house of worship for both. These days, it's decidedly Orthodox. Step into the humble interior (free, daily May-Oct 10:00-20:00, Nov-April 8:00-13:00 & 17:00-19:00).

The bigger and much newer **St. Nicholas' Church** (Crkva Sv. Nikola), at the far end of the square, was built in 1909—because of its Neo-Byzantine design, it has similarly spherical domes and slitlike windows (free, same hours as St. Luke's).

Notice how the Orthodox crosses on the steeples of St. Nicholas' Church differ from the cross seen in Roman Catholic churches (known as a Latin cross). In addition to the standard crossbar, Orthodox crosses often also have a second, smaller crossbar near the top (representing the *I.N.R.I.* plaque that was displayed above Jesus' head). Sometimes Orthodox crosses also feature a third, angled crossbar at the bottom. Many believe that rather than being nailed directly to the cross, Jesus' feet were nailed to a crossbar like this one to prolong his suffering. The slanted angle represents Jesus' forgiveness of the thief crucified to his right (the side that's pointing up)...and suggests where the unrepentant thief on his left ended up.

Stepping into these (or any other Orthodox) churches, you'll immediately notice some key differences from Catholic church-

es: no pews (worshippers stand through the service as a sign of respect), tall and skinny candles (representing prayers), and a screen of icons, called an iconostasis, in the middle of the sanctuary to separate the material world from the holy world (where the Bible is kept).

Before continuing on, enjoy this square's lazy ambience. The big building fronting the square is a music school, and the students practicing here fill this already pleasant public space with an appealing soundtrack.

• *If you go down the street to your left as you face St. Nicholas, you'll wind up back at the Square of Arms. But first try getting lost, then found again, in Kotor's delightful maze of streets.*

The town's final attraction is above your head. To go there directly, face St. Nicholas' Church, turn right, and walk straight for two blocks until you reach St. Mary's Church (named for one of four Catholic saints who came from the Bay of Kotor—which some faithful locals call the "Bay of Saints"). If you carry on straight past the church—down the narrow lane with two arches—you'll find the entrance to the town walls.

▲▲Town Walls (Gradske Zidine)

Kotor's fortifications begin as stout ramparts along the waterfront, then climb up the sheer cliff face behind town in a dizzying zigzag line. If there's a more elaborate city wall in Europe, I haven't seen it. A proud Kotorian bragged to me, "These fortifications cost more to build than any palace in Europe."

Imagine what it took to create this "Great Wall of Kotor"—it's nearly three miles long and sits on some extremely inaccessible

terrain. It was built in fits and starts over a millennium (9th-19th centuries, though most of it was completed during the Venetian occupation in the 17th and 18th centuries). Its thickness varies from 6 to 50 feet, and the tallest parts are 65 feet high. Sections higher on the hill—with thinner walls, built before the age of gunpowder—are the oldest, while the thick walls along the water are most recent. It was all worth it: The fortified town survived many attacks, including a two-month Ottoman siege in 1657.

MONTENEGRO

If you're in great shape, consider scrambling along the walls and turrets above the Old Town.

Cost and Hours: Entry to the walls is €3 May-Oct daily 8:00-20:00; otherwise they're free.

Hiking the Walls: If you go all the way up to the top fortress and back again, it'll take around an hour and a half round-trip (de-

pending on how fast you go). This involves climbing 1,355 steps (an elevation gain of more than 700 feet)—don't overestimate your endurance or underestimate the heat. ("Am-I-*that*-out-of-shape?" tourists routinely find themselves winded and stranded high above town.) Bring plenty of water, along with a hat and sunscreen, and wear sturdy shoes. Most of the way, there's both a ramp and uneven stairs, but the route is in poor repair, with a lot of rough, rocky patches.

It's best to tackle the walls clockwise. (Even if you're not doing the hike, you can visually trace this route.) Find the entrance at the back-left corner of town (near St. Mary's Church, through the alley with the two arches over it). Pay the entry fee and begin hiking up. On the way up, notice the sign explaining that the fortress reconstruction was funded by the United States (Nov 2004)—if you're a US taxpayer, consider this hike your tax dollars at work.

First climb as high as the **Church of Our Lady of Health** (Crkva Gospe od Zdravlj). This is the halfway mark—about 20 minutes from the base at a good pace. While some believe this church has miraculous healing powers, most everyone agrees it offers some of the best views down over Kotor.

From this church, you can either cut back down toward the Old Town, or—if you're not exhausted yet—keep hiking up to the tippy-top **Fortress of St. John** (figure another 25-30 minutes from the church, if you're in decent shape). Built on the remains of fortifications from the Illyrians (you can scan the third-century B.C. remains just beyond the fort), this was the headquarters for the entire wall network below it. There's not much to see here, but it is fun to play "king of the castle" exploring the ruined shell—and the views, with 360 degrees of Montenegrin cliffs, are spectacular.

Then head back down, enjoying your reward: a downhill walk with head-on views of the Bay of Kotor. On the way down, watch your step on the slippery-even-when-dry marble stairs, highly polished by the feet of centuries of visitors. At the round terrace below the church, you can head to the right (back the way you came); or,

MONTENEGRO

for a different path, head left following *powder magazine* signs, then down (right) at the fork. The ticket-seller warned me that he's often seen people wipe out on the very last step on their way down—so exhausted after the demanding hike that they let their guard down.

Sleeping in Kotor

Kotor is a delightful town and an enjoyable place to spend the night. (Given its popularity as a cruise port, and among side-trippers from Dubrovnik, only a tiny fraction of visitors bother to sleep here.) However, the town has two big disadvantages: inexplicably high prices (you'll sleep more affordably in Dubrovnik) and lots of nighttime noise—it seems that every street in town has at least two or three bars, cranking their music until the wee hours. In most towns, I take noise into consideration when recommending hotels—but here, I don't even bother and just assume it'll be loud everywhere. While it's noisiest in summer, pack earplugs (and patience) any time of year. Kotor's hotels feel very "Balkan" (a mix of colorful, tacky, and chaotic).

$$$ Boutique Hotel Hippocampus oozes class, with nine plush rooms tucked down a back lane at one end of the Old Town. The design—shiny gold/stone/ancient artifacts are everywhere—toes the line between stylish and gaudy. If you're going to splurge in Kotor, do it here (standard Db-€180/€160, fancier "lux" Db-€280/€260, gigantic "deluxe" suite-€300/€280, higher prices are for June-mid-Sept, air-con, elevator, free Wi-Fi, Stari Grad 489, tel. 078/106-160, www.hotelhippocampus.com, hotel.hippocampus@gmail.com).

$$$ Hotel Villa Duomo is a stylish refuge just down the street from the cathedral. The 13 stony-chic rooms share an interior terrace where breakfast is served in good weather (Db-€135/€120, Tb-€185/€170, more for bigger units, air-con, free Wi-Fi, Stari Grad 358, tel. 032/323-111, www.villaduomo.com, villaduomo@yahoo.com).

$$$ Hotel Vardar has 24 rooms with mod bathrooms smack-dab in the middle of the Old Town. This classic old copper-roofed hotel has been renovated from top to bottom, leaving it tastefully chic. While convenient, the dead-central location can come with some noise, especially on weekends—request a quieter room (Sb-€125/€115/€95, Db-€185/€155/€125; 15 percent less Fri-Sat nights for two people, pricier and larger apartments have views

MONTENEGRO

MONTENEGRO

Sleep Code

(€1 = about $1.30, country code: 382, area code: 032)
S = Single, **D** = Double/Twin, **T** = Triple, **Q** = Quad, **b** = bathroom. Unless otherwise noted, credit cards are accepted and breakfast is included, but the modest tourist tax (about €1 per person, per night) is not. Everyone listed here speaks English.

Rates: If I list two rates for an accommodation, the second rate applies off-season (generally Oct-May); if I list three rates, separated by slashes, the first is for peak season (July-Aug), the second is for shoulder season (May-June and Sept), and the third is for off-season (Oct-April). The dates for seasonal rates vary by hotel.

To help you sort easily through these listings, I've divided the accommodations into three categories, based on the highest price for a standard double room with bath during high season:

$$$ Higher Priced—Most rooms €100 or more.
  $$ Moderately Priced—Most rooms between €70-100.
    $ Lower Priced—Most rooms €70 or less.

Prices can change without notice; verify the hotel's current rates online or by email. For the best prices, always book direct.

---

on the square, air-con, elevator, free Wi-Fi, Stari Grad 476, tel. 032/325-084, www.hotelvardar.com, info@hotelvardar.com).

$$$ Hotel Cattaro offers a welcoming staff and 20 Balkan-plush rooms with dark wood, bold old-meets-new decor, and paintings of local sea captains who all seem to resemble George Washington. Lining a very long hallway that runs inside the city wall, all of the rooms face the boisterous Square of Arms—expect some noise (Sb-€99/€79, Db-€129/€109, cheaper rates are for Nov-April, pricier suites, air-con, elevator, free Wi-Fi, tel. 032/311-000, www.cattarohotel.com, cattarohotel@t-com.me).

$$ Hotel Marija, an Old World throwback on an Old Town square, offers 17 rooms and wood-paneled halls. Rooms overlooking the square come with noise and the windows are thin, so request a quieter room in the back (Sb-€65/€50, Db-€90/€70, Tb-€103/€90, Qb-€130/€110, air-con, free Wi-Fi, on Trg od Kina, Stari Grad 449, tel. 032/325-062, hotel.marija.kotor@t-com.me).

$ D&Sons Apartments has six good, modern apartments along an atmospheric, café-lined lane at the back edge of the Old Town (Db-€50-60/€40, no breakfast but kitchenette in each apartment, air-con, free Wi-Fi, Stari Grad 490, mobile 069-050-094, www.dandsons.com, dandsons@t-com.me, Dražan).

$ **Old Town Hostel** is the best budget option in the Old Town, filling a stony, labyrinthine 13th-century building with 10 rooms, ranging from private doubles to 10-bed dorms. Youthful conviviality fills the inviting lounge (D-€50/€30, Db-€60/€35; per-person rates in dorms: €14/€9 in 10-bed dorm, €18/€10 in 6-bed dorm, €19/€12 in 4-bed dorm; air-con, free Wi-Fi, no breakfast but kitchen in each room, Stari Grad 284, tel. 032/325-317, mobile 067-737-825, www.hostel-kotor.me, info@hostel-kotor.me).

Near Kotor, in Perast

If you're overnighting in Montenegro, tiny Perast is sleepier than Kotor—which is both good (quiet after dark) and bad (quiet after dark). It's also, if anything, more expensive than Kotor. These two hotels flank the main square along the waterfront road, right in the heart of town. Both have restaurant piers with fine seating on the water.

$$$ **Conte Hotel** has 10 modern apartments with stone accents. Most have sea views (non-view Db-€130/€100/€85, view Db-€150/€120/€95, more for larger apartments, air-con, free Wi-Fi, free parking in front, Obala Kapetana Marka Martinovića bb, tel. 032/373-687, mobile 067-257-387, www.hotel-conte.com, hotel-conte@t-com.me).

$$ **Admiral Hotel** has eight rooms in a historic officer's mansion. They may renovate soon, which will increase prices (older and smaller "attic" Db-€60/€50, standard Db-€85/€75, big Db with seaview balcony-€120/€100, lower rates are for Sept-Oct and May-June, closed Nov-April, air-con, free Wi-Fi, Obala Kapetana Marka Martinovića 82, tel. 032/373-556, mobile 069-958-920, www.hoteladmiralperast.com, hoteladmiral@t-com.me). They also rent four apartments farther inland.

Eating in Kotor

In coastal, Italian-influenced Kotor, the cuisine is very similar to Croatia's: seafood, pasta, and pizza. There are a few local specialties to look for, and at the top of the list is *Njeguški pršut*, the delicious smoked ham from the village of Njeguši high in the mountains above town (described later, under "The Montenegrin Interior"). While *pršut* (prosciutto) is beloved throughout the Balkans, *Njeguški pršut*'s rich, salty, smoky flavor is perhaps the best. It goes well with the local cow's cheese—smoked, of course.

Montenegro produces some surprisingly good (and expensive) wines. The biggest producer in the country—and one of the biggest in the Balkans—is Plantaže Podgorica, which corks up some 20 million bottles each year. While that kind of volume often doesn't come with quality, Plantaže's vintages are quite good and worth

MONTENEGRO

trying (if not impossible to avoid). The most popular red-wine grape is the dry, medium-bodied *vranac* (VRAH-nahts), which is distantly related to Italian *primitvo*, Californian zinfandel, and Croatian *plavac mali*. For white, you'll see the dry, fruity *krstač* (kur-STACH), similar to Riesling.

As far as choosing restaurants in Kotor, there's not much to recommend. Truly great cuisine is rare here—I'd just settle for something scenic and functional. For a better quality, memorable meal in a romantic setting, drivers can consider heading to Konoba Ćatovića Mlini or Restoran Stari Mlini (described later).

MONTENEGRO

Simple and Tasty near the Cathedral: **La Pasteria** has good pizzas, pastas, and other local dishes, but its main appeal is its breezy outdoor tables facing St. Tryphon's Cathedral (€6-9 pizzas and pastas, €11-15 main courses, daily 8:00-1:00 in the morning, Pjaca Sv. Tripuna/Trg od Katedrale, tel. 032/322-269). Nearby, **City Restaurant** lacks cathedral views but offers a fine, shady perch—its well-varnished picnic tables are set within the little forest in the Old Town, and more tables fill a small square out front (€6-10 pizzas, pastas, and salads; €8-18 main courses; daily 8:00-1:00 in the morning; mobile 069-049-653).

Local Fish: **Cesarica** offers unpretentious seafood in a casual, stony interior buried deep in the Old Town. They enjoy bragging that the owner, Petar, was a fisherman, so he has a line on the freshest ingredients (€7-12 salads, €8-15 main dishes, daily 9:00-23:00, Stari Grad 375, mobile 069-049-733).

Market: Just outside the Old Town wall, facing the harbor, is a lively open market that hops each morning (typically 9:00-14:00, busiest on Sat). This is a great place to gather ingredients for a picnic, including the delicious local smoked ham, *Njeguški pršut*.

Fresh Juices: **Yo!** offers a jolt of fresh modernity in antique-feeling Kotor. From fresh-squeezed juices to iced coffee to bubble tea and frozen yogurt, the menu is enticing. The main location is in the modern Kamelija shopping mall, a 10-minute walk north of the Old Town (along the water and over the two canals), but there's also a more convenient smaller branch (with a limited menu) in the kiosk just left of the TI (as you face the Old Town gate).

Wine Bar: **The Old Winery** (Stara Vinarija) fills an inviting stony-chic space on a tight Old Town lane with convivial indoor and outdoor seating. It's a chance to sample wines from throughout the former Yugoslavia—with an emphasis on Montenegrin vintages. You can hang out in the wine bar itself (about 20 wines available by the glass, €3-13/glass; frequent live music—piano in the morning, blues after 21:00), or stop in their wine shop—called Mon Ami—next door. Both are open long hours daily (Stari Grad 483, mobile 068-517-417, www.vinarija.me, Goran). You can sample three wines in the shop for €3, or spring for a more elaborate

five-wine tasting in the bar (€9/person, €12 with light food—call or drop by in advance to reserve).

Near Kotor

The first two restaurants sit in oasis-like settings near running water, which helps keep them cool during the hot summer months.

In Ljuta

Restoran Stari Mlini has a cozy interior and wonderful outdoor seating scattered around a spring-fed stream near an old, namesake water mill. Surrounded by trickling water, you'll dine on local cuisine, with an emphasis on local seafood. If you prefer freshwater fish, you can choose your own trout from the pond (€12-18 pastas, €13-22 main dishes, daily 12:00-24:00, tel. 032/333-555).

Near the Verige Strait, in Morinj

Konoba Ćatovića Mlini is a memorable restaurant worth going out of your way to reach. Hiding in a sparse forest off the main fjordside road, this oasis is situated amidst a series of ponds, streams, waterfalls, and bubbling springs. The traditionally clad waiters are stiffly formal, mindful of this place's good reputation. Choose between several different stony seating options, indoors and out. Family-run for 200 years, this place is a local institution, yet it feels like a well-kept secret. Reservations are essential in summer, when it can be crowded (€8-14 pastas, €10-24 fish dishes, extensive wine list, daily 11:00-23:00, tel. 032/373-030, www.catovi-camlini.me). The best plan might be to dine here on your way back to Dubrovnik from Kotor: At the town of Morinj, watch for burgundy *Konoba Ćatovića Mlini* signs and fish-shaped signs leading away from the water. You'll make several turns, but the signs will lead you right to the restaurant.

 Tramontana is a more affordable, still very scenic option overlooking a beach with grand fjord views, right along the main waterfront road on the way out of Morinj (€4-6 sandwiches, €5-9 salads, €7-9 pizzas and pastas, daily 8:00-24:00, mobile 068-737-737, www.tramontanabeachbar.me).

Kotor Connections

From Kotor by Bus to: Perast (hourly, usually at :15 past the hour, every 2 hours on Sun, departs from small bus stop near Old Town rather than bus station), **Herceg Novi** (2/hour, 1 hour), **Budva** (1-4/hour, 40 minutes), **Cetinje** (2/hour, 1 hour), **Dubrovnik** (daily at 8:30 and 15:55, one additional run in summer, 2.5 hours), **Mostar** (1/day via Dubrovnik, plus 1/day via Trebinje, both departing about the same time in the afternoon, 5.5 hours), **Zagreb** (daily at 14:45). Bus info: tel. 032/325-809, www.autobuskastani-cakotor.me.

The Montenegrin Interior

Although Montenegro is trying to cultivate a glitzy beach-break cachet, for most of its history it has been thought of as a rugged mountain kingdom. While the coast—the focus of most of this chapter—was traditionally Venetian or Austrian, the real heart of Montenegro beat behind the sheer wall of mountains rising up from that seafront. Romantics, caught up in outdated Balkan fantasies, still think of this inland area as the "real" Montenegro.

While the Bay of Kotor is the most accessible and appealing part of the country, if you have more time, consider a joyride up into the mountains. For a quick look at this area, the easiest loop takes you to the historic capital of Cetinje—a dull little town in its own right, but a fine excuse for a mountain drive. You could do this whole loop in about two and half hours without stopping (about an hour from Kotor to Cetinje, then another hour to Budva, then a half hour back to Kotor), but if you want to stretch your legs in Njeguši or Cetinje, allow more time.

Self-Guided Driving Tour

The Road into the Mountains

The road to Cetinje twists you up the mountain face that stretches high above Kotor—it's an incredibly scenic, white-knuckle drive.

From Kotor, leave town toward Budva (bearing left at the roundabout). At the edge of Kotor, after the cemetery but before the big tunnel, take a right (marked for *Cetinje*) and begin your ascent. Cresting the first hill, go left to get to Cetinje (also marked for *Njeguši*). You'll wind up and up (past a small Roma encampment) on 25 numbered switchbacks. The road is a souvenir from the Habsburg era (1884). While Venetian rule brought sea trade, Austrian rule brought fortresses and infrastructure. After switch-

back #13, you'll pass an old customs house marking the former border between the Austro-Hungarian Empire and the Kingdom of Montenegro—a reminder that the coastline was not historically an integral part of Montenegrin cultural identity. As you near the top, look across the canyon to the left to spot the impossibly rough little donkey path that once was Cetinje's connection with the coast... like a tenuous umbilical cord tethering the mountainous interior to the outside world.

As you crest the hill, the vegetation changes—you're high above the Adriatic, with commanding views of Kotor and its bay (and great photo-op pull-outs; the best is just after switchback #25). Continuing inland, you find yourself in another world: poor, insular, and more Eastern (you'll see more Cyrillic lettering). Country farmhouses sell smoked ham, mountain cheese, and *medovina* (honey brandy). Before long, you reach a broad plain and the hamlet of...

Njeguši

The humble-seeming village of Njeguši (NYEH-goo-shee) is actually well-known among Montenegrins, with two very important claims to fame. This was the hometown of the House of Petrović-Njegoš, the dynasty that ruled Montenegro for much of its history (1696-1918). The family's favorite son was Petar II Petrović-Njegoš (1813-1851). Aside from ruling the country, Petar II is remembered most fondly as a great poet and playwright—sort of the Montenegrin Shakespeare.

Njeguši is also famous for producing its own special type of air-dried ham, called *Njeguški pršut*. Locals explain that, because this meadow overlooks the sea on one side, and the mountains on the other, the wind changes direction 10 times each day, alternating between dry mountain breeze and salty sea air—perfect for seasoning and drying ham hocks. For good measure, the *pršut* is also smoked with beech wood. The blocky, white buildings lining the road that look like giant Monopoly houses are actually smokehouses, jammed with five layers of hanging ham hocks—thousands of euros' worth—silently aging. (More industry than you realize hides out in sleepy villages.) A couple of traditional restaurants at the heart of the village are happy to serve passing tourists a lunch of this local specialty.

From Njeguši to Cetinje

Continuing through Njeguši toward Cetinje, you'll twist up into more mountains—soon arriving in an even more rugged and inhospitable landscape than you passed on the road that brought you here from the coast. Eyeing this desolate scenery, you can understand why the visiting Lord Byron said of this place, "Am I in

paradise or on the moon?" Along the mountain road that drops you down into Cetinje, each rock has the phone number of a vulture-esque road repair service *(auto slep)* spray-painted onto it. Low-profile plaques mark the site of Tito-era ambush assassinations.

Keep an eye out (on the horizon to the right) for the pointy peak of the mountain called **Lovćen,** which is capped by an elaborate mausoleum, designed by the great Croatian sculptor Ivan Meštrović, and devoted to King Petar II Petrović-Njegoš. With more time, you could actually drive up to the top of this mountain for sweeping views across Montenegro.

When you get into Cetinje, take a right when you hit a fork and find a place to park. To find your way into the old center, ask "guh-DEH yeh TSEHN-tar?"

Cetinje

Cetinje (TSEH-teen-yeh)—the historic capital of Montenegro—is a fine but fallen-on-hard-times little burg that sits cradled in a desolate valley surrounded by mighty peaks. Run-down as Cetinje is, it's still more pleasant than the current, drab capital, Podgorica.

Observing Cetinje from afar, it seems made to order as the historic capital of a remote and rustic people. It was the home of the Montenegrin king since the 15th century, but has always been pretty humble. In fact, it's said that when the Ottomans conquered it and moved in ready to rampage, they realized there wasn't much to pillage and plunder—so they just destroyed the town and moved on. The town was destroyed several other times, as well—and each time, the local people rebuilt it.

This "Old Royal Capital," once the leading city in the realm, is today recovering from its status as a victim of Tito's quirky economic program for Yugoslavia. It used to provide shoes and refrigerators for the country, but when Yugoslavia disintegrated, so did the viability of Cetinje's economy. As you explore the two-story town today, it seems there's little more than a scruffy dollop of tourism to keep its 17,000 people housed and fed. Many of its younger generation have left for employment along the coast in the tourism industry.

Stroll the main street (Njegoševa) past kids on bikes, old-timers with hard memories, and young adults with metabolisms as low as the town's. At the end of this drag is the main square (Balšića Pazar), surrounded by low-key sights with sporadic opening hours: the **Ethnographic Museum** (traditional costumes and folk life), **Historical Museum** (tracing the story of Montenegro), **Njegoš Museum** (dedicated to the beloved poet-king Petar II Petrović-Njegoš), and **National Museum,** which honors King Nikola I, who ruled from 1860 until 1918. While his residence is as poor and humble a royal palace as you'll see in Europe, Nikola I thought big.

He married off five of his daughters into the various royal families of Europe.

A short walk from the palace is the birthplace of the town, **Cetinje Monastery.** It's dedicated to St. Peter of Cetinje, a legend-

ary local priest who carried a cross in one hand and a sword in the other, established the first set of laws among Montenegrins, and in-spired his people to defend Chris-tianity against the Muslims. The monastery also holds the supposed right hand of St. John the Baptist. You are free to wander respectfully through the courtyard and church of this spiritual capital of Ser-bian Orthodox Montenegro.

From Cetinje Back to the Coast

To avoid backtracking down the same twisty road you came up, consider heading more directly back toward the coast from Cetinje. Just follow signs for *Budva.* A few miles outside of Cetinje along this road, look for the good **Restoran Konak,** which serves up tasty traditional dishes with indoor and outdoor seating (open long hours daily, tel. 041/761-011).

Continuing along this road, you'll pop out high above the **Budva Riviera.** Looking out to sea, you'll spot the distinctive pen-insula of Sveti Stefan off to the left, and the town of Budva to the right. If you have even more time, linger along the coast to visit these sights (described next). Otherwise, head right to return to Kotor or Dubrovnik.

The Budva Riviera

Montenegrins boast, "Croatia's got islands, but we've got beaches!" Long swaths of coarse-sand and fine-pebble beaches surround the resort town of Budva, just south of Kotor. This 15-mile stretch of coast, called the "Budva Riviera," is unappealingly built up, with endless strings of cheap resort hotels (and quite a few new five-star ones)—making it pale in comparison to the jagged saltiness of the Bay of Kotor or the romantic tidiness of Dalmatia. This region has recently become a mecca for super-wealthy Russians, staking their claim to this patch of Adriatic seafront. But the area isn't without its charm. Aside from the pleasant Old Town of the region's unoffi-cial capital, Budva, you'll discover a near-mythical haunt of the rich and famous: the highly exclusive resort peninsula of Sveti Stefan

(not possible to visit, but alluring from afar). For me, more time in Kotor or an earlier return to Dubrovnik would be more satisfying than the trek to the Budva Riviera. But beach lovers who have plenty of time and a spirit of adventure will find this area merits a look.

Getting to the Budva Riviera

Budva is about a 30-minute drive south of **Kotor.** The easiest approach is to continue past Kotor along the fjord, left at the roundabout, then through the tunnel (following *Budva* signs; exiting the tunnel, notice the sign in Cyrillic letters for Russki Radio 107.3—catering to the Russian jet-setters). For a more scenic route, take a right before the tunnel for the upper road to Budva, which twists over the mountain (described earlier, under "The Montenegrin Interior"). After winding up several switchbacks (with giddy views back over the Bay of Kotor) and cresting the hill, go right (again following *Budva* signs). You'll coast down into a valley, through the town of Lastva, then back over another mild hill that deposits you above the beaches of Budva.

First you'll reach the town of **Budva** (turn right at traffic light, following brown *Stari Grad* signs to the Old Town; parking is well-marked in modern complex next to Old Town). Continuing around the bay, you'll pass the busy, modern resort cluster of Bečići before reaching **Sveti Stefan.**

Sights on the Budva Riviera

Between the strings of resort hotels are two towns that deserve a quick visit.

Budva

The Budva Riviera's best Old Town has charming Old World lanes crammed with souvenir shops and holiday-making Serbs and Russians. While far less appealing than Kotor (and Dalmatian towns such as Korčula, Hvar, and Trogir), Budva at least offers a taste of romance between the resort sprawl.

Budva's ancient history (dating back at least to the fifth century B.C.) is arguably more illustrious than Kotor's. It began as an "emporium" (market and trading center) for Greek seamen, and extremely valuable jewelry uncovered here indicates that some pretty important people spent time in Budva. And yet, Budva isn't about history; it's about today. As in many Mexican vacation areas, the Old Town is

just one more part of the resort experience—it's basically treated as a backdrop for outdoor dining and nightclubs.

A 10-minute stroll tells you all you need to know about Budva. The layout is simple and intuitive—a peninsula (flanked by beaches) with a big Venetian-style bell tower. From the parking lot, a pedestrian-only, tree-and-café-lined boulevard runs away from the Old Town. But to see the historic core of town, go instead through the Old Town walls and wander up the main drag, Njegoševa. Out at the tip of town, you'll pop out into a small café-lined square with a **Catholic church** (on the left, with an unusually modern 1970s mosaic behind the altar depicting St. John preaching on the Montenegrin coast) facing the Orthodox **Holy Trinity Church,** with gorgeous and colorful Orthodox decorations inside. Beyond that is a huge **citadel** that's imposing on the outside but dull on the inside; it's not worth paying the €2 to tour its museum of model ships, antiquarium (old library), restaurant, and less-than-thrilling sea views (long hours daily).

Sveti Stefan

Like a mirage hovering just offshore, the famously exclusive luxury hotel that makes up the resort peninsula of Sveti Stefan beckons curious travelers to come, see, snap a photo...and then wish they'd spent more time elsewhere. While scenic, there's not much to actually experience at Sveti Stefan (unless you've got a thousand bucks to rent a room); while it's a great photo op, it disappoints many who make the trip. But for those caught up in Robin Leach-ian memories of this hotel's glory days, it's worth a pilgrimage.

Once an actual, living town (connected to the mainland only by a narrow, natural causeway), Sveti Stefan was virtually abandoned after World War II. The Yugoslav government developed it into a giant resort hotel in the 1950s. As old homes were converted to hotel rooms, the novelty of the place—and its sterling location, surrounded by pebbly beaches and lush scenery—began to attract some seriously wealthy guests.

During this resort's heyday in the 1960s and 1970s, it ranked with Cannes or St-Tropez as *the* place to see or be seen on Europe's beaches. You could rent a room, a house, an en-

tire block of houses, or even the entire peninsula. Anonymity was vigilantly protected, as the nicest "rooms" had their own private pools (away from public scrutiny), lockable gates, and security guards. Lured by Sveti Stefan's promise of privacy, celebrities, rock stars, royalty, and dignitar-

ies famously engaged in bidding wars to decide who'd be grant-ed access to the best suites: Whoever put the most money in a sealed envelope and slipped it to the manager, won. (Accord-ing to local legend, Sly Stallone's money talked.) Guests were pampered—indulged no matter how outrageous their requests. Sophia Loren, Kirk Douglas, Doris Day, and Claudia Schiffer are just a few of the big names who basked on Sveti Stefan's beaches.

By the late 2000s, Sveti Stefan had experienced a dramat-ic decline. Warfare in nearby places (such as Dubrovnik and Kosovo) kept visitors away, its cachet faded, and the resort grew a bit rough around the edges. Then the Indian company Aman Resorts swept in with ambitious plans to restore the island to its former status as one of the world's most exclusive, crème-de-la-crème resorts (cheapest Db-€950 in high season, www.amansvetistefan.com). These days, no-neck thugs guard the causeway, letting only guests (no exceptions) cross over into the fantasy world of Sveti Stefan. If you're desperate to check it out, you can reserve a meal at the restaurant (€25/person mini-mum, but count on paying far more). If you want to relax on the beaches flanking the causeway, most areas charge €30-50 per person for the day, but there are a few free areas—ask the guard for pointers.

Even if you can't enter the peninsula, let your imagination run as you gaze upon it. Strolling through the dead town, peek-ing through gates, visitors hope to spot a withered old celebrity who forgot to go home. "Rooms" come with varying degrees of privacy (each more expensive than the last): no fence, small fence, big fence. At the far end is the biggest and most famous "suite," where guests have an entire corner of the peninsula to themselves. At the top of the peninsula is a big Russian Orthodox church and a smaller Serbian Orthodox church—though both are little more than hotel decorations today.

Across the water from Sveti Stefan, on its own little cove, is one of Tito's former vacation villas (Villa Miločer, also part of the Aman resort). From here, you can enjoy the newly completed promenade that runs from the beach in front of the villa and to the next cove; eventually, this path will let you stroll along the water all the way to Budva.

Getting to Sveti Stefan: Sveti Stefan is just three miles be-yond Budva. Coming around the bay from Budva (following signs toward *Bar*), you'll pass above the peninsula on the main road, watching for the well-marked pull-out on the right that offers clas-sic views. After snapping your photos, if you want to get closer, continue down and turn off to the right, following signs to *Hotel*

Sveti Stefan; you can park in the pay lot (€1/hour) and walk along the beach as far as the causeway.

From Sveti Stefan to Dubrovnik: Figure 1.5 hours to the Croatian border (if you go via Tivat—rather than Kotor—and use the shortcut ferry across the Bay of Kotor), then another 45 minutes to Dubrovnik.

BOSNIA-HERZEGOVINA

Bosna i Hercegovina

BOSNIA-HERZEGOVINA

The mid-1990s weren't kind to Bosnia-Herzegovina: War. Destruction. Genocide. But apart from the tragic way it separated from Yugoslavia, the country has long been—and remains—a remarkable place, with ruggedly beautiful terrain, a unique mix of cultures and faiths, kind and welcoming people who pride themselves on their hospitality, and some of the most captivating sightseeing in southeastern Europe.

Little Bosnia-Herzegovina is a country with three faiths, three languages, and two alphabets. While the rest of Yugoslavia has splintered into countries dominated by one ethnicity, Bosnia remains an uneasy mix of scattered communities, with large contingents of all three major Yugoslav groups: Muslim Bosniaks, Eastern Orthodox Serbs, and Catholic Croats. These same three factions fought each other in that brutal war just two decades ago, and today they're struggling to reconcile, work together, and put the country back on track.

A visit here offers a fascinating opportunity to sample the cultures of these three major faiths within a relatively small area. In the same day, you can inhale incense in a mystical-feeling Serbian Orthodox church, hear the subtle clicking of rosary beads in a Roman Catholic church, and listen to the Muslim call to prayer echo across a skyline of prickly minarets. Few places in Europe—or the world—cram so much diversity into such a small space.

About half of the people in Bosnia are "Bosniaks"—that is, Muslims. Travel in Bosnia offers an illuminating and unique glimpse into a culture that's both devoutly Muslim and fully European. Here, just a short drive from the touristy Dalmatian Coast, you can step into a mosque and learn about Islam directly from a Muslim. The country also holds one of the most important pilgrimage sites of the Roman Catholic world: Međugorje, where six residents have reported seeing visions of the Virgin Mary.

Bosnian coffee *(bosanska kafa)* is not just a drink, but a complex ritual that captures this culture's deliberate, stop-and-smell-the-tulips approach to life. Similar to what you might call "Turkish coffee," what defines Bosnian coffee is how it's prepared: unfiltered, with

Bosnia-Herzegovina Political Regions
- Republika Srpska
- Muslim-Croat Federation

a thick layer of "mud" at the bottom of the cup. First, the coffee must be ground to just the right coarseness, which takes quite some time when using an old-fashioned, hand-cranked grinder. Then the coffee is added to water and vigorously stirred in a copper pot as it comes to a boil. Even when it's ready to drink, it's done slo-o-o-owly: Carefully decant the coffee—easy now, don't pour off too many grounds—into a small ceramic cup. If you take sugar, Bosnians stress that you should put the sugar cube in the cup first, then pour the coffee over it. Sip your coffee gradually, to allow the grounds to continually re-settle to the bottom. Swirl the cup to agitate and recaffeinate your brew. Nibble on the Turkish delight candy *(rahatlokum)* that usually accompanies Bosnian coffee, and take time to chat with your travel partner or a new Bosnian friend. The point is not to slam down caffeine—as it is with many European coffee cultures—but to have an excuse to slow down and focus on where you are and who you're with.

Bosnian coffee is just one of the many facets of local culture that were adopted from the Ottomans (from today's Turkey) who ruled here for centuries. Thanks largely to the Turkish influence, Bosnian culture (particularly among Muslim Bosniaks) is permeated with a deep and abiding soulfulness that's rare in Europe. The Bosnian language features an entire lexicon of words that have no clear translation in other tongues or cultures. Sarajevans embrace the concept of *raja*, meaning an unpretentious humility that involves being one with a community or a circle of friends. *Merak* is enjoyment, particularly a relaxed atmosphere that arises when you're among friends—perhaps while listening to *sevdah* music (explained below) and sipping Bosnian coffee. Enjoying the company of friends while going out for snacks is called *mezetluk* (related to the Greek *mezedes*, or tapas-like small plates). And *ćejf* is a sense of well-being, typically while engaged in an enjoyable—and often highly idiosyncratic—routine. These rituals—from the way someone spins their worry beads, to their own unique procedure for preparing and drinking coffee or smoking a water pipe, to a dervish whirling in a worshipful trance—may seem like OCD (or simply "annoying") to many Americans...but Bosnians understand that it's simply *ćejf.*

Sevdah—sometimes called "the Bosnian blues"—is a traditional folk music that mingles powerful emotions: sad and happy, convivial and nostalgic. Bosnians explain how the passionate, mournful strains of *sevdah* (which sounds distinctly eastern) pair perfectly with falling in love, drinking with friends, or contemplating loss. *Sevdah* is also the word for a poignant, melancholic mood—sort of the counterpoint to *merak*. Balancing these moods, Bosniaks explain, is key to emotional satisfaction.

To strike up a conversation, ask your new Bosnian friend to tell you more about what any of these terms means. All of them are examples of how Bosnians celebrate the "little things" that make life worth living...things that mainstream American and European cultures, all too often, see as barriers to progress.

In keeping with their generally relaxed culture, Bosnians are known for their gregarious sense of hospitality and their sharp sense of humor. Even during the darkest days of the war, they found ways to joke about the horrors unfolding around them. And today, they're willing and able to chuckle at their complicated political system and shambolic economy. Pointing to an ATM, your new Bosnian friend may say, "That's what we call our 'wailing wall.'" And they like to quip about their unfortunate circumstances in life: "Just our luck. Bosnia has so many Muslims—but no oil."

This unique Muslim culture seems fitting in this porous and mountainous land, where streams and rivers trickle endlessly. After all, the very name "Bosnia" comes from a term that means "running water" or "saturated"—and Muslim culture prizes constantly

flowing water. While Christians bless still water and call it holy, for Muslims, the power of nature is in its movement; they prefer water to be continually flowing, cleansing, replenishing, circulating. Just as a dervish whirls to connect with the spirituality of the earth and the heavens, so, too, should water be in motion. When the Ottomans arrived here from their Turkish homeland, they must have felt right at home.

Bosnia rearranges your mental furniture more than any other country in this book. It offers an enticing glimpse at a completely different, very eastern worldview. And it comes with some in-your-face lessons about recent history.

While repairs are ongoing, you'll still be confronted by vivid and thought-provoking scars of the recent war, especially outside of the tourist zones. Poignant roadside memorials to fallen soldiers, burned-out husks of buildings, unmistakable starburst patterns in the pavement, and bullet holes in walls are a constant reminder that the country is still recovering—physically and psychologically. Driving through the countryside, you'll pass between Muslim, Croat, and Serb towns—each one decorated with its own provocative sectarian symbols. In an age when we watch news coverage of conflicts abroad with the same detachment we accord Hollywood blockbusters, Bosnia teaches an essential lesson about how real—and destructive—war and interethnic strife truly are.

In this book I focus on a few key destinations, including several fascinating, user-friendly places within easy reach of the Dalmatian Coast: the Turkish-flavored city of Mostar (with its restored Old Bridge—one of Europe's most inspiring sights), some nearby attractions offering a more complete view of Herzegovina (Blagaj, Počitelj, and Stolac), and the Catholic shrine at Međugorje. A longer trip from Dalmatia—but well worth the trek—is the Bosnian capital of Sarajevo, with a spectacular mountain-valley setting, a multilayered history, powerful wartime stories, and a resilient populace of proud Sarajevans eager to show you their fine city.

Bosnia is highly recommended as a detour—both geographical and cultural—from the Croatian and Slovenian mainstream. Inquisitive visitors come away from a visit to Bosnia with a more nuanced understanding of the former Yugoslavia. Practically speaking, Bosnia offers lower prices and a warmer welcome than you'll find on the Croatian coast.

Nervous travelers might be tempted to give Bosnia-Herzegovina a miss. The country can be unsettling, because of

Bosnia-Herzegovina Almanac

Official Name: Bosna i Hercegovina (abbreviated "BiH"); the *i* means "and"—Bosnia and Herzegovina (the country's two regions). For simplicity, I generally call the whole country "Bosnia" in this book. "Bosna" (literally "running water") is the name of a major river here, while the tongue-twisting name "Herzegovina" (hert-seh-GOH-vee-nah) comes from the German word for "dukedom" (Herzog means "duke").

Snapshot History: Bosnia-Herzegovina's early history is similar to the rest of the region: Illyrians, Romans, and Slavs (oh, my!). In the late 15th century, Turkish rulers from the Ottoman Empire began a 400-year domination of the country. Many of the Ottomans' subjects converted to Islam, and their descendants remain Muslims today. Bosnia-Herzegovina became part of the Austro-Hungarian Empire in 1878, then Yugoslavia after World War I, until it declared independence in the spring of 1992. The bloody war that ensued came to an end in 1995. (For details, see the Understanding Yugoslavia chapter.)

Population: About 3.9 million. (There were about 100,000 identified casualties of the recent war, but many estimates of total casualties are double that number.) Someone who lives in Bosnia-Herzegovina, regardless of ethnicity, is called a "Bosnian." A southern Slav who practices Islam is called a "Bosnlak." Today, about half of all Bosnians are Bosniaks (Muslims), a little more than a third are Orthodox Serbs, and about 15 percent are Catholic Croats.

Area: 19,741 square miles (about the size of West Virginia). In both size and population, Bosnia is comparable to Croatia.

Geography: Bosnia and Herzegovina are two distinct regions that share the same mountainous country. Bosnia constitutes the majority of the country (in the north, with a continental climate), while Herzegovina is the southern tip (about a fifth of the total area, with a hotter Mediterranean climate). The nation's capital,

its in-your-face war damage and exotic mélange of cultures that seems un-European. But to me, for exactly these reasons, Bosnia ranks alongside Croatia and Slovenia as a rewarding destination. Overcome your jitters and dive in.

Bosnian History

With its mountainous landscape, remote from the more mainline areas of the western Balkans, Bosnia's evolution has followed a unique course. Even now, the people of Bosnia struggle with being outsiders—afloat on an oddball cultural island flanked by the Roman Catholic West (Croatia) and the Orthodox East (Serbia), borrowing elements from both but not fully belonging to either.

After periods of rule by the Illyrians (ancestors of today's Al-

Sarajevo, has an estimated 310,000 people; Mostar is Herzegovina's biggest city (with approximately 130,000 people) and unofficial capital.

Red Tape: To enter Bosnia-Herzegovina, Americans and Canadians need only a passport (no visa required).

Economy: The country's economy has struggled since the war—the per capita GDP is just $8,400, and the official unemployment rate is around 43 percent.

Currency: The official currency is the Convertible Mark (Konvertibilna Marka, abbreviated KM locally, BAM internationally). The official exchange rate is $1 = about 1.40 KM. But merchants are usually willing to take euros, and (in Mostar) they'll often accept Croatian kunas, roughly converting prices with a simple formula:

2 KM = €1 = 8 kn (= about $1.30)

Telephones: Bosnia-Herzegovina's country code is 387. If calling from another country, first dial the international access code (00 in Europe, 011 in the US), then 387, then the area code (minus the initial zero), then the number.

Flag: The flag of Bosnia-Herzegovina is a blue field with a yellow triangle along the top edge. The three points of the triangle represent Bosnia-Herzegovina's three peoples (Bosniaks, Croats, Serbs), and the triangle itself resembles the physical shape of the country. A row of white stars underscores the longest side of the triangle. These stars—and the yellow-and-blue color scheme—echo the flag of the European Union (a nod to the EU's efforts to bring peace to the region). While this compromise flag sounds like a nice idea, almost no Bosnian embraces it as his or her own; each group has its own unofficial but highly prized symbols and flags (such as the fleur-de-lis for the Bosniaks, the red-and-white checkerboard shield for the Croats, and the cross with the four C's for the Serbs)—many of which offend the other groups.

BOSNIA-HERZEGOVINA

banians) and the Romans, Bosnia fostered its own thriving Slavic culture during the Middle Ages. This was the time of the Bogomil culture: A homegrown branch of Christianity that was neither Catholic nor Orthodox—and was viewed with suspicion by both faiths. The Bogomil (literally "dear to God") faith was simple, ascetic, and somewhat mystic, combining elements of Slavic, Illyrian, and Celtic traditions. The Bogomils—who comprised a majority of the population of medieval Bosnia—had a thriving civilization. Vivid artifacts of the Bogomil kingdom are still around, such as their engraved burial grave markers, called *stećaks* (some of the best-preserved are in Stolac, near Mostar).

When the Ottomans (from what's now called Turkey) took over this land in the 15th century, they tolerated different faiths...

but offered generous economic and political incentives to those who converted to Islam. In negotiating their religious freedoms with the sultans, Bosnia's Roman Catholics (who identified as Croats) and Eastern Orthodox (who identified as Serbs) both had the support of larger church hierarchies outside of Bosnia. But the Bogomils had no bargaining power, and were more likely to swap one monotheistic faith for another—creating the Muslim South Slav ethnicity that would come to be known as "Bosniak."

Under the Ottomans, Bosnia flourished. The Ottoman sultans invested in infrastructure (primarily bridges—including Mostar's Old Bridge—and fountains) and architecture, including many mosques, hammams (baths), caravanserais (inns), madrassas (theological schools), and so on. Bosnian Muslims rose through the ranks of the empire, becoming military generals, religious leaders, beloved poets, and even grand viziers (top-level advisers to the sultans).

After four centuries of rule, the Ottoman Empire entered a steep decline. The Bosniak military hero Husein Gradaščević—nicknamed "The Dragon of Bosnia" (Zmaj od Bosne)—led an armed uprising in the 1830s. Though he died in battle, his movement eventually brought about the end of the archaic Ottoman system of rule in Bosnia, leading to a greater degree of autonomy.

But Bosnia was bound for even bigger changes. Unable to continue to rule over its vast holdings, in 1878 the Ottomans passed control of Bosnia-Herzegovina to their Habsburg rival, the Austro-Hungarian Empire (which already controlled neighboring Croatia and Slovenia). The Habsburgs quickly moved to modernize Bosnia, erecting buildings and investing in infrastructure. Sarajevo, Mostar, and many other Bosnian cities still show the impressive results of these efforts, which pulled Bosnia from their antiquated Ottoman ways into the modern world. Habsburg rule piped in mainstream European culture—which, until then, had scarcely penetrated Bosnian soil. Now Bosnian urbanites and aristocrats exchanged their ornate Turkish gowns for snazzy Austrian business suits...which they wore, proudly, with their old fezzes and turbans.

Of course, not everybody bought what the Habsburgs were selling. Fierce underground resistance movements—such as the Black Hand—emerged, determined to bring about self-rule for the South Slavs, who had been under control of the Ottomans, and then the Austrians, for centuries. Just 40 years after the Habsburgs took over, their empire began to topple—losing a Great War that began when the Habsburg heir, Archduke Franz Ferdinand, was assassinated in Sarajevo.

Following World War I, Bosnia was swept up in the movement to create a union of the South Slavs. The original incarnation of Yugoslavia, called "the Kingdom of the Serbs, Croats, and Slo-

venes," ignored the Bosniaks both in name and in political influence—they were merely along for the ride.

During World War II, Bosnia was part of the so-called "Independent State of Croatia" (run by the Nazis' puppet Ustaše
government). Hitler's right-hand man, Heinrich Himmler, came
to Bosnia to assess where the Bosniaks might fit into the Führer's
ethnic vision. He determined that they were "Croats with Muslim
culture"—that is, good ol' Aryans, who would be conscripted to
fight. Himmler and the Ustaše leader, Ante Pavelić (a Bosnian-
born Croat), squabbled over whether the Bosniaks would fight
for the SS or the Ustaše. Ultimately they created an SS Hanjar/
Handschar unit (named for a Turkish knife), issuing the con-
scripts a Germanic-style uniform with a ceremonial fez. The unit
fought fiercely against Tito's Partisan Army, and participated in
the Ustaše's genocidal efforts against Serbs, Jews, and other "un-
desirables." But as the war wore on, more and more of these troops
became disillusioned with the Nazi cause, and deserted in large
numbers.

Some of the most dramatic WWII battles between the Yugoslav Partisans and the Nazis took place here in Bosnia—including
the Battle of the Neretva, in which Tito ingeniously saved more
than 4,000 of his wounded troops—effectively turning the tide of
the war.

The postwar communist country of Yugoslavia was born in
the Bosnian town of Jajce on November 29, 1943, when Partisan
generals met to outline the future of a hoped-for post-Nazi state.
But in the new incarnation of Yugoslavia, many Bosniaks still felt
like second-class citizens. Local Muslims recall that Yugoslav
government-issued textbooks reinforced negative stereotypes. For
example, they might say "Sasha [a typically Serb name] is working,"
but "Mujo [a typically Muslim name] is a bad boy."

Even after the outbreak of violence between breakaway republics Slovenia and Croatia and Serb-dominated Yugoslavia in 1991,
things stayed strangely calm in Bosnia. But when the Bosnian conflict finally erupted in 1992, it was war of the most brutal kind.
A three-way war exploded between Bosnian Croats (supported by
Croatia proper), Bosnian Serbs (supported by Serbia proper), and
Bosniaks (who, caught in the crossfire, realized they had no real
European lobby to support them). The early to mid-1990s saw the
worst human, architectural, and cultural devastation in Bosnian
history. Sarajevo, Srebrenica, and Mostar became synonymous
with sectarian strife, horrific sieges, and shocking genocide. (For
more details on the war, see the Understanding Yugoslavia chapter.)

The Dayton Peace Accords that ended the conflict here in 1995
gerrymandered the nation into three separate regions: the Federa-

tion of Bosnia and Herzegovina (FBiH, shared by Bosniaks and Croats, roughly in the western and central parts of the country), the Republika Srpska (RS, dominated by Serbs, generally to the north and east), and the Brčko District (BD, a tiny corner of the country, with a mix of the ethnicities). For the most part, each of the three native ethnic groups stay in "their" part of this divided country, but tourists can move freely between them.

On your visit, tune into the many ways that the Bosniaks, Croats, and Serbs of Bosnia are working to coexist. To satisfy the

country's various factions, the currency uses both the Roman and the Cyrillic alphabets, and bills have different figureheads and symbols (some bills feature Bosniaks, others Serbs). Until very recently, the alphabet used on road signs changed with the territory: Roman alphabet in Muslim and Croat areas, Cyrillic alphabet in Serb lands. But now all road signs throughout Bosnia-Herzegovina are required to appear in both alphabets—though that doesn't prevent vandals from spray-painting over the alphabet they don't like. License plates also used different alphabets, but this led to vandalism to cars that crossed into the "other side." Today's license plates use only letters that are common to both alphabets.

Towns with mixed populations are either effectively divided in half, or have buildings clearly marked with symbols indicating the ethnicity of the occupant. Small-town schoolhouses often operate "two schools under one roof," with separate entrances and staggered shifts for the Bosniak and Croat kids...who, virtually from birth, are constantly told they are very different from each other. In some towns, a beautifully restored Orthodox church may sit across from the battered footprint of a long-gone mosque (or vice versa).

Bosnia has a central government, but each population group also has its own autonomous government and sub-agencies, resulting in four different, essentially redundant bureaucracies. The country is also divided into 10 state-like cantons, each of which also has some governmental authority. What's more, these various levels of governments refuse to cooperate—imagine the inefficiency. (For example, nobody knows how many people live in Bosnia, because there's no agreement on how to conduct a national census.) On top of all this, Bosnia is still navigating the complex transition

Fundamentalist Islam in Bosnia?

Islam is a hot topic in today's Europe, where some citizens blame Muslim immigrants for society's woes. And even though Bosnia's Muslims are indigenous, they're not immune to the criticism—especially from their Serb and Croat rivals. While Bosniaks have a long history as a peace-loving people, critics allege that elements of the population are experimenting with some alarming fundamentalist Islamic ideologies.

These allegations do have some basis in fact. During the war and genocide of the 1990s, many Bosniaks felt abandoned by their western allies in Europe and the US, who were too timid to step in and "take sides" to end the violence. In his people's darkest hour, desperate Bosnian President Alija Izetbegović recruited assistance from the only group willing to offer help: Muslim fundamentalists from the Middle East and North Africa. Several hundred mujahideen (Islamic jihadists) came to Bosnia to train Bosniak soldiers—and participated in bloody massacres of Serbs and Croats. They brought with them the dangerous ideas of Wahhabism, an ultraconservative movement bent on "purifying" Islam, often through violent means. According to reports, Izetbegović was even in contact with Osama bin Laden. In some cases, the mujahideen offered donations to widows of šehids (Bosniak martyrs).

Today, while waning, these groups' influence persists. Muslim countries have helped to fund the postwar reconstruction of Bosnia, especially the building and rebuilding of mosques and madrassas. Just as the end of atheistic, communist Yugoslav rule kick-started a passion for Catholicism in Croatia and the Orthodox faith in Serbia, many Muslims in Bosnia are today actively pursuing their faith. You may even see women wearing traditional Muslim headscarves—a rare sight before the war, when most Bosniaks dressed just like their Serb and Croat neighbors. (But note that some women you see wearing headscarves are likely Muslim tourists from elsewhere in the world.)

Meanwhile, some of the fundamentalist Muslims who came to fight in the war are still here (although they were supposed to leave the country under the Dayton Peace Accords). Mujahideen who fought were initially rewarded with Bosnian citizenship (these passports were revoked in 2007). Some married local women, however, and are pursuing a Wahhabist agenda in Bosnia. Small pockets of Wahhabists live in remote areas high in the mountains, separate from mainstream Bosnian society—indeed, the typical Bosniak on the street is as wary of them as you might be. The violent element of Bosnian Wahhabists is just one more example of a terrorist "cell" in a country that doesn't want them. The majority of practicing Muslims in Bosnia explicitly denounce the Wahhabists. As in any country, Bosnia has its share of fanatics—but they make up a tiny fringe in this predominantly peaceful nation.

from communism to capitalism, and rebuilding from a devastating war. It's a miracle that things here work as well as they do.

Nearly 20 years later, the delicate compromises that were necessary to end a horrifying war have become almost too complicated to maintain. For Bosnia-Herzegovina to fully recover, all three groups must learn to truly set aside their differences and work together. Pessimists (who are abundant in this region) don't like Bosnia's chances, and Bosnian Serbs still talk loudly about secession (their president, Milorad Dodik, is a separatist who has floated several proposals to hold a referendum for independence). But others see signs of hope, such as the young people from the three faiths now beginning to cautiously intermingle, as their ancestors did for centuries. Will Bosniak, Serb, and Croat youth manage to transcend the fear and anger that tainted their parents' and grandparents' country in the 20th century? That history is yet to be written.

Bosnian Food

Bosnia-Herzegovina dines on grilled meat, stewed vegetables, soft cheeses, and other foods you may think of as "Turkish" or "Greek." On menus, look for the word *domaća*—"homemade." For a rundown of the most common items you'll eat in Bosnia—and throughout the Balkans—see the "Balkan Flavors" sidebar.

Beyond the mainstays listed there, another specialty is *dolma*—a pepper stuffed with minced meat, vegetables, and rice. A *sarma* or *sarmica* is similar, but stuffed in cabbage rather than a pepper, while *japrak* is stuffed grape leaves. *Begova čorba* ("nobleman's stew") is a meaty vegetable soup. *Grah* is bean soup.

While Balkan cuisine favors meat, a nice veggie complement is *đuveđ* (JOO-vedge)—a spicy mix of stewed vegetables, flavored with tomatoes and peppers. And the best salad option is *šopska salata*—a Greek-style salad of tomatoes, cucumbers, onions, and peppers, smothered in grated feta-like sirene cheese. *Srpska salata* ("Serb salad") is often the same thing, but may have extra cheese.

Bosnian desserts—typically sweetened with honey rather than sugar—are another local treat. Drop by a sweets shop and peruse your options. *Baklava*, a phyllo dough pastry with nuts and honey, is a familiar choice. *Kadaif* is similar, but made with shredded sheets of dough. *Tulumba* is a pastry cylinder drenched in honey, and *tufahija* is an apple stuffed with walnuts, soaked in honey, and topped with whipped cream. *Smokvača* is a dense, very sweet fig pie. You also may see blocks of nougat-like *halva*, made from sesame paste.

Bosnia produces some wine, but it's mostly consumed domestically. Sarajevso Pivo, brewed in the capital, is the favored brand of beer. In Bosnia, "coffee" is *kafa* (not *kava,* as in Croatia and Slovenia). While you can easily get espresso-style coffee, *bosanska kafa*

Balkan Flavors

All of the countries of the Balkan Peninsula—basically from Slovenia to Greece—have several foods in common: The Ottomans from today's Turkey, who controlled much of this territory for centuries, imported some goodies that remained standard fare here long after they left town. Whether you're in Bosnia-Herzegovina, Slovenia, Croatia, Montenegro, Serbia, Kosovo, or Albania, it's worth seeking out some of these local tastes.

A popular, cheap fast food you'll see everywhere is **burek** (BOO-rehk)—phyllo dough filled with meat, cheese, spinach, or apples. *Burek* rivals pizza-by-the-slice as the most popular take-away snack food in the former Yugoslavia.

Grilled meats are a staple of Balkan cuisine. You'll most often see **ćevapčići** (cheh-VAHP-chee-chee), or simply **ćevapi** (cheh-VAH-pee)—minced meat (typically a mix of lamb and beef) formed into a sausage-link shape, then grilled. It's similar—and similarly named—to a kebab. *Ćevapi* enthusiasts (a group that includes pretty much everyone in the Balkans) distinguish between different variations. For example, Sarajevo-style *(sarajevski ćevapi)* is typically eaten with grilled onions and stuffed into a pita-like flatbread called *somun*; Banja Luka-style *(banjalučki ćevapi)* is one long, continuous *ćevap* with hot peppers on the side.

Ražnjići (RAZH-nyee-chee) is small pieces of steak on a skewer, like a shish kebab. **Pljeskavica** (plehs-kah-VEET-suh) is similar to **ćevapčići,** except the meat is in the form of a hamburger-like patty. **Pileći** is chicken, and **piščančje** is grilled chicken breast. **Sudžukice** are sausages, and **ćufte** are meatballs.

You just can't eat any of this stuff without the ever-present condiment **ajvar** (EYE-var). Made from red bell pepper and eggplant, *ajvar* is like ketchup with a kick. Many Americans pack a jar of this distinctive sauce to remember the flavors of the Balkans when they get back home. (You may even be able to find it at specialty grocery stores in the US—look for "eggplant/red pepper spread.")

Particularly in Bosnia, another side-dish you'll see is the soft, spreadable—and tasty—cheese called **kajmak. Lepinje** is a pita-like grilled bread, which is often wrapped around *ćevapčići* or *pljeskavica* to make a sandwich. **Uštipci** is a fry bread that's especially popular throughout Bosnia-Herzegovina.

Ajvar, kajmak, lepinje, and diced raw onions are the perfect complement to a **"mixed grill"** of various meats on a big platter—the quintessence of Balkan cuisine on one plate.

(unfiltered "Bosnian coffee") is more local—and more fun to drink. (For tips on this ritual, see earlier.)

Bosnian Language

Technically, Bosnia-Herzegovina has three languages—Bosnian, Serbian, and Croatian. But all three are mutually intelligible variants of what was until recently considered a single language: Serbo-Croatian. Bosniaks and Croats use basically the same Roman alphabet we do, while Serbs use the Cyrillic alphabet. You'll see both alphabets on currency, official documents, and road signs, but the Roman alphabet predominates in virtually every destination covered in this book. Many people also speak English.

MOSTAR AND NEARBY

Mostar • Blagaj • Počitelj • Stolac • Međugorje

Mostar (MOH-star) encapsulates the best and the worst of the former Yugoslavia. During the Tito years, its residents—Catholic Croats, Orthodox Serbs, and Muslim Bosniaks—enjoyed an idyllic mingling of cultures, all living together in harmony, their differences spanned by an Old Bridge that epitomized an optimistic vision of a Yugoslavia where ethnicity didn't matter. But then, as the country unraveled in the early 1990s, Mostar was gripped by a gory three-way war among those same peoples...and that famous bridge crumbled into the Neretva River.

Mostar is still rebuilding, and the bullet holes and destroyed buildings are ugly reminders that the last time you saw this place, it was probably on the nightly news. Western visitors may also be struck by the immediacy of the Muslim culture that permeates Mostar—at this crossroads of civilizations, minarets share the horizon with church steeples. During the Ottomans' 400-year control of this region, many Slavic subjects converted

to Islam. And, although they retreated in the late 19th century, the Ottomans left behind a rich architectural, cultural, and religious legacy that has forever shaped Mostar. Five times each day, loudspeakers on minarets crackle to life, and the call to prayer warbles through the streets. In many parts of the city, you'd swear you were in Turkey.

If these images intrigue you, read on—Mostar has so much

MOSTAR & NEARBY

Mostar

To
"Kolodvor"
Bus Stop

WALK ENDS

Masala
Square

H. MASALA

To Main
Bus Station

To
Sarajevo

PJES MOST BUNUP.

To Medugorje

Neretva

River

BRAČE

MARŠALA

M-17

ADEMA BUĆA

N

MUSLIBEGOVIĆ
HOUSE

Cemetery

ĐIKIĆA

KARAĐOZBEG
MOSQUE

BIŠĆEVIĆ
TURKISH
HOUSE

FEJIĆA

TITA

To the
Rondo &

BULEVAR

RADE BITANGE

Radobolja

River

Cemetery

ORTHODOX
CHURCHES
(CONSTRUCTION
SITE)

TEPA
MARKET

BAJATOVA

MUSEUM OF
HERZEGOVINA

KUJUNDŽILUK

P

FRANCISCAN
CHURCH

KOSKI MEHMET-
PASHA MOSQUE

COPPERSMITHS'
STREET

M-17

TURKISH
BATHHOUSE

GALLERY ON THE
BRIDGE & MUSEUM
OF THE OLD BRIDGE

ONEŠĆUKOVA

WALK
BEGINS

CROOKED
BRIDGE

OLD
BRIDGE

MUJE BJELAVCA

KAJTAZ
HOUSE

P

G. VUKOVIĆA

BULEVAR

200 Meters

200 Yards

LUČKI BRIDGE

To
Dubrovnik

To H.M. Brkiċa Bridge,
M-17, Airport, Blagaj,
Počitelj & Stolac

1 Muslibegović House

2 Hotel Bristol

3 Hotel Kriva Ćuprija

4 Hotel Kriva Ćuprija II

5 Villa Anri

6 Motel Emen

7 Villa Fortuna

8 Pansion Čardak & Pansion Nur

9 B&B Shangri La

10 Villa Botticelli

11 Bridge View Eateries

12 Restoran Hindin Han

13 Nacionalni Restoran
Aščinica Balkan (2)

14 Saray Restaurant

15 Urban Grill

16 To Pivnica Štefanijino
Šetalište Brewpub

17 Ali Baba Nightclub

18 Oscar Nightclub

19 Fortuna Tours

20 Future Synagogue Site

more to offer. Despite the scars of war, its setting is stunning: straddling the banks of the gorgeous Neretva River, with tributaries and waterfalls carving their way through the rocky landscape. The sightseeing—mosques, old Turkish-style houses, and that spine-tingling Old Bridge—is more engaging than much of what you'll find in Croatia or Slovenia. And it's cheap: Hotels, food, and museums cost less than half of what you'll pay in Dubrovnik or Ljubljana.

In this chapter, I've also included some nearby attractions in Herzegovina that are worth trying to squeeze into your itinerary. Near Mostar is a trio of other mostly Bosniak sights: the river spring and whirling dervish house at Blagaj, the striking fortified hill town of Počitelj, and workaday Stolac, which sits upon some very impressive history. I've also included the top Croat sight in Bosnia-Herzegovina: Međugorje, where Catholic pilgrims flock from around the world to hear tales of a Virgin Mary apparition. All of these places are within a half-hour's drive of Mostar, and all are more or less on the way between Mostar and coastal destinations.

While a visit to Mostar was depressing not that long ago, the city gets more uplifting all the time: Mostarians are rebuilding at an impressive pace, tentatively re-integrating, and working hard to make Mostar tourist-friendly. Before long, Mostar will reclaim its status as one of the premier destinations in the former Yugoslavia. Visit now, while it still has its rough-around-the-edges charm—you'll get to see it before it really takes off.

Planning Your Time

Because of its cultural hairiness, a detour into Bosnia-Herzegovina feels like a real departure from a Dalmatian vacation. And yet, Mostar is easier to reach from Dubrovnik or Split than many popular Dalmatian islands (it's within a three-hour drive or bus ride from either city).

The vast majority of tourists in Mostar are day-trippers from the coast, which means the Old Town is packed at midday, but empty in the morning and evening. You can get a good feel for Mostar in just a few hours, but a full day—and, ideally, an overnight—gives you time to linger and ponder. My self-guided walk provides a framework for a visit of any duration. With extra time, be sure to venture to the western part of the city, which most tourists miss.

You have three basic options for getting here: take a package tour from Dalmatia; rent a car for a one-day side-trip into Mostar; or (my favorite) spend the night here en route between Croatian destinations. To work a Mostar overnight into your itinerary, consider a round-trip plan that takes you south along the coast, then back north via Bosnia-Herzegovina (for example, Split-Hvar-

Korčula-Dubrovnik-Mostar-back to Split). And if you're coming to Mostar, keep in mind that Sarajevo is just down the road.

Getting Around Herzegovina

The destinations I've covered in this chapter are accessible from the Dalmatian Coast, but non-drivers may have to get creative to connect the dots.

By Car: Coming with your own car gives you maximum flexibility, and a number of interesting routes connect Mostar to the coast. If you do plan to drive here, let your car-rental company know in advance, to ensure you have the appropriate paperwork for crossing the border. If you're not up for driving yourself, consider splurging on a **driver** to bring you here. Drivers may suggest several detours en route. Do your homework to know which ones interest you (for example, Međugorje isn't worth the extra time for most visitors), and don't hesitate to say you want to just max out on time in Mostar itself.

By Bus: Especially if you're spending the night in Mostar, public buses work well to connect Mostar with destinations on the Dalmatian Coast (particularly Split and Dubrovnik).

By Package Tour: Taking a package excursion from a Dalmatian resort town seems like an efficient way to visit Mostar or Međugorje. Unfortunately, in reality it can be less rewarding than doing it on your own—count on lots of hours on a crowded bus, listening to a lackluster, multilingual tour guide reading from a script, and relatively little time in the destinations themselves. But if you just want a quick one-day look at these places, an excursion can be a necessary evil. These all-day tours are sold from Split, Hvar, Korčula, Dubrovnik, and other Croatian coastal destinations for about €50-60. The best tours focus almost entirely on Mostar (it still won't be enough time); avoid tours that include a pointless boat trip on the Neretva River or time in Međugorje. Those that add a quick visit to the worthwhile town of Počitelj are a better deal. Ask for details at any travel agency in Dalmatia.

Orientation to Mostar

Mostar—a mid-sized city with around 130,000 people—is situated in a basin surrounded by mountains and split down the middle by the emerald-green Neretva River. Bosniaks live mostly on the east side of the river (plus a strip on the west bank) and Croats in the modern sprawl to the west. The populations are beginning to mix again, albeit tentatively. Virtually all of the sights are in the Bosniak zone, but visitors move freely throughout the city, and most don't even notice the division. The cobbled, Turkish-

feeling Old Town (called the "Stari Grad" or—borrowing a Turkish term—the "Stara Čaršija") surrounds the town's centerpiece, the Old Bridge.

The skyline is pierced by the minarets of various mosques, but none is as big as the two major Catholic (Croat) symbols in town, both erected since the recent war: the giant white cross on the hilltop (marking the place from where Croat forces shelled the Bosniak side of the river, including the Old Bridge); and the enormous (almost 100-foot-tall) bell tower of the Franciscan Church of Sts. Peter and Paul. A monumental Orthodox cathedral on the hillside across the river was destroyed in the war, but is now being rebuilt.

A note about safety: Mostar is as safe as any city its size, but it doesn't always *feel* safe. You'll see bombed-out buildings everywhere, even in the core of the city. Some are marked with *Warning! Dangerous Ruin* signs, but for safety's sake, never wander into any building that appears damaged or deserted. In terms of petty theft, the Old Town has as many pickpockets as any tourist zone in Europe: Watch your valuables, especially on the Old Bridge.

Tourist Information

The virtually worthless TI shares a building with a tour office, but it does give out a free town map and a few other brochures on Mostar and Herzegovina (sporadic hours, generally May-Oct daily 9:00-12:00, maybe later in busy times, likely closed Nov-April, a block from the Old Bridge at Rade Bitange 5, tel. 036/580-275, www.turizam.mostar.ba).

Arrival in Mostar

By Bus or Train: The **main bus station** (where most buses arrive in town) sits next to the giant but mostly deserted **train station,** north of the Old Town on the east side of the river. At the bus station, you'll find ticket windows and a left-luggage counter (2 KM/bag) in the Autoprevoz lobby facing the bus stalls. You can check schedules and buy tickets in this office for most buses *except* the many connections operated by Globtour, whose office is nearby (exit Autoprevoz, turn left, and walk to the end of the bus-station area). Because these two companies don't cooperate well, you may have to check with both to get the complete schedule. To find your way to the town center, walk through the bus stalls and parking lot and turn left at the big road, which leads you to the Old Town area in about 15 minutes. A taxi into town costs about 7-10 KM.

If you're arriving by bus it's possible (though unlikely) that you'll arrive at Mostar's makeshift secondary bus station, called **"Kolodvor,"** on the west/Croat side of town. From here, it's a drea-

ry 20-minute walk into town: Turn right out of the bus station area, turn left down the busy Dubrovačka street, and head straight to the river (which you can follow south into the Old Town).

For details on both stations, see "Mostar Connections," later.

Helpful Hints

Local Cash: Need Convertible Marks? The most convenient ATM in town is to the left of Fortuna Tours' door, right at the top of Coppersmiths' Street (but on a short visit, you can generally skip a trip to the ATM, as most vendors here also accept Croatian kunas and euros).

Travel Agency: The handy **Fortuna Tours** travel agency, right in the heart of the Old Town (at the top of Coppersmiths' Street), sells all the tourist stuff, can book a local guide or arrange a transfer, and answers basic questions (long hours daily, Kujundžiluk 2, tel. 036/551-887, main office tel. 036/552-197, www.fortuna.ba, headoffice@fortuna.ba).

Local Guides: Hiring a guide is an excellent investment to help you understand Mostar. I've enjoyed working with **Alma Elezović,** a warm-hearted Bosniak who loves sharing her city and her wartime stories with visitors (€20/person, up to €70/group for 2-3-hour tour, mobile 061-467-699, http://almas-guidedtours.blogspot.com, aelezovic@gmail.com). If Alma is busy, she may send you with her son **Jaz** (pronounced "yahz"), a well-trained guide who speaks perfect English and offers a younger generation's perspective. Other companies around town can arrange for a local guide at extremely reasonable prices (2-hour tour—€30/2 people, €40/4 people, includes entry to mosque and/or Turkish house); try **Fortuna Tours,** listed previously.

Local Driver: Ermin Elezović, husband of local guide Alma (see above), is a gregarious, English-speaking driver who enjoys taking visitors on day trips from Mostar. You can also hire him for a transfer between Mostar and destinations anywhere in Croatia (prices for a van for up to 6 people: €120 for one-way transfer to Sarajevo, Split, or Dubrovnik with a few brief sightseeing stops on the way; €240 for an all-day round-trip from Mostar to Sarajevo, Split, or Dubrovnik; also available for longer trips—contact Ermin and Alma for help planning out a multiday itinerary; mobile 061-908-597, elezovicermin@gmail.com).

Updates to This Book: Check www.ricksteves.com/update for any significant changes that have occurred since this book was published.

Sights in Mostar

Mostar's major sights line up along a handy L-shaped axis. I've laced them together as an enjoyable orientation walk: From the Franciscan Church, you'll walk straight until you cross the Old Bridge. Then you'll turn left and walk basically straight (with a couple of detours) to the big square at the far end of town. This walk is designed to help you see both the main tourist zones, and the parts of workaday Mostar that many visitors miss.

• *Begin at the...*

▲Franciscan Church of Sts. Peter and Paul

In a town of competing religious architectural exclamation points, this spire is the tallest. The church, which adjoins a working Franciscan monastery, was built in 1997, after the fighting subsided (the same year as the big cross on the hill). The tower, which looks at first glance like a minaret on steroids, is actually modeled after typical Croatian/Venetian campanile bell towers. Step inside to see the cavernous interior, still not fully decorated. (Sunday Mass here is an inspiration.)

• *The church fronts the busy boulevard called...*

▲Bulevar

"The Boulevard" was once the modern main drag of Mostar. In the early 1990s, this city of Bosniaks, Croats, and Serbs began to frac-

ture under the pressure of politicians' propaganda. In October of 1991, Bosnia-Herzegovina—following Croatia's and Slovenia's example, but without the blessing of its large Serb minority—began a process of splitting from Yugoslavia. Soon after, the Serb-dominated Yugoslav People's Army invaded. Mostar's Bosniaks and Croats joined forces to battle the Serbs and succeeded in claiming the city as their own, forcing out the Serb residents.

But even as they fended off the final, distant bombardments of Serb forces, Mostar's Bosniaks (Muslims) and Croats (Catholics) began to squabble. Neighbors, friends, and even relatives took up arms against each other. As fighting raged between the Croat and Bosniak forces, this street became the front line—and virtually all

of its buildings were destroyed. Then as now, the area to the east of here (toward the river) was held by Bosniaks, while the western part of town was Croat territory.

While many of the buildings along here have been rebuilt, some damage is still evident. Stroll a bit, imagining the hell of a split community at war. Mortar craters in the asphalt leave poignant scars. During those dark war years, the Croats on the hill above laid siege to the Bosniaks on the other side, cutting off electricity, blocking roads, and blaring Croatian rabble-rousing pop music and Tokyo Rose-type propaganda speeches from loudspeakers. Through '93 and '94, when the Bosniaks dared to go out, they sprinted past exposed places, for fear of being picked off by a sniper. Local Bosniaks explain, "Night was time to live" (in black clothes). When people were killed along this street, their corpses were sometimes left here for months, because it wasn't safe to retrieve the bodies. Tens of thousands fled. Scandinavian countries were the first to open their doors, but many Bosnians ended up elsewhere in Europe, the US, and Canada.

The stories are shocking, and it's difficult to see the war impartially. But looking back on this complicated war, I try not to broadly cast one side as the "aggressors" and another as the "victims." Bosniaks were victimized in Mostar, just as Croats were victimized during the siege of Dubrovnik. And, as the remains of a destroyed Orthodox cathedral on the hillside above Mostar (not quite visible from here) attest, Serbs also took their turn as victims. Every conflict has many sides, and it's the civilians who often pay the highest toll—no matter their affiliation.

Cross the boulevard and head down Onešćukova street. A few steps down on the left, the vacant lot with the menorah-ornamented metal fence will someday be the **Mostar Synagogue.** While the town's Jewish population has dwindled to a handful of families since World War II, many Jews courageously served as aid workers and intermediaries when Croats and Bosniaks were killing each other. In recognition of their loving help, the community of Mostar gave them this land for a new synagogue.

• *Continue past the synagogue site, entering the Old Town and following the canyon of the...*

Radobolja River Valley

Cross the small river called Radobolja, which winds over waterfalls and several mills on its way to join the Neretva, and enter the city's cobbled historic core (keeping the river on your right). As you step upon the smooth, ankle-twisting river stones, you suddenly be-

come immersed in the Turkish heritage of Mostar. Around you are several fine examples of Mostar's traditional heavy limestone-shingled roofs. From the arrival of the Ottomans all the way through the end of World War II, Mostar had fewer than 15,000 residents—this compact central zone was pretty much all there was to the city. It wasn't until the Tito years that it became industrialized and grew like crazy. As you explore, survey the atmospheric eateries clinging to the walls of the canyon—and choose one for a meal or drink later in the day (I've noted a couple under "Eating in Mostar," later).

Walk straight ahead until you reach a square viewpoint platform on your right. It's across from a charming little mosque and above the stream (you may have to squeeze between souvenir stands to get there). The mosque is one of 10 in town. Before the recent war there were 36, and before World War II there were even more (many of those damaged or destroyed in World War II were never repaired or replaced, since Tito's communist Yugoslavia discouraged religion). But the recent war inspired Muslims to finally rebuild. Each of the town's reconstructed mosques was financed by a Muslim nation or organization (this one was a gift from an international association for the protection of Islamic heritage). Some critics (read: Croats) allege that these foreign Muslim influences—which generally interpret their faith more strictly than the typically progressive and laid-back Bosniaks—are threatening to flood the country with a rising tide of Islamic fundamentalism.

• *Look upriver. Spanning the river below the mosque (partly obscured by trees) is the...*

▲Crooked Bridge (Kriva Ćuprija)

This miniature Old Bridge was built nearly a decade before its more famous sibling, supposedly to practice for the real deal. Damaged—but not destroyed—during the war, the original bridge was swept away several years later by floods. The bridge you see today is a reconstruction.

• *Continue on the same street deeper into the city center. After a few steps, a street to the left (worth a short detour) leads to the **TI**, then a copper-domed hammam (Turkish bathhouse), which was destroyed in World War II and only recently rebuilt. A happening nightlife and restaurant scene tumbles downhill toward the river from here, offering spectacular views of the Old Bridge.*

Back on the main drag, continue along the shopping zone, past several market stalls, to the focal point of town, the...

▲▲▲Old Bridge (Stari Most)

One of the most evocative sights in the former Yugoslavia, this iconic bridge confidently spanned the Neretva River for more than

MOSTAR & NEARBY

four centuries. Mostarians of all faiths love the bridge and speak of "him" as an old friend. Traditionally considered the point where East meets West, the Old Bridge is as symbolic as it is beautiful. Dramatically arched and flanked by two boxy towers, the bridge is stirring—even if you don't know its history.

Before the Old Bridge, the Neretva was spanned only by a rickety suspension bridge, guarded by *mostari* ("watchers of the bridge"), who gave the city its name. Commissioned in 1557 by the Ottoman Sultan Süleyman the Magnificent, and completed just nine years later, the Old Bridge was a technological marvel for its time..."the longest single-span stone arch on the planet." (In other words, it's the granddaddy of the Rialto Bridge in Venice.) Because of its graceful keystone design—and the fact that there are empty spaces inside the structure—it's much lighter than it appears. And yet, nearly 400 years after it was built, the bridge was still sturdy enough to support the weight of the Nazi tanks that rolled in to occupy Mostar. Over the centuries, it became the symbol of the town and region—a metaphor in stone for the way the diverse faiths and cultures here were able to bridge the gaps that divided them.

All of that drastically changed in the early 1990s. Beginning in May of 1993, as the city became engulfed in war, the Old Bridge frequently got caught in the crossfire. Old tires were slung over its sides to absorb some of the impact from nearby artillery and shrapnel. In November of 1993, Croats began shelling the bridge from the top of the mountain (where the cross is now—you can just see its tip peeking over the hill from the top of the bridge). The bridge took several direct hits on November 8; on November 9, another shell caused the venerable Old Bridge to lurch, then tumble in pieces into the river. The mortar inside, which contained pink bauxite, turned the water red as it fell in. Locals said that their old friend was bleeding.

The decision to destroy the bridge was partly strategic—to cut off a Bosniak-controlled strip on the west bank from Bosniak forces on the east. (News footage from the time shows Bosniak soldiers scurrying back and forth over the bridge.) But there can be no doubt that, like the Yugoslav Army's siege of Dubrovnik, the attack was also partly symbolic: the destruction of a bridge representing the city's Muslim legacy.

After the war, city leaders decided to rebuild the Old Bridge. Chunks of the original bridge were dredged up from the river. But the limestone had been compromised by soaking in the water for

so long, so it couldn't be used (you can still see these pieces of the old Old Bridge on the riverbank below). Having pledged to rebuild the bridge authentically, restorers cut new stone from the original quarry, and each block was hand-carved. Then they assembled the stones with the same technology used by the Ottomans 450 years ago: Workers erected wooden scaffolding and fastened the blocks together with iron hooks cast in lead. The project was overseen by UNESCO and cost over $13 million, funded largely by international donors.

It took longer to rebuild the bridge in the 21st century than it did to build it in the 16th century. But on July 23, 2004, the new Old Bridge was inaugurated with much fanfare and was immediately embraced by both the city and the world as a sign of reconciliation.

Since its restoration, another piece of bridge history has fully returned, as young men once again jump from the bridge 75 feet down into the Neretva (which remains icy cold even in summer). Done both for the sake of tradition and to impress girls, this custom carried on even during the time when the destroyed bridge was temporarily replaced by a wooden one. Now the tower on the west side of the bridge houses the office of the local "Divers Club," a loosely run organization that continues this long-standing ritual. On hot summer days, you'll see divers making a ruckus and collecting donations at the top of the bridge. They tease and tease, standing up on the railing and pretending they're about to jump... then getting down and asking for more money. (If he's wearing trunks rather than Speedos, he's not a diver—just a teaser.) Once they collect about €30, one of them will take the plunge.

Before moving on, see how many of the town's 10 mosques you can spot from the top of the bridge (I counted seven minarets).

Inside the Halebija Tower at the near end of the bridge, up the stairs (above the Divers Club), the **War Photo Exhibition** displays 50 somber, poignant wartime images taken by photojournalist Wade Goddard. While small, the collection of black-and-white images puts a human face on the suffering by focusing not on the conflict itself, but on the everyday people whose lives were ripped apart by the war (6 KM, daily mid-July-mid-Oct 9:00-21:00; April-mid-July and mid-Oct-Nov 11:00-18:00, closed Dec-March, mobile 062-345-789).

• *If you'd like to see one of the best* **views** *in town—looking up at the Old Bridge from the riverbank below—backtrack the way you came into the shopping zone, take your first left (at the Šadrvan restaurant—a good*

MOSTAR & NEARBY

place to try the powerful "Bosnian coffee"), then find the steps down to the river on the left.

When you're ready to continue, hike back up to the Old Bridge and cross to the other side. After the bridge on the right are two different exhibits worth a quick visit.

Gallery on the Bridge

This excellent bookstore—operated by the local Islamic cultural center—has a good, free photo exhibition of powerful images of war-torn Mostar, displayed inside a former mosque for soldiers who guarded the bridge. They play a montage of videos and photos of the bridge—before, during, and after the war—that's nearly as good as the similar film shown at the Museum of Herzegovina (described later). The shop also sells an impressively wide range of books about the former Yugoslavia and its troubled breakup.

Cost and Hours: Free, daily 7:00-24:00.

• *Just beyond the bookstore, tucked into the corner on the right, look for the stairs leading up to the...*

Museum of the Old Bridge (Muzej Stari Most)

Located within one of the Old Bridge's towers, this museum features a film and photos about the reconstruction of the bridge, archaeological findings, and a few other paltry exhibits about the history of the town and bridge, all in English. First climb up the stairs just after the bridge and buy your ticket, before hiking the rest of the way up to the top of the tower, where you can enjoy fine views through grubby windows. Then go around below to the archaeological exhibit. The museum offers more detail than most casual visitors need; consider just dropping into the smaller, free photo exhibition described previously, then moving along.

Cost and Hours: 5 KM, daily April-Aug 8:00-18:00, Feb-March and Sept-Nov 8:00-16:00, closed Dec-Jan, lots of stairs, Bajatova 4, tel. 036/551-6021.

• *After the Old Bridge, the street swings left and leads you along...*

▲▲Coppersmiths' Street (Kujundžiluk)

This lively strip, with the flavor of a Turkish bazaar, offers some of the most colorful shopping this side of Istanbul. You'll see Mostar's characteristic bridge depicted in every possible way, along with blue-and-white "evil eyes" (believed in the Turkish culture to keep bad spirits at bay), old Yugoslav Army kitsch (including spent bullet and shell casings engraved with

images of Mostar), and hammered-copper decorations (continuing the long tradition that gave the street its name). Partway up, the homes with the colorfully painted facades double as galleries for local artists. The artists live and work upstairs, then sell their work right on this street. Pop into the *atelier d'art* ("Đul Emina") on the right to meet Sead Vladović and enjoy his impressive iconographic work (daily 9:00-20:00). This is the most touristy street in all of Bosnia-Herzegovina, so don't expect any bargains. Still, it's fun. As you stroll, check out the fine views of the Old Bridge.

• *Continue uphill. After the street levels out, about halfway along the street on the left-hand side, look for the entrance to the...*

▲Koski Mehmet-Pasha Mosque (Koski Mehmet-Paša Džamija)

Mostar's Bosniak community includes many practicing Muslims. Step into this courtyard for a look at one of Mostar's many mosques. This mosque, dating from the early 17th century, is notable for its cliff-hanging riverside location, and because it's particularly accessible for tourists. But Mostar's other mosques share many of its characteristics—much of the following information applies to them as well.

Cost and Hours: 4 KM to enter mosque, 4 KM more to climb minaret, daily April-Oct 9:00-18:00, until 19:00 at busy times, Nov-March 9:00-15:00; if it seems crowded with tour groups, you can enter a very similar mosque later on this walk instead.

Visiting the Mosque: The **fountain** *(šadrvan)* in the courtyard allows worshippers to wash before entering the mosque, as directed by Islamic law. This practice, called ablution, is both a literal and a spiritual cleansing in preparation for being in the presence of Allah. It's also refreshing in this hot climate, and the sound of running water helps worshippers concentrate.

The **minaret**—the slender needle jutting up next to the dome—is the Islamic equivalent of the Christian bell tower, used to call people to prayer. In the old days, the *muezzin* (prayer leader) would climb the tower five times a day and chant, "There is only one God, and Muhammad is his prophet." In modern times, loudspeakers are used instead. Climbing the minaret's 89 claustrophobic, spiral stairs is a memorable experience, rewarding you at the top with the best views over Mostar—and the Old Bridge—that you can get without wings (entrance to the right of mosque entry).

Because this mosque is accustomed to tourists, you don't need to take off your shoes to enter (but stay on the green carpet), women don't need to wear scarves, and it's fine to take photos inside. Near the front of the mosque, you may see some of the small, overlapping rugs that are below this covering (reserved for shoes-off worshippers).

The Muslims of Bosnia

While Muslim immigrants have only recently become a fixture in many European cities, Bosnia-Herzegovina is one place where Muslims have continuously been an integral part of the cultural tapestry for centuries.

During the more than 400 years that Bosnia was part of the Ottoman Empire, the Muslim Turks did not forcibly convert their subjects (unlike some Catholic despots at the time). However, it was advantageous for non-Turks to adopt Islam (for lower taxes and better business opportunities), so many Slavs living here became Muslims. In fact, within 150 years of the start of Ottoman rule, half of the population of Bosnia-Herzegovina was Muslim.

The Ottomans became increasingly intolerant of other faiths as time went on, and uprisings by Catholics and Orthodox Christians eventually led to the end of Ottoman domination in the late 19th century. But even after the Ottomans left, many people in this region continued practicing Islam, as their families had been doing for centuries. These people constitute an ethnic group called "Bosniaks," and many of them are still practicing Muslims today (following the Sunni branch of the Muslim faith). Most Bosniaks are Slavs—of the same ethnic stock as Croats and Serbs—and look pretty much the same as their neighbors; however, some Bosniaks have ancestors who married into Turkish families, and they may have some Turkish features.

The actions of a small but attention-grabbing faction of Muslim extremists have burdened Islam with a bad reputation in the Western world. But judging Islam based on Osama bin Laden and al-Qaeda is a bit like judging Christianity based on the Oslo gunman and the Ku Klux Klan. Visiting Mostar is a unique opportunity to get a taste of a fully Muslim society, made a bit less intimidating because it wears a more-familiar European face.

Once **inside,** notice the traditional elements of the mosque. The niche *(mihrab)* across from the entry is oriented toward Mecca

(the holy city in today's Saudi Arabia)—the direction all Muslims face to pray. The small stairway *(mimber)* that seems to go nowhere is symbolic of the growth of Islam—Muhammad had to stand higher and higher to talk to his growing following. This serves as a kind of pulpit, where the cleric gives a speech, similar to a sermon or homily in Christian church services. No priest ever stands on the top stair, which is symbolically reserved for Muhammad.

The balcony just inside the door is

Here's an admittedly basic and simplistic outline (written by a non-Muslim) designed to help travelers from the Christian West understand a very rich but often misunderstood culture that's worthy of respect:

Muslims, like Christians and Jews, are monotheistic. They call God "Allah." The most important person in the Islamic faith is Muhammad, Allah's most important prophet, who lived in the sixth and seventh centuries A.D.

The "five pillars" of Islam are the same among Muslims in Bosnia-Herzegovina, Turkey, Iraq, Indonesia, the US, and everywhere else. Followers of Islam should:

1. Say and believe, "There is only one God, and Muhammad is his prophet."

2. Pray five times a day, while facing Mecca. Modern Muslims explain that it's important for this ritual to include several elements: washing, exercising, stretching, and thinking of God.

3. Give to the poor (one-fortieth of your wealth, if you are not in debt).

4. Fast during daylight hours through the month of Ramadan. Fasting is a great social equalizer and helps everyone to feel the hunger of the poor.

5. Visit Mecca. This is interpreted by some Muslims as a command to travel. Muhammad said, "Don't tell me how educated you are, tell me how much you've traveled."

Good advice for anyone, no matter what—or if—you call a higher power.

traditionally where women worship. For the same reason I find it hard to concentrate on God at yoga classes, Muslim men decided prayer would go better without the enjoyable but problematic distraction of bent-over women between them and Mecca. These days, women can also pray on the main floor with the men, but they must avoid physical contact.

Muslims believe that capturing a living creature in a painting or a sculpture is inappropriate. (In fact, depictions of Allah and the prophet Muhammad are strictly forbidden.) Instead, mosques are filled with ornate patterns and Arabic calligraphy (of the name "Muhammad" and important prayers and sayings from the Quran). You'll also see some floral and plant designs, which you'd never see in a more conservative, Middle Eastern mosque.

Before leaving, ponder how progressive the majority of Mostar's Muslims are. Most of them drink alcohol, wear modern Eu-

ropean clothing (you'll see very few women wearing head scarves or men with beards—and those you do see are likely tourists from the Middle East), and almost never visit a mosque to pray. In so many ways, these people don't fit our preconceived notions of Islam...and yet, they consider themselves Muslims all the same.

The mosque's **courtyard** is shared by several merchants. When you're done haggling, head to the terrace behind the mosque for the best view in town of the Old Bridge.

• *Just beyond this mosque, the traffic-free cobbles of the Old Town end. Take a right and leave the cutesy tourists' world. Walk up one block to the big...*

▲▲New Muslim Cemetery

In this cemetery, which was a park before the war, every tomb is dated 1993, 1994, or 1995. As the war raged, more exposed cemeteries were unusable. But this tree-covered piece of land was relatively safe from Croat snipers. As the casualties mounted, locals buried their loved ones here under cover of darkness. Many of these people were soldiers, but some were civilians. Strict Muslim graves don't display images of people, but here you'll see photos of war dead who were young, less-traditional members of the Muslim community. The fleur-de-lis shape of many of the tombstones is a patriotic symbol for the nation of Bosnia. The Arabic squiggles are the equivalent of an American having Latin on his or her tombstone—old-fashioned and formal.

• *Go up the wide stairs to the right of the cemetery (near the mosque). At #4 (on the right, just before and across from the bombed-out tower), you'll find the...*

Museum of Herzegovina (Muzej Hercegovine)

This humble little museum is made worthwhile by a deeply moving **film** that traces the history of the town through its Old Bridge: fun circa-1957 footage of the diving contests; harrowing scenes of the bridge being pummeled, and finally toppled, by artillery; and a stirring sequence showing the bridge's reconstruction and grand reopening on that day in 2004—with high-fives, Beethoven's *Ode to Joy*, fireworks, and more divers. (This includes much of the same footage as the similar film at the Gallery on the Bridge, described earlier, but doesn't focus solely on the wartime damage.)

The museum itself displays fragments of this region's rich history, including historic photos and several items from its Ottoman period. There are sparse English descriptions, but without a tour

guide the exhibits are a bit difficult to appreciate. Topics include the Turkish period, Herzegovina under the Austro-Hungarian Empire, village life, and (in the basement) local archaeology. One small room commemorates the house's former owner, Dzemal Bijedić, who was Tito's second-in-command during the Yugoslav period until he was killed in a mysterious plane crash in 1977. (If Bijedić had lived, many wonder whether he might have succeeded Tito...and succeeded in keeping Yugoslavia together.)

Cost and Hours: 5-KM museum entry includes 12-minute film, no narration—works in any language, ask about "film?" as you enter; Mon-Fri 9:00-16:00, Sat 10:00-15:00, closed Sun; often closed in winter—call first; Bajatova 4—walking up these stairs, it's the second door that's marked for the museum, under the over-hanging balcony, tel. 036/551-602, www.muzejhercegovine.com.

• *Backtrack to where you left the Old Town. Notice the* **Tepa Market**, *with locals buying clothing and produce, in the area just beyond the pedestrian zone. Now walk (with the market on your left) along the lively street called* **Braće Fejića**. *(There's no sign, but the street is level and busy with cafés.) You're in the "new town," where locals sit out in front of boisterous cafés sipping coffee while listening to the thumping beat of distinctly Eastern-sounding music.*

Stroll down this street for a few blocks. At the palm trees (about 50 yards before the minaret—look for sign to Ottoman House*), you can side-trip a block to the left to reach...*

▲Bišćević Turkish House (Bišćevića Ćošak)

Mostar has three traditional Turkish-style homes that are open for tourists to visit. The Bišćević House is the oldest, most interesting, and most convenient for a quick visit, but two others are described at the end of this listing. Dating from 1635, the Bišćević House is typical of old houses in Mostar, which mix Oriental style with Mediterranean features.

Cost and Hours: 4 KM, March-Nov Mon-Fri 8:00-19:00, Sat-Sun 9:00-18:00, generally closed Dec-Feb—but you can arrange a visit by calling ahead to Fortuna Tours, tel. 036/552-197, Bišćevića 13.

Visiting the House: First you'll step through the outer (or animals') garden, then into the inner (or family's) garden. This inner zone is surrounded by a high wall—protection from the sun's rays, from thieves...and from prying eyes, allowing women to take off the veil they were required to wear in public. Enjoy the geometrical patters of the smooth river stones in the floor (for example, the five-sided star), and keep an eye out for the house's pet

turtles. It's no coincidence that the traditional fountain *(šadrvan)* resembles those at the entrance to a mosque—a reminder of the importance of running water in Muslim culture. The little white building is a kitchen—cleverly located apart from the house so that the heat and smells of cooking didn't permeate the upstairs living area.

Buy your ticket and take off your shoes before you climb up the wooden staircase. Imagine how a stairway like this one could be pulled up for extra protection in case of danger (notice that this one has a "trap door" to cover it). The cool, shady, and airy living room is open to the east—from where the wind rarely blows. The over-hanging roof also prevented the hot sun from reaching this area. The loom in the corner was the women's workplace—the carpets you're standing on would have been woven there. The big chests against the wall were used to bring the dowry when the home-owner took a new wife. Study the fine wood carving that decorates the space.

Continue back into the main gathering room *(divanhan)*. This space—whose name comes from the word "talk"—is designed in a circle so people could face each other, cross-legged, for a good conversation while they enjoyed a dramatic view overlooking the Neretva. The room comes with a box of traditional costumes—great for photo fun. Put on a pair of baggy pants and a fez and really lounge.

Other Turkish Houses: If you're intrigued by this house, consider dropping by Mostar's two other Turkish houses. The **Muslibegović House** (Muslibegovića Kuća) feels newer because it dates from 1871, just a few years before the Ottomans left town. This homey house—which also rents out rooms to visitors (see "Sleeping in Mostar," later)—has many of the same features as the Bišćević House. If they're not too busy, Sanela or Gabriela can give you an English tour (4 KM, mid-April-mid-Oct daily 10:00-18:00, closed to visitors off-season, just two blocks uphill from the Karađozbeg Mosque at Osman Đikića 41, tel. 036/551-379, www.muslibegovichouse.com). To find it, go up the street between the Karađozbeg Mosque and the cemetery, cross the busy street, and continue a long block uphill on the alley. The wall with the slate roof on the left marks the house.

The **Kajtaz House** (Kajtazova Kuća), hiding up a very residen-tial-feeling alley a few blocks from the Old Bridge, feels lived-in because it still is (in the opposite direction from most of the other sights, at Gaše Ilića 21).

• *Go back to the main café street and continue to the...*

▲Karađozbeg Mosque (Karađozbegova Džamija)

The city's main mosque was completed in 1557, the same year work began on the Old Bridge. This mosque, which welcomes visitors, feels less touristy than the one back in the Old Town. Before entering the gate into the complex, look for the picture showing the re-

cent war damage sustained here. You'll see that this mosque has most of the same elements as the Koski Mehmet-Pasha Mosque (described earlier), but some of these decorations are original. Across the street is another cemetery with tombstones from that terrible year, 1993.

Cost and Hours: 4 KM to enter mosque (free for Muslims), 4 KM more to climb minaret, daily May-Sept 9:00-19:30, Oct-April 10:00-15:00. Inside the mosque, either stay on the designated area or remove your shoes. Women can choose whether to cover their heads, but women wearing shorts will be asked to cover their legs with a loaner scarf.

• *Now leave the tourists' Mostar and continue into modern, urban Mostar along the street in front of the Karađozbeg Mosque. This grimy, mostly traffic-free street is called...*

▲Braće Fejića

Walking along the modern town's main café strip, enjoy the opportunity to observe this workaday Bosniak town. You'll see the humble offices of the ragtag B&H Airlines; a state-run gambling office (Lutrija BIH) taxing its less-educated people with a state lottery; and lots of cafés that serve drinks but no food. People generally eat at home before going out to nurse an affordable drink. (Café ABC has good cakes and ice cream; the upstairs is a popular pizza hangout for students and families.)

At the small mosque on the left, obituary announcements are tacked to the tree, listing the bios and funeral times for locals who have recently died. A fig tree grows out of the mosque's minaret, just an accident of nature illustrating how that plant can thrive with almost no soil (somehow, the Bosniaks can relate). Walking farther, look back and up to see a few ruins—still ugly nearly two decades after the war. There's a messy confusion about who owns what in Mostar. Surviving companies have no money. Yugo Bank, which held the mortgages, is defunct. No one will invest until clear ownership is established. Until then, the people of Mostar sip their coffee in the shadow of these jagged reminders of the warfare that wracked this town a couple of decades ago.

The Dawn of War in Mostar

Mostar was always one of the most stubbornly independent parts of the former Yugoslavia. It had one of the highest rates of mixed-ethnicity marriages in all of Bosnia-Herzegovina. In the early 1990s, Mostar's demographics were proportioned more or less evenly—about 35 percent of its residents were Bosniaks, 34 percent Croats, and 19 percent Serbs. But this delicate balance was shattered in a few brutal months of warfare.

On April 1, 1992, Bosnia-Herzegovina—led by Muslim president Alija Izetbegović—declared independence from Yugoslavia. Very quickly, the Serb-dominated Yugoslav People's Army moved to stake their claim on territory throughout the country, including the important city of Mostar. On April 3, Serb forces occupied the east end of town (including the Ottoman Old Town), forcing many residents—predominantly Croats and Bosniaks—to hole up in the western part of the city. Meanwhile, Serbian and Croatian leaders were secretly meeting to divvy up Bosnian territory, and by early May, they'd agreed that Croatia would claim Mostar. Several weeks later, when the joint Croat-Bosniak forces crossed back over the river, the Serb forces mysteriously withdrew from the city (having been directed to capitulate), and retreated to the mountaintops above town. The Croats and Bosniaks, believing they'd achieved peace, began putting their city back together. During this time, some factions also rounded up, tortured, and killed Serbs still living in Mostar. Many Bosniaks moved back to their homes on the east side of town, but, rather oddly, many of the Croats who had previously resided there instead stayed in the west—in many cases, moving into apartments vacated by Serbs who had fled.

On May 9, 1993—the Yugoslav holiday of "Victory over Fascism Day"—Mostarians were rocked awake by the terrifying sounds of artillery shells. Croat military forces swept through the city, forcibly moving remaining Bosniaks from the west part of town into the east. Throughout that summer, Bosniak men were captured and sent to concentration camps, while the Croats virtually sealed off the east side of town—creating a giant ghetto with no way in or out. The long and ugly siege of Mostar had begun.

Near the end of the pedestrian zone, through the parking lot on the right, look for the building with communist-era reliefs of 12th-century Bogomil tomb decor—remembering the indigenous culture that existed here even before the arrival of the Ottomans.

When you finally hit the big street (with car traffic), head left one block to the big **Masala Square** (literally, "Place for Prayer"). Historically, this was where pilgrims gathered before setting off for Mecca on their hajj. This is a great scene on balmy evenings, when

it's a rendezvous point for the community. The two busts near the fountain provide perfect goal posts for budding soccer stars.

• *For a finale, you can continue one block more out onto the bridge to survey the town you just explored. From here, you can backtrack to linger in the places you found most inviting. Or you can venture into...*

Western (Croat) Mostar

Most tourists stay on the Bosniak side of town. But for a complete look at this divided city, it's well worth strolling to the west side. While there's not much in the way of sightseeing here, and much of this urban zone isn't particularly pretty, it does provide an interesting contrast to the Muslim side of town. As this is the location of some of Mostar's new shopping malls, this area feels more vital each year, and a few of the tree-lined streets seem downright elegant.

Crossing the river and the Bulevar, the scarred husks of destroyed buildings begin to fade away, and within a block you're immersed in concrete apartment buildings—making it clear that, when the city became divided, the Muslims holed up in the original Ottoman Old Town, while the Croats claimed the modern Tito-era sprawl. The relative lack of war damage here (aside from a few stray bullet holes) emphasizes that it was the Croats laying siege to the Muslims of Mostar. You'll also notice some glitzy new shopping centers and more pizza and pasta restaurants than *ćevapčići* joints (in other words, even the food over here is more Croatian than Bosnian).

Looking at a map, you'll notice that many streets on this side of town are named for Croatian cities (Dubrovačka, Splitska, Vukovarska) or historical figures (Kneza Branimira, Kralja Tomislava, and Kralja Petra Krešimira—for the dukes who first united the Croats in the ninth and tenth centuries). This side of town also has several remnants of Mostar's brief period of Habsburg rule (1878-1918). During this time, the empire quickly expanded what had been a sleepy Ottoman backwater, laying out grand boulevards and erecting genteel buildings that look like they'd be at home in Vienna.

All streets converge at the big roundabout (about a 15-minute walk from the Old Town) called the **Rondo,** which is a good place to get oriented to this neighborhood. Overlooking this lively intersection is the stately Hrvatski Dom ("Croatia House") cultural center. In this part of town, notice how even the street signs are politically charged: *Centar* signs pointedly direct traffic *away* from the (Bosniak) Old Town, and many road signs point toward Široki Brijeg—a Croat stronghold in western Herzegovina.

The adjacent **Park Zrinjevac** is a pleasant place to stroll, and was the site of an infamously ill-fated attempt at reconciliation.

In the early 2000s, idealistic young Mostarians formed the Urban Movement of Mostar, which searched for a way to connect the still-feuding Catholic and Muslim communities. As a symbol of their goals, they chose Bruce Lee, the deceased kung-fu movie star, beloved by both Croats and Bosniaks for his characters' honorable struggle against injustice. A life-size bronze statue of Lee was unveiled with fanfare in this park in November of 2005—but was almost immediately vandalized. The statue was repaired, and may or may not have been returned to its pedestal (which you'll still find in the park).

Several interesting sights lie close to this roundabout. A block toward the Old Town from the Rondo (on Kralja Višeslava Humskog), look for the big **Muslim cemetery** with tombstones from the early 1990s. These are the graves of those killed during the first round of fighting, when the Croats and Bosniaks teamed up to fight the Serbs.

If you head from the Rondo down Kneza Branimira (across from the park), you'll enjoy an inviting boulevard shaded by plane trees. When first built, this street was called **Štefanijino Šetalište**—"Stéphanie's Promenade," after the Belgian princess who married Austria's Archduke Rudolf (the heir apparent of the Habsburg Empire until he died in a mysterious murder-suicide pact with his mistress). Partway down the street on the left is the recommended Pivnica Štefanijino Šetalište, a good place for a microbrew or a meal.

If you head up Kralja Petra Krešimira IV from the Rondo, after two long blocks on the left you'll see an abandoned, derelict park leading to a gigantic **Partisan Cemetery and Monument**. This socialist-style monument spreads all the way up the hill. It oozes with symbolism trumpeting the pivotal WWII Battle of the Neretva, when Tito and his Partisan Army turned the tables on Nazi forces (just 30 miles north of here). It was designed by Bogdan Bogdanović, who created many such monuments and memorials throughout Yugoslavia, and dedicated by Tito himself in 1965. From the terrace at the top, which is scattered with symbolic gravestones for those who gave their lives to free Yugoslavia from the Nazis, small streams once trickled down to the large enclosure at the bottom, ultimately flowing beneath a stylized broken bridge representing the Bridge at the Neretva. Today the monument is overgrown and ignored—a tragic symbol of post-Tito ethnic discord. Local Croats—who have little nostalgia for the Yu-

goslav period, which they now view as a time of oppression—seem to intentionally neglect the place. This formerly hallowed ground is a mess of broken concrete and a popular place for drunken benders, garbage dumping, and drug deals (be careful if you decide to explore, and avoid it after dark). A pensive stroll here comes with a poignant reflection on how one generation's honored war dead can become the next generation's unwanted burden.

Nightlife in Mostar

Be sure to enjoy the local scene after dark in Mostar. Though the town is touristy, it's also a real urban center with a young population riding a wave of raging hormones. The meat market in the courtyard next to the old Turkish bathhouse near the TI is fun to observe. The Old Bridge is a popular meeting place for locals as well as tourists (and pickpockets). A stroll from the Old Bridge

down the café-lined Braće Fejića boulevard to the modern Masala Square at the far end of town (described earlier) gives a great peek at Mostarians socializing away from the tourists. Wherever you wind up, order a cocktail or try a Turkish-style hubbly-bubbly (*šiša*, SHEE-shah). Ask to have one of these big water pipes fired up for you and choose your flavored tobacco: apple, cappuccino, banana, or lemon.

Ali Baba is an actual cave featuring a fun, atmospheric, and youthful party scene. While this place has gone in and out of business over the past few years, it's worth checking to see if it's open to enjoy a drink in

a unique and very cool space (look for low-profile entrance along Coppersmiths' Street, just down from the Old Bridge—watch for signs tucked down a rocky alley).

Oscar Nightclub is a caravanserai for lounge lizards—an exotic world mixing babbling streams, terraces, lounge chairs, and big sofas where young and old enjoy cocktails and *šiša* (June-Aug open "non-stop," closed Sept-May, up from the Old Bridge on Onešćukova street, near the Crooked Bridge at the end of the pedestrian zone).

Sleeping in Mostar

Most of my listings are small, friendly, accessible, affordable guest houses in or very near the Old Town. Many hotels and pensions in town promise "parking," but it's often street parking out front—private lots are rare. Mostar's Old Town can be very noisy on weekends, with nightclubs and outdoor restaurants rollicking into the wee hours. If you're a light sleeper, consider Villa Fortuna, the Muslibegović House, or Shangri La, which are quieter than the norm.

$$$ The **Muslibegović House,** a Bosnian national monument that also invites tourists in to visit during the day, is in an actual Turkish home dating from 1871. The complex houses 10 homey rooms and two suites, all of which combine classic Turkish style (elegant and comfortable old beds, creaky wooden floors with colorful carpets, lounging sofas; guests remove shoes at the outer door) with modern comforts (air-con, free Wi-Fi, flatscreen TVs). Situated on a quiet residential lane just above the bustle of Mostar's main pedestrian drag and Old Town zone, this is a memorable experience (Sb-€60, Db-€90/€75, "pasha suite"-€105, includes a tour of the house, closed Nov-Feb, 2 blocks uphill from the Karađozbeg Mosque at Osman Đikića 41, tel. 036/551-379, www.muslibegovichouse.com, muslibegovichouse@gmail.com; Taž, Sanela, and Gabriela).

$$$ **Hotel Bristol** is the only business-class place near central Mostar. Its 47 rooms don't quite live up to their four stars, but the location is handy, overlooking the river a 10-minute walk from the heart of the Old Town (Sb-€51, Db-€82, apartment-€90, extra bed-€15, air-con, elevator, free guest computer and Wi-Fi, some street noise, limited parking, Mostarskog Bataljona, tel. 036/500-100, www.bristol.ba, info@bristol.ba).

$$ **Hotel Kriva Ćuprija** ("Crooked Bridge"), by the bridge of the same name, is tucked between waterfalls in a picturesque valley a few steps from the Old Bridge. It's an appealing oasis with 10 stylish rooms and a restaurant with atmospheric outdoor seating (Sb-€39, Db-€65, apartment-€75, extra bed-€18, 10 percent discount on rooms and food with this book, can be noisy, air-con, free Wi-Fi, free parking, call to reconfirm if arriving after 19:00, enter at Onešćukova 23 or Kriva Ćuprija 2, tel. 036/360-360, mobile 061-135-286, www.motel-mostar.ba, info@motel-mostar.ba, Sami). Their second location—**Hotel Kriva Ćuprija II**—offers 10 modern rooms in a restored Habsburg-style building on a dreary urban

Sleep Code

($1 = about 1.40 KM, €1 = about $1.30, country code: 387, area code: 036)

S = Single, **D** = Double/Twin, **T** = Triple, **Q** = Quad, **b** = bathroom. Unless otherwise noted, prices include breakfast.

Rates: If I've listed three sets of rates, separated by slashes, the first is for peak season (typically mid-July through late Aug), the second is for shoulder season (roughly June-mid-July and late Aug-Sept), and the third is for off-season (Oct-May). If I've listed only two rates, the first is for peak season and the second for shoulder/off-season. The dates for seasonal rates vary by hotel.

Price Ranges: To help you sort easily through these listings, I've divided the accommodations into three categories based on the price for a double room with bath during peak season:

$$$ Higher Priced—Most rooms €80 or more.
$$ Moderately Priced—Most rooms between €60-80.
$ Lower Priced—Most rooms €60 or less.

Prices can change without notice; verify the hotel's current rates online or by email. For the best prices, always book direct.

MOSTAR & NEARBY

street, about 200 yards to the south. As it's a less convenient location and lacks soul, I prefer the original (same prices, discount, amenities, and contact information as main hotel; some traffic noise, Maršala Tita 186, next to the Lučki Bridge, reception tel. 036/554-125).

$$ Villa Anri, a bit more hotelesque than other pensions in Mostar, sits a block farther from the bustle near the Bulevar. The stony facade hides eight rooms (six with balconies) combining old Herzegovinian style and bright colors. The big draw is the rooftop terrace, shared by two rooms, which enjoys grand views over the Old Bridge area (Db-€70/€60/€55, Db with grand terrace-€95/€80/€60, Tb-€95/€80/€60, Tb with grand terrace-€115/€90/€70, cash only, air-con, free Wi-Fi, free parking, Braće Đukića 4, tel. 036/578-477, www.villa-anri-mostar.ba, villa. anri@gmail.com).

$$ Motel Emen has six modern, sleek rooms overlooking a busy café street a few cobbled blocks from the Old Bridge (Sb-€50, Db-€70, bigger Db with balcony-€80, all rooms €10 less Oct-May, air-con, free guest computer and Wi-Fi, free parking, Onešćukova 32, tel. 036/581-120, www.motel-emen.com, info@motel-emen. com).

$ **Villa Fortuna** is an exceptional value, located in a nondescript urban neighborhood a few minutes' walk farther away from the Old Bridge. Owners Nela and Mili Bijavica rent eight tasteful, modern rooms above the main office of Fortuna Tours. The courtyard in front offers free, secure parking, and in back there's a pleasant garden with a traditional Herzegovinian garden cottage (Sb-€30, Db-€40, apartment-€80, these prices if you book direct by email, breakfast-€5, non-smoking, air-con, free Wi-Fi, Rade Bitange 34, tel. 036/580-625, mobile 063-315-017 or 063-299-189, www.villafortuna.ba, villa_fortuna@bih.net.ba). Fortuna Tours can also put you in touch with locals renting rooms and apartments.

$ **Pansion Čardak,** run by Suzana and Nedžad Kasumović, has five straightforward rooms sharing a kitchen and Internet nook in a stone house set just back from the bustling Crooked Bridge area (Db-€50-60/€45, higher price is for bigger room or room with terrace, Tb-€75/€60, Qb-€90/€70, cash only, breakfast at nearby restaurant-€3-4, air-con, free Wi-Fi, free parking, Jusovina 3, tel. 036/578-249, mobile 061-385-988, www.pansion-cardak.com, info @pansion-cardak.com).

$ **Pansion Nur,** run by Feđa, a relative of Suzana and Nedžad (above), has four simpler but cheaper rooms and a shared kitchen (twin Db-€40/€35, Db-€50/€40, Tb-€60/€50, suite-€70/€60, cash only, no breakfast, air-con, free Wi-Fi, free parking, Jusovina 8b, tel. 036/580-296, mobile 062-160-872, www.pansion-nur.com, info@pansion-nur.com).

$ **B&B Shangri La** fills a gorgeously restored Austro-Hungarian building on a hill above the Old Town, squeezed between war ruins. The eight rooms come in all different sizes, but all of them are modern and nicely appointed (Db-€41-58 depending on size and amenities, breakfast-€6, air-con, free Wi-Fi, free parking, Kalhanska 10, mobile 061-169-362, www.shangrila.com.ba, info@ shangrila.com.ba, Nijaz).

$ **Villa Botticelli,** overlooking a charming waterfall garden just up the valley from the Crooked Bridge, has five colorful rooms at affordable prices (Sb-€30, Db-€40, breakfast-€3, air-con, free Wi-Fi, Muje Bjelavca 6, enter around back along the alley, mobile 063-319-057, www.villabotticelli.com, info@villabotticelli.com, Snježana and Zoran).

Eating in Mostar

Most of Mostar's tourist-friendly restaurants are conveniently concentrated in the Old Town. If you walk anywhere that's cobbled, you'll stumble onto dozens of tempting restaurants charging the same reasonable prices and serving rustic, traditional Bosnian

food. In my experience, the menus at most places are virtually identical—though quality and ambience can vary greatly. As eateries
tend to come and go quickly here, and little distinguishes these
places anyway, don't be too focused on a particular spot. Grilled
meats are especially popular. As for local wines, most are made
with one of two indigenous grapes: *blatina* (literally "muddy"; a
thick, heavy, earthy red) and *žilavka* (literally "root"; a bright, fairly
acidic white).

On the Embankment, with Old Bridge Views

For the best atmosphere, find your way into the several levels of
restaurants that clamber up the riverbank and offer perfect views
of the Old Bridge. In terms of the setting, this is the most memorable place to dine in Mostar—but be warned that the quality of
the food along here is uniformly low, and prices are relatively high
(figure 8-18 KM for a meal). If you want a good perch, it's fun and
smart to drop by earlier in the day and personally reserve the table
of your choice.

To reach two of the most scenic eateries, go over the Old
Bridge to the west side of the river,
and bear right on the cobbles until
you get to the old Turkish bathhouse
(with the copper domes on the roof).
To the right of the bathhouse is the
entrance to a lively courtyard surrounded by cafés. Crossing straight
through the courtyard, you'll find
stairs leading down to several river-
front terraces belonging to two dif-
ferent restaurants: **Babilon** (my choice for better food) and **Teatar.**
Poke around to find your favorite bridge panorama before settling
in for a drink or a meal.

Two other places (including a pizzeria) are a bit closer to the
bridge—to reach these, look for the alley on the left just before the
bridge tower.

Near the Old Bridge

While they lack the Old Bridge views, these places are just as central as those listed above, and serve food that's generally a step up.
The first three places are in the atmospheric Old Town, while the
last one is in the modern part of town.

Restoran Hindin Han is pleasantly situated on a woody terrace over a rushing stream. It's respected locally for its good cooking and fair prices (big 12-16-KM salads, 7-15-KM grilled dishes,
12-20-KM fish and other main dishes, Sarajevsko beer on tap,
daily 11:00-24:00, Jusovina 10, tel. 036/581-054). To find it, walk

west from the Old Bridge, bear left at the Šadrvan restaurant, cross the bridge, and you'll see it on the left.

Nacionalni Restoran Aščinica Balkan ("Balkan National Restaurant/Cafeteria") is a convenient cafeteria-style eatery with two handy locations. They serve up tasty, home-cooked Bosnian specialties; you can order from the menu, but it's more fun to order a "mix" *(mješanac)* plate from the display case—the small 10-KM plate is plenty for a light meal (16-KM "medium" and 20-KM "large" plates also available, 3-KM salads, Bosnian coffee, tempting dessert display case, daily 10:00-22:00, one location right at the end of the Old Town cobbles before the market, the other a couple of blocks away on the new town's main drag at Braće Fejića 57, tel. 036/551-868).

Saray is an untouristy, nondescript little eatery just uphill from the Karađozbeg Mosque in the modern part of town. They have a basic menu of cheap and very tasty grilled meats—specializing in the classic *ćevapčići* (little sausage-shaped meat patties)—and outdoor seating overlooking a playground that offers good people- and kid-watching while you eat (4-10-KM grilled meat dishes, big 7-KM salads, daily 7:00-23:00, Karađozbegova 3, mobile 062-062-301).

Urban Grill's food is nothing special—it has basically the same menu as other places in town—but its terrace enjoys one of Mostar's best unobstructed views of the Old Bridge (8-17-KM grilled meat and other meals, 10-12-KM pastas and salads, Bosnian coffee, daily 8:00-22:00, enter along the main cobbled Old Town drag at Mala Tepa 26, tel. 036/552-235).

In the West (Croat) Side of Town

While less charming and romantic, a stroll to the west side of town (still inhabited primarily by Croats) offers an interesting contrast to the cutesy Old Town—and a completely different array of restaurants. Here you'll find more pizza and pasta places than grilled meats, as well as shiny new shopping centers with modern food courts.

Pivnica Štefanijino Šetalište ("Stéphanie's Promenade Brewpub"), named for the onetime Austro-Hungarian crown princess, mingles modern Croat class with Habsburg grandeur. It fills a stylish cellar and an inviting outdoor terrace with happy diners, sipping beers and digging into international fare. It sits along its gorgeous, tree-lined namesake boulevard (9-15-KM main dishes, Mon-Fri 8:00-23:00, Sat-Sun 15:00-23:00, Kneza Branimira 11, tel. 036/319-319, www.stefanija.info).

Mostar Connections

By Bus

Not surprisingly for a divided city, Mostar has two different, autonomous bus terminals, each served by different companies. Mostar's **main bus station** (called "Autobusna Stanica") is on the east/Bosniak side of the river, about a 15-minute walk north of the Old Town (for details, see "Arrival in Mostar," earlier). Most buses you're likely to take use this station; for information on the other station (on the west/Croat side of town), see the end of this section.

Schedules and Tickets: At the main station, two primary companies (one Bosniak, one Croat) operate independent offices, providing schedule information and tickets only for their own buses. Because the companies are reluctant to cooperate, there's no single information or ticket office for all Mostar buses—visit both companies to know your options before buying tickets. As you face the bus station, near the left end is the Bosniak company **Autoprevoz** (tel. 036/551-900, www.autoprevoz-bus.ba); they also sell tickets for a few other companies (including Eurolines and Bogdan Bus). Near the right end is the Croat-owned **Globtour** (look for *Mediteran Tours* sign, tel. 036/550-065, www.globtour.com), which sells tickets only for its own buses. Local and regional connections (not listed below) are operated by Mostar Bus, whose buses depart from across the street from the main bus station (www.mostarbus.ba).

Tracking down reliable **schedule** information in Mostar is tricky, but you can start by checking the websites listed above, then calling or visiting both companies at the station to confirm your options and buy tickets. Note that buses to seasonal destinations (such as along the Dalmatian Coast) run more frequently in peak season, roughly June through mid-September.

From Mostar's Main Bus Station: Both Autoprevoz and Globtour operate buses to **Sarajevo** (6/day on Autoprevoz, 4/day on Globtour, 2.5 hours). Globtour exclusively handles buses to **Međugorje** (6-7/day, 40 minutes), **Zagreb** (4/day, 9 hours, includes a night bus), **Split** (5/day, 4-4.5 hours; additional departures by Eurolines in summer), and **Dubrovnik** (3/day, 4-5 hours). That important Dubrovnik connection is tricky: Most days, all Dubrovnik buses depart early in the day, making an afternoon return from Mostar to Dubrovnik impossible. However, in summer (June-Aug), Eurolines adds two more departures each day—including a handy 17:30 departure, which makes day-tripping from Dubrovnik workable (tickets sold at Autoprevoz office). Globtour also runs a handy bus to Montenegro's **Bay of Kotor** (departs Mostar at 7:00, arrives at Kotor at 12:30 and Budva at 13:30, then returns the same day); a second bus runs on a similar schedule, via Croatia.

From Mostar's West/Croat Bus Station: A few additional buses, mostly to Croatian destinations and to Croat areas of Bosnia-Herzegovina, depart from the west side of town. These use a makeshift "station" (actually a gravel lot behind a gas station) on Vukovarska street, called "Kolodvor." It's about a 15-minute walk due west of the main bus station. Most buses using the Kolodvor station are operated by the Euroherc company. In addition to one daily bus apiece to **Zagreb, Split,** and **Sarajevo,** this station has several departures to **Metković** (at the Croatian border, with additional connections to Croatian destinations; 8/day) and to **Međugorje** (7/day Mon-Fri, 3/day Sat, none Sun). Additionally, some Croat buses leave from a bus stop near the Franciscan Church. But since the connections are sparse, the location is inconvenient, and the "station" is dreary, I'd stick with the main bus station and ignore this option unless you're desperate.

By Train

Mostar is on the train line that runs from Ploče (on the Croatian coast between Split and Dubrovnik) to Zagreb, via Mostar and Sarajevo. But I'd avoid the train, which tends to be cramped and slow; buses are typically much more efficient and comfortable. The train schedule changes frequently, but it's usually possible to go by train to **Ploče** (with good bus connections to elsewhere in Dalmatia; 2 hours) and **Sarajevo** (2.5 hours). Some trains continue from Sarajevo all the way to **Zagreb** (11.5 hours from Mostar; bus is faster). Train info: Tel. 036/550-608.

Route Tips for Drivers:
From Dubrovnik to Mostar

You have two options for the drive between Dubrovnik and Mostar: easy and straightforward along the coast, or adventurous and off the beaten path through the Herzegovinian mountains. I've narrated each route as you'd encounter it driving from Dubrovnik to Mostar, but you can do either one in reverse—just hold this book upside-down.

The Main Coastal Road

The vast majority of traffic from Dubrovnik to Mostar follows the coastal road north, then cuts east into Bosnia. Because this is one of the most direct routes, it can be crowded (allow about 2.5 hours). It's also a bit inconvenient, as you have to cross the border three times (into and out of Bosnia at Neum, and into Bosnia again at Metković).

Begin by driving north of Dubrovnik, passing some of the places mentioned in the Near Dubrovnik chapter: **Trsteno** (with its arboretum), and **Ston** and **Mali Ston** (with a mighty wall and

waterfront restaurants, respectively). After passing the Ston turn-off, you'll see the long, mountainous, vineyard-draped **Pelješac Peninsula** across the bay on your left.

Soon you'll come to a surprise border crossing, at **Neum.** Here you'll cross into Bosnia-Herzegovina—then, six miles later, cross back out again.

You won't be back in Croatia for long. Just north of Neum, the main coastal road jogs away from the coast and around the striking **Neretva River Delta**—the extremely fertile "garden patch of Croatia," which produces a significant portion of Croatia's fruits and vegetables. The Neretva is the same river that flows under Mostar's Old Bridge upstream—but in Metković, it spreads out into 12 branches as it enters the Adriatic, flooding a vast plain and creating a bursting cornucopia in the middle of an otherwise rocky and arid region. Enjoying some of the most plentiful sunshine on the Croatian coast, as well as a steady supply of water for irrigation, the Neretva Delta is as productive as it is beautiful.

At the Neretva Delta, turn off for the town of **Metković;** at the far end of that town, you'll cross the border into **Bosnia-Herzegovina,** then continue straight on the main road (M-17) directly into Mostar. As you drive, you'll see destroyed buildings and occasional roadside memorials bearing the likenesses of fresh-faced soldiers who died in the recent war.

Along the way are a few interesting detours: In Čapljina, you can turn off to the left to reach **Međugorje**. If you stay on the main road, keep your eyes peeled soon after the Čapljina turnoff for a mountaintop castle tower (on the right side of the road), which marks the medieval town of **Počitelj**. With extra time, just before Mostar (in Buna), you can detour a few miles along the Buna River into **Blagaj**.

Approaching **Mostar** on M-17, you'll pass the airport, then carry on straight toward *Sarajevo* (ignoring the first turn-off to the left for *Centar*). As you skirt the city, take the left turn for *Centar* and *Posušje*. When you come to the traffic light, you can turn right to reach the east side of the river (for the Muslibegović House or Hotel Kriva Ćuprija II); or continue straight to reach the west side of the river (for my other accommodations). If you continue straight, you'll bear right onto Bulevar street, and continue on that main artery for several blocks (passing several destroyed buildings). At the street called Rade Bitange (just after the giant church bell tower), turn right to find the public parking lot (2 KM/hour, 10 KM/8 hours)—less than a 10-minute walk from the Old Bridge. Be warned that signage is poor; if you get lost, try asking for directions to "Stari Most" (STAH-ree most)—the Old Bridge.

MOSTAR & NEARBY

Rugged-but-Scenic Backcountry Journey Through Serb Herzegovina

While the coastal route outlined above is the most common way to connect Dubrovnik to Mostar, I enjoy getting out of the tourist rut by twisting up the mountains behind Dubrovnik and cutting across the scenic middle of Herzegovina. (If you're traveling by road between Dubrovnik and Split at another point in your trip, you'll see the coastal road anyway—so this alternative helps you avoid the rerun.) This route feels much more remote, but the roads are good and the occasional gas station and restaurant break up the journey. I find this route particularly interesting because it offers an easily digestible taste of the **Republika Srpska** part of Herzegovina—controlled by the country's Serb minority, rather than its Bosniak and Croat majority. You'll see Orthodox churches and monasteries, the Cyrillic alphabet, and various symbols of the defiantly proud Serb culture (such as the red, white, and blue flag with the four golden C's). You can't get a complete picture of the former Yugoslavia without sampling at least a sliver of Serb culture. (Because this road goes through the Serbian part of Herzegovina, it's not popular among Bosniaks or Croats—in fact, locals might tell you this road "does not exist." It does.) If you want a little taste of Republika Srpska, consider just day-tripping into Trebinje—especially on Saturday, when the produce market is at its liveliest.

The first step is to climb up into the mountains and the charming market town of Trebinje. From there, two different roads lead to Mostar: via Stolac or via Nevesinje. If you take the Stolac route, the whole journey from Dubrovnik to Mostar takes about as long as the coastal road (and potentially even faster, thanks to the light traffic and lack of an extra border). The Nevesinje route takes a good hour longer than the Stolac route, and immerses you in an even more remote landscape.

Dubrovnik to Trebinje: From Dubrovnik, head south toward Cavtat, the airport, and Montenegro. Shortly after leaving Dubrovnik, watch for—and follow—signs on the left directing you to *Brgat Gornji*. (Signage completely ignores the large Serb town of Trebinje, just past this obscure border village.) As you drive through the border into Bosnia-Herzegovina, notice the faint remains of a long-abandoned old rail line cutting sharp switchbacks up the hill. This once connected Dubrovnik to Mostar and Sarajevo. The charred trees you may see are not from the war, but from more recent forest fires.

Carry on across the plateau, where you may begin to notice Cyrillic lettering on signs: You've crossed into the Republika Srpska. About 20 minutes after the border, you'll come upon **Trebinje** (Требиње)—a pleasant and relatively affluent town that's a good place to stretch your legs, get some Convertible Marks (ATMs

are scattered around the town center), and maybe nurse a coffee while people-watching on the big, leafy, inviting main square. Out on the square, a smattering of humble open-air market stalls sell local produce (Saturday is the biggest market day, but there's

always some action). There's a welcoming TI on the square, but in this small-time town, they don't have much to do (Mon-Fri 8:00-20:00, Sat 9:00-15:00, closed Sun, shorter hours off-season, Jovana Dučića b.b., tel. 059/273-410, www.trebinjeturizam.com). From the bottom of the square, you can stroll through the fortified gate into the sleepy, almost completely untouristy Old Town (called Kaštel), with more cafés and the town mosque (vengefully demolished during the war, but later rebuilt). The Trebišnjica River is spanned by the graceful, Ottoman-built Arslanagica Bridge. Overlooking the town from its hilltop perch is the striking Orthodox Church of Nova Gračanica, built to resemble the historically important Gračanica Monastery in Kosovo. If you have time, drive up to the church's viewpoint terrace for great views over Trebinje and the valley, and step inside the church to immerse yourself in a gorgeously vibrant world of Orthodox icons.

From Trebinje, you have two options for getting to Mostar: The faster route via Stolac, or the very rugged slower route via Nevesinje.

Stolac Route: As you enter Trebinje, after crossing the river, follow signs for *Mostar* and *Ljubinje*. Follow the Trebišnjica River into a high-altitude karstic basin, where evocative old waterwheels power a primitive irrigation system. From here, the river flows down to the coast—providing hydroelectric power for Dubrovnik—before detouring south and emptying into the sea near Herceg Novi, Montenegro...one river, three countries, in just a few miles. This area is blanketed with vineyards and dotted with old monasteries. Passing the village of Mesari ("Butchers"), you'll also see flocks of sheep. In this part of the Balkans, Croats were traditionally the city-dwellers, while Serbs were the farmers. There used to be sheep like these in the pastures near Dubrovnik, but when the Serbs left during the war, so did the sheep.

Pull over at one of the humble, slate-roofed Orthodox chapels by the road. (There's one in Staro Slano.) In the cemeteries, many of the gravestones are from 1991—when soldiers from this area joined the war effort against Dubrovnik.

The large, flat, sunken field you're driving along is called **Popovo Polje** ("Priests' Field"). Because it floods easily, the canal was

built to remove floodwater. Watch for the turnoff to **Vjetrenica** (near Zavala), a karstic cave that was a big draw in Yugoslav times. Closed down during the war, it recently re-opened. It's less spectacular than the famous caves in Slovenia, but has interesting water features that may be worth touring for spelunkers with time to kill (www.vjetrenica.ba).

At the fork, carry on straight to Ljubinje. Climbing up into the mountains, you'll see garbage along the side of the road—an improvised dump in this very poor land, where a fractured government struggles to provide even basic services. Twisting up through even higher mountains, you'll wind up in the town of **Ljubinje** (Љубиње). In this humble burg, roadside stands with *med* signs advertise homegrown honey. Also keep an eye out for drying tobacco. The partially built houses are not signs of war damage (the war didn't reach here); they're a form of "savings" in the Balkans, where people don't trust banks: Rather than deposit money in an account, they spend many years using any extra funds to gradually add on to a new house.

Continuing toward Mostar, you'll pass through more desolate countryside, then your ears will pop (and you'll pass a red, white, and blue sign marking the "border" of Republika Srpska) as you drop down into the town of **Stolac** (Столац); the town's defiant mosque minaret tells you that you've crossed from Serb territory into Bosnia's Muslim-Croat Federation. Stolac is home to some fascinating history, and worth a stroll if you have the time. Leaving Stolac, keep an eye out (on the left, just before the *Poprati* sign) for its interesting **necropolis**—a cluster of centuries-old traditional Bosnian tombstones (worth a quick photo-op stop).

Past Stolac, you'll climb up the hill, going through the village of Poprati. Soon you'll have the option of either turning off to the right to head directly to **Mostar,** or continuing along the main road to reach Čapljina, where you'll turn right to go past **Počitelj** on your way into Mostar. Either way, **Blagaj** is worth considering as a detour before ending in Mostar. (If you want to go to **Međugorje,** go through Čapljina and follow signs.) For arrival tips in Mostar, see the end of the driving directions above.

Nevesinje Route: This longer, more remote, middle-of-nowhere routing takes about an hour longer than the Stolac route. But if you're adventurous, it's a fun ride. From Trebinje, drive north toward **Bilećko Lake**—a vast, aquamarine lake you'll see on your right (the Vikiovac Restaurant offers a great viewpoint). Then you'll go through the town of **Bileća** (Билећа), turning west at the gloomy industrial town of **Gacko** (Гацко, with a giant coal mine), and onward to the humble but proud little town of **Nevesinje** (Невесиње). From Nevesinje, it's a quick drive up over the moun-

tains, then down into Mostar—passing spectacular views of Herzog Stjepan's imposing castle over the town of Buna. Follow signs on into Mostar.

Near Mostar

While Mostar has its share of attractions, there's also plenty to see within a short drive. Ideally try to splice one or two of these stops into your trip between Mostar and the coast (see my "Route Tips for Drivers," earlier, for tips on linking them up).

Blagaj

Blagaj (BLAH-gai, rhymes with "pie") was the historical capital of this region until the arrival of the Ottomans. This is the site of a mountain called Hum, which is topped by the ruins of a hilltop castle that once belonged to Herzog ("Duke") Stjepan, who gave Herzegovina its name.

Deep in Blagaj is an impressive cliff face with a scenic house marking the source of the Buna River. The building, called the **Tekija,** is a former monastery for Turkish dervishes (an order that emphasizes poverty and humility, famous for the way they whirl in a worshipful trance). Built in the 15th century and recently restored, the house is surrounded by a modern visitors center complex with a café, gift shop, and coin-op WCs. It's free to enter

and look around the Tekija, which feels similar to the tourable Turkish houses in Mostar. You'll take your shoes off and tiptoe across a patchwork of small rugs from room to room. Gazing out the windows at the towering cliff stretching to heaven, and hearing the constant, steady flow of water, it's easy to imagine how this could be considered a very spiritual place.

After seeing the house, stroll a bit along the river, which is crossed by several footbridges offering a grand view back on the Tekija and cliff. A handful of sprawling, touristy restaurants—with open-air terraces right along the refreshing river—serve up traditional Bosnian food, including trout pulled from their own river-fed ponds.

Getting There: Blagaj is easiest to see on the way to or from Mostar—just turn off from the main road and follow the Buna River, following *tekija* signs to the big parking lot.

Počitelj

Počitelj (POTCH-ee-tell) is an artists' colony filled with a compelling mix of Christian and Muslim architecture. Ideally situated right along the main Mostar-to-Croatia road, it's one of the most popular rest stops for passing tour buses, so it's hardly undiscovered. But it's still worth a stop for its dramatically vertical townscape and beautifully restored Ottoman architecture.

Park your car and hike across the riverstone cobbles to the open square at the base of town, with a handy restaurant, lots of gift shops, and aggressive vendors. The multidomed building is an old hammam (bathhouse). Then hike up the steep stairs (dodging costumed vendors, and enjoying fine aerial views on those hammam domes) to reach the **mosque.** It's free to enter (women must cover their heads). The interior is bigger, though not necessarily better decorated, than the mosques in downtown Mostar. A photo on the porch shows the building circa 1993, destroyed to its foundation.

Continue up the stairs behind the mosque, which lead steeply all the way up to the fortress, which was originally built in the 15th century by Hungarian King Mátyás Corvinus (who pushed the

Ottomans back, briefly reclaiming some territory—including this region—for the forces of Christian Europe). There's virtually nothing to see inside (the stairs inside the tower are extremely steep and narrow—tread carefully), but the views are sensational. The best views are from the flat terrace out front. It's clear just how strategic this location is, with perfect views up and down the Neretva Valley, constricted as it is here between steep cliffs.

Stolac

One of the most historic spots in Herzegovina, Stolac (STOH-lats) was a cradle of early Balkan civilization. Unless you're fascinated by archaeology, Stolac isn't worth a long detour—but since it's on the way between Mostar and Dubrovnik (on the back-roads route), consider stopping off if you have a little time to spare.

About 15,000 to 16,000 years ago—long before the Greeks or Romans arrived in this region—the Illyrians (ancestors of today's Albanians) lived in this area's caves, where they left behind some drawings. On a hill above the modern town are the overgrown remains of the once-fearsome dry-stone Illyrian fortress that

watched over this strategic road in the third and fourth centuries B.C. The Romans were later supplanted by the local Bogomil civilization, an indigenous Christian society. Stolac's most impressive attraction dates from this era: On the outskirts of town (on the road toward Mostar), you'll find a **necropolis** with a bonanza of giant tombstones called *stećak*s (from the 13th-15th centuries), engraved with evocative reliefs. Soon after these were erected, the Ottomans arrived, and conversions to Islam followed.

Archaeological treasures aside, today's Stolac is a workaday village with little tourism—it trudges along, largely oblivious to the ancient treasures embedded all around. The town was particularly hard-hit during the recent war, when it was taken over by Croat forces and its majority Muslim residents forced to flee to Mostar. Today the war crimes tribunal in The Hague has an entire division devoted to "Stolac Crimes"—at least 80 civilians were killed here. The mosque and surrounding area were completely leveled; it's now rebuilt, and the town's population is divided evenly between Croats and Bosniaks. Tension still hangs heavy in the air. Local Croats have erected crosses in front of several buildings in town, and the main square features a giant monument engraved with the names of Croats killed in the fighting here. The new, super-modern Catholic church spire rockets up over town, evoking the one-upsmanship of the similar steeple in Mostar. In a recent soccer match between the Croatian and Turkish national teams, local Bosniaks backed the Turks...and things got very tense.

If you're interested in learning more, it's well worth hiring local guide **Sanel Marić** to show you around. Sanel is an industrious young man who works for a local organization that strives to

help the people of Stolac transcend the scars of the recent war. He can both show you some of the ancient sights around town, and fill you in on recent events (€30 for a tour around town, mobile 061-071-830, sanell_m@yahoo.com).

Međugorje

Međugorje is an unassuming little village "between the hills" (as its name implies) that ranks with Lourdes, Fátima, and Santiago de Compostela as one of the most important pilgrimage sites in all of Christendom. To the cynical non-Catholic, it's just a strip of

crassly commercial hotels, restaurants, and rosary shops leading up to a dull church, all tied together by a silly legend about a hilltop apparition. But if you look into the tear-filled eyes of the pilgrims who've journeyed here, it's clear that to some, this place offers much more than what you see on the surface. Strolling through the grounds, you can hear the hushed sounds of prayer whispering through the bushes.

For true believers, Međugorje represents a once-in-a-lifetime opportunity to tread on sacred soil: a place where, over the past three-plus decades, the Virgin Mary has appeared to six local people. Even though the Vatican has declined to recognize the apparitions, that doesn't stop hundreds of thousands of Catholics from coming here each year. More than 30 million pilgrims have visited Međugorje since the sightings began—summer and winter, war (which didn't touch Međugorje) and peace, rain and shine. People make the trek here from Ireland, Italy, Germany, Spain, the US, and just about anywhere else that has Catholics.

Planning Your Time

Unless you're a pilgrim (or think you might be a pilgrim), skip Međugorje—it's an experience wasted on nonbelievers. (The only "attractions" are an unexceptional modern church, a couple of hilltop hikes, and pilgrim-spotting.)

If you do go, the easiest way is to take a day-trip excursion from the Dalmatian Coast (sold from Split, Dubrovnik, and Korčula). By public bus, you can day-trip into Međugorje from Split, but not from Dubrovnik. Consider spending the night here, or sleep in Mostar two nights and day-trip into Međugorje.

Međugorje Mary

What compels millions to flock to this little village in the middle of nowhere? The official story goes like this: On the evening of June 24, 1981, two young women were gathering their sheep on the hillside above Mostar. They came across a woman carrying a baby who told them to come near. Terrified, they

fled, only to realize later that this might have been a vision of the Virgin Mary. They returned the next night with some friends and saw the apparition again.

In the three-plus decades since, six different locals (including the two original seers) claim to have seen the vision, and some of them even say they see it regularly to this day. They also say that Mary has given them 10 secrets—predictions of future events that will portend Judgment Day. Written on a piece of parchment, these are kept safely at the home of one of the seers. They have said they will reveal each of these secrets, 10 days before the event occurs, to the local parish priest, who will then alert the world.

But official representatives of the Vatican are not among the believers. According to Catholic law, such visions must be "certified" by the local bishop—and the one around here didn't buy it. One cause for suspicion is that the six seers, before witnessing the visions, were sometimes known to be troublemakers. (In fact, they later admitted that they went up the hill that fateful night not to chase wayward sheep, but to sneak a smoke.) One investigator even suggested that they invented the story as a prank, only to watch it snowball out of control once they told it to the local priest. After decades of reluctance, in mid-2010 the Vatican formed a commission to determine whether to officially endorse this "miracle." (For now, priests are allowed to accompany pilgrimages to Međugorje, but not to *lead* them.)

Whether or not the story is true is, to a certain extent, beside the point—that people *believe* it's true is why they come here.

Orientation to Međugorje

Međugorje (MEDGE-oo-gor-yeh, sometimes spelled "Medjugorje" in English) is basically a one-street town—most everything happens in the half-mile between the post office (where the bus stop is) and the main church, St. James (Crkva Sv. Jakova). On the hills behind the church are two trails leading to pilgrimage sites. Many travel agencies line the main strip; at any of these, you can

find a room, rent a car, hire a local guide, buy ferry tickets for Croatia, and use the Internet.

By the way, Međugorje is clearly a "Croat" sight. While this may seem odd (after all, you're in Bosnia-Herzegovina, not Croatia), remember that any Catholic from the former Yugoslavia is called a Croat. Virtually every local person you'll meet in Međugorje is, strictly speaking, a Bosnian Croat.

Sights in Međugorje

The center of pilgrim activity is **St. James' Church** (Crkva Sv. Jakova), which was built before the apparitions. The exterior and interior are both pretty dull, but that doesn't stop pilgrims from worshipping here at all times of day (inside and outside). The inside, like the outside, is modern and monochromatic—with a soothing yellow color, and modern stained-glass windows lining the nave. Out in front of the church are posted maps that are useful for getting oriented, and a white statue of the Virgin Mary that attracts a lot of attention from pilgrims. Outside, along the left side of the church, notice the long row of multilingual confessional booths—each one marked with the language spoken by the priest inside, who stands at the ready.

As you face the church, you'll see two trails leading up to the hills. Behind and to the left of the church is **Apparition Hill** (at Podbrdo), where the sightings occurred (a one-mile hike, topped by a statue of Mary). Directly behind the church is the **Great Hill** (Križevac, or "Cross Mountain"), where a giant hilltop cross, which predates the visions, has become a secondary site of pilgrimage (1.5-mile hike). Note that the paths up to the hilltops are embedded with rocks. If you wonder why they don't make it easier to climb up, remember that an act of pilgrimage is supposed to be challenging. In fact, pilgrims often do one or both of these hikes barefoot, as an act of penitence.

Around back of the church is a makeshift amphitheater with

benches, used for outdoor services. Beyond that is a path, lined with scenes from the life of Jesus. Farther along, on the right, is a giant statue of the **Resurrected Savior** (Uskrsli Spasitelj), also known as the "Weeping Knee." While the elongated, expressionistic sculpture—exemplifying Christ's suffering—is inherently striking, the eternal dampness of its right knee attracts the most attention from pilgrims. Miraculously (or not), it's always wet—go

ahead and touch the spot that's been highly polished by worshippers and skeptics alike.

Believers and nonbelievers both appreciate the parade of kitsch that lines the **main street** leading up to the church. While rosaries are clearly the big item, you can get basically anything you want stamped with Catholic imagery (Mary is particularly popular, for obvious reasons).

Eating in Međugorje

The main street is lined with straightforward, crank-'em-out eateries catering to tour groups. For something a little more atmospheric and fun, head for **Gardens Restaurant** (near the post-office end of the main drag). The ground-floor bar, which feels a bit like a transplanted British pub, serves only drinks; you can order tasty international cuisine in the classy dining room upstairs, and the namesake garden terrace out back. Somewhat youthful, but still respectable, it's a nice place to unwind at the end of a long pilgrimage (10-14-KM pastas and pizzas, 14-24-KM main courses, daily 10:00-23:00, Antunovića 66, tel. 036/650-499, www.clubgardens. com).

Sleeping and Eating near Međugorje

Considering how drab the town itself is, if you're determined to sleep or eat near Međugorje, you might as well do it at a pleasant facility just outside of town (leaving town, follow signs for *Split/ Ljubuški*, and look for it on the left between warehouses). **$$ Herceg Etno Selo** (Herceg Ethno Village) is a completely artificial but undeniably appealing faux-village of new but old-looking Bosnian dry-stone buildings wedged between industrial areas and office parks. With slate roofs, inviting ponds, playgrounds, a vineyard, a small farm, and a big amphitheater, this sprawling complex includes 50 buildings, housing a restaurant, a big hotel, gift shops, and more. Designed as a retreat center for church groups on pilgrimage, it's a restful place. If Epcot had a low-rent "Croat Herzegovina" pavilion, it would look a lot like this—completely artificial but utterly charming. The industrial-size, smoky restaurant has a menu of very well-executed Bosnian and Croatian food (6-15-KM starters, 13-25-KM main dishes), while the hotel has 71 rooms (Db-€72, Tromeđa b.b., tel. 036/653-400, www.etno-herceg.com, info@etno-herceg.com).

UNDERSTANDING YUGOSLAVIA

Americans struggle to understand the complicated breakup of Yugoslavia—especially when visiting countries that rose from its ashes. Here's an admittedly oversimplified, as-impartial-as-possible history to get you started. (For a longer version, see www.ricksteves.com/yugo.)

For starters, it helps to have a handle on the different groups who've lived in the Balkans—the southeastern European peninsula between the Adriatic and the Black Sea, stretching from Hungary to Greece. The Balkan Peninsula has always been a crossroads of cultures. The Illyrians, Greeks, and Romans had settlements here before the Slavs moved into the region from the north around the seventh century. During the next millennium and a half, the western part of the peninsula—which would become Yugoslavia—was divided by a series of cultural, ethnic, and religious fault lines.

The most important influences were three religions: Western Christianity (i.e., Roman Catholicism, first brought to the western part of the region by Charlemagne and later reinforced by the Austrian Habsburgs), Eastern Orthodox Christianity (brought to the east from the Byzantine Empire), and Islam (in the south, from the Ottomans).

Two major historical factors made the Balkans what they are today: The first was the split of the Roman Empire in the fourth century A.D., dividing the Balkans down the middle between Roman Catholic (west) and Byzantine Orthodox (east)—roughly along today's Bosnian-Serbian border. Then the Ottoman victory at the Battle of Kosovo Polje (1389) began five centuries of Islamic influence in Bosnia-Herzegovina and Serbia, further dividing the Balkans into Christian (north) and Muslim (south).

Because of these and other events, several distinct ethnic identities emerged. Confusingly, the major "ethnicities" of Yugoslavia

Yugoslav Succession

AUSTRIA   HUNGARY

ITALY

Ljubljana   SLOVENE   Zagreb

SLOVENIA   CROATIA

VOJVODINA

Novi Sad

ROMANIA

BOSNIA-
Banja Luka
HERZEGOVINA

SERBO-CROATIAN

Belgrade

SERBIA

Adriatic Sea

Knin

Sarajevo

ITALY

MONTE-
NEGRO
Podgorica

Priština

KOSOVO

BULGARIA

Skopje

ALBANIAN

MACEDONIA

ALBANIA

GREECE

Former Yugoslavia Border

Current Borders

Province within Serbia

SLOVENE   Language

"Serbian Krajina"
(Serb-Controlled Croatia
1991-1995)

Republika Srpska (Serb
territory in Bosnia-Herz.)

100 Kilometers

100 Miles

are all South Slavs—they're descended from the same ancestors
and speak closely related languages, but they practice different
religions. Roman Catholic South Slavs are called **Croats** or **Slo-
venes**; Orthodox South Slavs are called **Serbs** or **Montenegrins**;
and Muslim South Slavs are called **Bosniaks** (whose ancestors
converted to Islam under the Ottomans). The region is also home
to several non-Slavic minority groups, including **Hungarians, Albanians,** and others. The groups overlapped a lot—which is exactly
why the eventual breakup of Yugoslavia was so contentious.

The Kingdom of Yugoslavia ("Land of the South Slavs"—*yugo*
means "south") was first formed after the Austro-Hungarian Empire fell at the end of World War I. It was an arbitrary union of the
various, mostly Slavic groups of southeast Europe. But from the
very beginning, the different ethnicities struggled for power within
the new Yugoslavia. This continued through the interwar period,
until the region was occupied by the Nazis during World War II.

At the end of World War II, the rest of Eastern Europe was
"liberated" by the Soviets, but the Yugoslavs regained their inde-

pendence on their own, as their communist Partisan Army forced out the Nazis. After the short but rocky Yugoslav union between the World Wars, it seemed that no one could hold the southern Slavs together in a single nation. But there was one man who could, and did: Communist Party president and war hero Josip Broz, better known as Tito. With a Slovene for a mother, a Croat for a father, a Serb for a wife, and a home in Belgrade, Tito was a true Yugoslav. Tito had a compelling vision that this fractured union of the South Slavs could function.

Tito's new incarnation of Yugoslavia aimed for a more equitable division of powers. It was made up of six republics, each with its own parliament and president: **Croatia** (mostly Catholic), **Slovenia** (mostly Catholic), **Serbia** (mostly Orthodox; also included the "autonomous provinces" of **Kosovo** and **Vojvodina**), **Bosnia-Herzegovina** (the most diverse—mostly Muslim Bosniaks, but with very large Croat and Serb populations), **Montenegro** (mostly Orthodox—a sort of a Serb/Croat hybrid), and **Macedonia** (with about 25 percent Muslim Albanians and 75 percent Orthodox Macedonians). Each republic managed its own affairs...but always under the watchful eye of president-for-life Tito, who said that the borders between the republics should be "like white lines in a marble column."

Tito's Yugoslavia was communist, but it wasn't Soviet communism. Despite strong pressure from Moscow, Tito refused to ally himself with the Soviets—and therefore received good will (and $2 billion) from the United States. Tito's vision was for a "third way," in which Yugoslavia could work with both East and West, without being dominated by either. While large industry was nationalized, Tito's system allowed for small businesses. This experience with a market economy benefited Yugoslavs when Eastern Europe's communist regimes eventually fell.

After Tito died in 1980, it did not take long for his union to unravel. In the late 1980s, squabbles broke out in the autonomous province of Kosovo between the Serb minority and the ethnic-Albanian majority. Serbia, led by Slobodan Milošević, annexed Kosovo—causing other republics (especially Slovenia and Croatia) to fear that he would gut their nation to create a "Greater Serbia," instead of a friendly coalition of diverse Yugoslav republics. Over the next decade, Yugoslavia broke apart, with much bloodshed.

Slovenia declared independence from Yugoslavia on June 25, 1991. After 10 days of fighting and fewer than a hundred deaths, they were granted their freedom. But the situation in other republics—which were far more ethnically diverse—was not so simple.

In April 1990, a historian named Franjo Tuđman won Croatia's first free elections. Tuđman invoked the spirit of the last group that led an "independent" Croatia—the Ustaše, who had ruthlessly

run Croatia's puppet government under the Nazis (and had killed many Serbs in their concentration camps). The 600,000 Serbs living in Croatia began to rise up.

By the time Croatia formally declared its independence (also on June 25, 1991), it was already embroiled in the beginnings of a bloody war. Croatia's Serb residents immediately declared their own independence from Croatia. The Serb-dominated Yugoslav National Army swept in, supposedly to keep the peace between Serbs and Croats—but it soon became obvious that they were there to support the Serbs.

Fighting raged through the region. In a surprise move, the Yugoslav National Army even attacked the tourist resort of Dubrovnik. By early 1992, the Serbs had gained control over the parts of inland Croatia where they were in the majority, and a tense ceasefire began. Then, in 1995, the Croats swept back through Serb territory to reclaim it for Croatia. During this period, both the Serbs and the Croats carried out "ethnic cleansing"—systematically removing an ethnic group from a territory, by displacing or killing them. Finally, the 1995 Erdut Agreement brought peace.

Bosnia-Herzegovina declared its independence from Yugoslavia four months after Croatia and Slovenia did. But Bosnia-Herzegovina was even more diverse than Croatia, as it was populated predominantly by Muslim Bosniaks (mostly in the cities) but also by large numbers of Serbs and Croats (many of them farmers).

At first, the Bosniaks and Croats teamed up to fight against the Serbs. But even before the first wave of fighting had subsided, Croats and Bosniaks turned their guns on each other. A bloody war raged for years between the three groups: the Serbs led by Radovan Karadžić (with support from Serbia proper), the Croats (with support from Croatia proper), and—squeezed between them—the internationally recognized Bosniak government, led by President Alija Izetbegović, who desperately worked for peace.

Bosnia-Herzegovina was torn apart. Even the many mixed families were forced to choose sides. If you had a Serb mother and a Croat father, you were expected to pick one ethnicity or the other—and your brother might choose the opposite. As families and former neighbors trained their guns on each other, proud and beautiful cities such as Sarajevo and Mostar were turned to rubble, and people throughout Bosnia-Herzegovina lived in a state of constant terror.

Finally, in 1995, the Dayton Peace Accords carefully divided Bosnia-Herzegovina among the different ethnicities. And today—following the peaceful declarations of independence in Montenegro (2006) and Kosovo (2008)—there are seven countries where once was a single, united Yugoslavia. While tension still exists, the region is peaceful, stable, and welcoming to visitors.

Travelers to this region quickly realize that the vast majority of people they meet here never wanted these wars. And so finally comes the inevitable question: Why did any of it happen in the first place?

Explanations tend to gravitate to two extremes. Some observers consider this part of the world to be inherently warlike—a place where deep-seated hatreds and age-old ethnic passions unavoidably flare up. Others believe that this theory is an insulting oversimplification. Sure, animosity has long simmered in the Balkans, but the conflict broke out because of the single-minded, self-serving actions of a few selfish leaders who exploited existing resentments to advance their own interests. It wasn't until Milošević, Karadžić, Tuđman, and others expertly manipulated the people's grudges that the country fell into war.

Many of the people you'll meet here are eager to tell you their own story. But keep in mind that everyone in the former Yugoslavia seems to have a slightly different version of events. A very wise Bosniak told me, "Listen to all three sides—Muslim, Serb, and Croat. Then decide for yourself what you think."

UNDERSTANDING YUGOSLAVIA

PRACTICALITIES

This section covers just the basics on traveling in Croatia (for much more information, see *Rick Steves' Croatia & Slovenia*). You can find free advice on specific topics at www.ricksteves.com/tips.

This book also includes destinations that are in different countries: Bosnia-Herzegovina and Montenegro. You'll find most of the practicalities about traveling in each of those places (such as the local currency and telephone tips) in their chapters.

Money

Croatia uses a currency called the kuna: 5 Croatian kunas (kn) = about $1. A kuna is broken into 100 smaller units, called lipas. To roughly convert Croatian kunas into dollars, double the amount and drop the final zero (e.g., 5 kn = about $1; 70 kn = about $14; 200 kn = about $40).

The standard way for travelers to get kunas is to withdraw money from a cash machine (called a *bankomat* in Croatia) using a debit or credit card, ideally with a Visa or MasterCard logo. Before departing, call your bank or credit-card company: Confirm that your card will work overseas, ask about international transaction fees, and alert them that you'll be making withdrawals in Europe. Also ask for the PIN number for your credit card in case it'll help you use Europe's "chip-and-PIN" payment machines (see below); allow time for your bank to mail your PIN to you. To keep your valuables safe, wear a money belt.

Dealing with "Chip and PIN": While much of Europe is shifting to a "chip-and-PIN" security system for credit and debit cards, the countries in this region still use the old magnetic-stripe technology. (European chip-and-PIN cards are embedded with an electronic security chip, and require the purchaser to punch in a PIN rather than sign a receipt.) If you happen to encounter chip and PIN, it will probably be at automated payment machines, such as those at toll roads or self-serve gas pumps. On the outside

chance that a machine won't take your card, find a cashier who can make your card work (they can print a receipt for you to sign), or find a machine that takes cash. But don't panic. Most travelers who are carrying only magnetic-stripe cards never encounter any problems. You can always use an ATM to withdraw cash with your magnetic-stripe card, even in countries where people predominantly use chip-and-PIN cards.

Phoning

Smart travelers use the telephone to reserve or reconfirm rooms, reserve restaurants, get directions, research transportation connections, confirm tour times, phone home, and lots more.

To call Croatia from the US or Canada: Dial 011-385 and then the phone number, minus its initial zero. (The 011 is our international access code, and 385 is Croatia's country code.)

To call Croatia from a European country: Dial 00-385 followed by the phone number, minus its initial zero. (The 00 is Europe's international access code.)

To call within Croatia: If you're dialing within an area code, just dial the local number; but if you're calling outside your area code, you have to dial both the area code (which starts with a 0) and the local number.

To call from Croatia to another country: Dial 00 followed by the country code (for example, 1 for the US or Canada), then the area code and number. If you're calling European countries whose phone numbers begin with 0, you'll usually have to omit that 0 when you dial.

Tips on Phoning: A mobile phone—whether an American one that works in Croatia, or a European one you buy when you arrive—is handy, but can be pricey. If traveling with a smartphone, switch off data-roaming until you have free Wi-Fi. With Wi-Fi, you can use your smartphone to make free or inexpensive domestic and international calls by taking advantage of a calling app such as Skype or FaceTime.

To make cheap international calls from any phone (even your hotel-room phone), you can try to buy an international phone card. These work with a scratch-to-reveal PIN code at any phone, allow you to call home to the US, and also work for domestic calls. Although common throughout much of Europe, prepaid phone cards are relatively rare in Croatia, and the savings aren't that enticing (calls to the US generally cost around 25-50 cents per minute). A phone card works only in the country where you bought it.

Another option is buying an insertable phone card. These work only at pay phones, are reasonable for making calls within the country, and can be used to make international calls as well. Note that insertable phone cards work only in the country where

From:	rick@ricksteves.com
Sent:	Today
To:	info@hotelcentral.com
Subject:	Reservation request for 19-22 July

Dear Hotel Central,

I would like to reserve a room for 2 people for 3 nights, arriving 19 July and departing 22 July. If possible, I would like a quiet room with a double bed and a bathroom inside the room.

Please let me know if you have a room available and the price.

Thank you!
Rick Steves

you buy them and—with the prevalence of mobile phones—public phones are getting harder to find.

Calling from your hotel-room phone is usually expensive, unless you use an international phone card. For more on phoning, see www.ricksteves.com/phoning.

Croatian Accommodations

For most travelers, Croatian hotels are a bad value; instead, I focus my recommendations on what locals call "private accommodations": a rented apartment *(apartman)* or a room in a private home *(soba,* pronounced SOH-bah; plural *sobe,* SOH-bay). Private accommodations offer travelers a characteristic and money-saving alternative for a fraction of the price of a hotel. While most Croatian accommodations quote their rates in euros, when you check out, payment is expected in kunas (or, occasionally, by credit card).

Generally the more you pay for your *soba,* the more privacy and amenities you get: private bathroom, TV, air-conditioning, kitchenette, and so on (though telephones are rare). Apartments are bigger and cost more than *sobe,* but they're still far cheaper than hotels. The prices for private accommodations generally fluctuate with the seasons, and stays of fewer than three nights usually come with a 20–50 percent surcharge (though this is often waived outside of peak season).

For the *sobe* listed in this book, **always book direct with your host**—it saves you and them money. You can reserve most *sobe* in advance online or by phone. Since the best-value *sobe* understandably book up early, reservations are highly recommended. For most of my recommended accommodations, I provide a website (which may have a built-in booking form) and an email address; you can expect a response in English within a day and often sooner. Email the *sobe* host with the following key pieces of information: number and type of rooms; number of nights; date of arrival; date of depar-

PRACTICALITIES

ture; and any special requests. (For a sample form, see the sidebar.) Use the European style for writing dates: day/month/year.

Most *sobe* hosts may ask for your credit-card number to secure the reservation (though you'll pay in cash when you're there). A few hosts might ask you to mail or wire money to them as a deposit; to avoid bank fees, it's better to mail a check or travelers check than to wire money. If the *sobe* host's request seems too complicated for you, reserve elsewhere.

Given the economic downturn, *sobe* hosts and hoteliers may be willing to make a deal—try emailing several to ask for their best price. In general, prices can soften if you do any of the following: offer to pay cash, stay at least three nights, or travel off-season.

If you like to travel without reservations, during most of the year you'll have no problem finding *sobe* as you go (though late July and August are the exceptions). Locals hawking rooms meet each arriving boat and bus. The quality can be hit or miss, but many of these are good options. Be sure you understand exactly where the room is located (i.e., within easy walking distance of the attractions) before you go to take a look. Because Europeans tend to dramatically lowball walking estimates, ask to see the location on a map. You can also keep an eye out for rooms as you walk or drive through town—blue *sobe* and *apartmani* signs are everywhere.

As a last resort, enlist the help of a travel agency on the ground to find you a room—but you'll pay 10–30 percent extra (to search from home, try www.dubrovnikapartmentsource.com).

Eating

Croatian food has a distinct Mediterranean flavor; you'll enjoy locally produced wine, olive oil, and *pršut* (air-dried ham, similar to prosciutto). The budget standby is pizza and pasta. For a splurge, try seafood: fish, scampi, mussels, squid, octopus, and more. Prices for fish dishes are listed either by the kilogram (1,000 grams) or by the 100-gram unit; figure about a half-kilo, or 500 grams—that's about one pound—for a large portion. Try the octopus salad, a flavorful mix of octopus, tomatoes, onions, and spices.

You'll find similar fare in Bosnia-Herzegovina and Montenegro, but there you're also likely to come across some pan-Balkan elements. One staple is phyllo dough pastries—both honey-drenched baklava and its savory cousin, *burek* (stuffed with cheese, meat, or spinach). But the big item is grilled meat: čevapčići (cheh-VAHP-chee-chee), grilled minced meat shaped like a sausage link; *pljeskavica* (plehs-kah-VEET-suh), grilled minced meat shaped like a patty; and *ražnjići* (RAZH-nyee-chee), skewered grilled steak similar to a shish kebab. Any kind of meat goes perfectly with the eggplant/red-pepper condiment called *ajvar* (EYE-var).

Good service is relaxed (slow to an American). You won't get

the bill until you ask for it: *"Računʔ»* (RAH-choon). To tip at restaurants that have a waitstaff, round up the bill 5 to 10 percent if you're happy with the service.

Transportation

Since Dubrovnik has no train access, you'll generally get around by car, bus, or boat.

By Car: A car is a headache to drive and park in Dubrovnik, but is the most convenient way to side-trip to this book's other destinations. You can arrange a short-term rental on the fly in Dubrovnik (ask any travel agency), or—often cheaper—reserve it in advance from the US (several big rental-car companies have offices in Dubrovnik). For tips on your insurance options, see www.ricksteves.com/cdw. Bring your driver's license; in Bosnia, it's required to carry an International Driving Permit (IDP), available at your local AAA office ($15 plus two passport-type photos, www.aaa.com). As you approach any town, follow the signs to *Centar* (usually also signed with a bull's-eye symbol). Follow this book's parking advice, and get additional tips from your hotelier. If you want someone else to do the driving, hire a local driver (listed on page 16).

It's mandatory to wear seat belts. For other rules of the Croatia road, ask your car-rental company, or check the US State Department website (www.travel.state.gov, search for your country in the "Learn about your destination" box, then click on "Travel and Transportation").

By Bus: If you lack a car, buses are the best way to connect most of the destinations in this book (and beyond). Confusingly, a single bus route can be operated by a variety of different companies, making it difficult to find comprehensive timetables; confirm schedules with a local TI or bus station (or try www.libertasdubrovnik.com or www.autobusni-kolodvor.com). For popular routes during peak season, drop by the station to buy your ticket a few hours—or even days—in advance to ensure getting a seat (ask the bus station ticket office or the local TI how far ahead you should arrive). You'll pay about $2 per bag to stow your luggage under the bus.

By Boat: Slow car ferries and speedy catamarans inexpensively shuttle tourists between major coastal cities and quiet island villages. The big ferries are operated by the national boat company, Jadrolinija (www.jadrolinija.hr). Walk-on passengers riding these boats don't need reservations, but drivers will want to line up their cars in advance (get advice locally about how early you need to arrive). A faster, private catamaran called *Nona Ana*—which takes only passengers (no cars)—also connects Dubrovnik to nearby islands (www.gv-line.hr). Because space is limited on this boat, in peak season it's smart to show up 1.5 hours ahead to be sure you get on the boat.

Helpful Hints

Emergency Help: For medical or other emergencies, dial 112 in Croatia, Montenegro, and Bosnia-Herzegovina. If you have a minor illness, do as the locals do and go to a pharmacist for advice. Or ask at your hotel for help—they'll know of the nearest medical and emergency services. For passport problems, call the **US Embassy** (for Croatia it's in Zagreb—tel. 01/661-2200, http://zagreb.usembassy.gov; for Montenegro it's in Podgorica—tel. 020/410-500, http://podgorica.usembassy.gov; for Bosnia it's in Sarajevo, tel. 033/704-000, http://sarajevo.usembassy.gov). For other concerns, get advice from your hotelier.

Theft or Loss: To replace a passport, you'll need to go in person to an embassy (see above). Cancel and replace your credit and debit cards by calling these 24-hour US numbers collect: Visa—tel. 303/967-1096, MasterCard—tel. 636/722-7111, American Express—tel. 336/393-1111. In Croatia, to make a collect call to the US, dial 0800-220-111; press zero or stay on the line for an operator. In Bosnia, call 00-800-0010. In Montenegro, dial 1201 for an international service operator. File a police report either on the spot or within a day or two; it's required if you submit an insurance claim for lost or stolen railpasses or travel gear, and can help with replacing your passport or credit and debit cards. Precautionary measures can minimize the effects of loss—back up your digital photos and other files frequently. For more information, see www.ricksteves.com/help.

Borders: You'll have to stop and show your passport when you cross the border between Croatia, Bosnia-Herzegovina, and Montenegro. Drivers may be asked to show proof of car insurance ("green card"), so be sure you have it when you pick up your rental car. When you change countries, you change phone cards, postage stamps, and, in most cases, money.

Time: All three countries use the 24-hour clock. It's the same through 12:00 noon, then keep going: 13:00, 14:00, and so on. Croatia, Bosnia-Herzegovina, and Montenegro, like most of continental Europe, are six/nine hours ahead of the East/West Coasts of the US.

Business Hours: Business hours can fluctuate wildly, based on demand—shops are open long hours daily in summer, but might be closed entirely in winter. Most businesses close on Sundays.

Holidays and Festivals: All three nations celebrate many holidays, which can close sights and attract crowds (book hotel rooms ahead). For information on holidays and festivals, check these websites: Croatia—http://us.croatia.hr, Bosnia-Herzegovina—www.bhtourism.ba, Montenegro—www.montenegro.travel. For a simple list showing major—though not all—events, see www.ricksteves.com/festivals.

Numbers and Stumblers: What Americans call the second

floor of a building is the first floor in Europe. Europeans write dates as day/month/year, so Christmas is 25/12. Commas are decimal points and vice versa—a dollar and a half is 1,50, and there are 5.280 feet in a mile. All three nations use the metric system: A kilogram is 2.2 pounds; a liter is about a quart; and a kilometer is six-tenths of a mile.

Smoking: Croatia has enacted smoking bans in most public places, though patrons at outdoor tables can still smoke. Bosnia-Herzegovina and Montenegro have no such bans.

Resources from Rick Steves

This Snapshot guide is excerpted from my latest edition of *Rick Steves' Croatia & Slovenia,* which is one of more than 30 titles in my series of guidebooks on European travel. I also produce a public television series, *Rick Steves' Europe,* and a public radio show, *Travel with Rick Steves.* My website, www.ricksteves.com, offers free travel information, a forum for travelers' comments, guidebook updates, my travel blog, an online travel store, and information on European railpasses and our tours of Europe. If you're bringing a mobile device on your trip, you can download free information from Rick Steves Audio Europe, featuring podcasts of my radio shows, free audio tours of major sights in Europe, and travel interviews about the Balkans (via www.ricksteves.com/audioeurope, iTunes, Google Play, or the Rick Steves Audio Europe free smartphone app). You can also follow me on Facebook and Twitter.

Additional Resources

Tourist Information: Croatia—http://us.croatia.hr; Bosnia-Herzegovina—www.bhtourism.ba; Montenegro—www.montenegro.travel

Passports and Red Tape: www.travel.state.gov

Packing List: www.ricksteves.com/packing

Cheap Flights: www.kayak.com

Airplane Carry-on Restrictions: www.tsa.gov

Updates for This Book: www.ricksteves.com/update

How Was Your Trip?

If you'd like to share your tips, concerns, and discoveries after using this book, please fill out the survey at www.ricksteves.com/feedback. Thanks in advance—it helps a lot.

Croatian Survival Phrases

In the phonetics, ī sounds like the long *i* in "light," and bolded syllables are stressed.

English	Croatian	Pronunciation
Hello. (formal)	Dobar dan.	**doh**-bahr dahn
Hi. / Bye. (informal)	Bok.	bohk
Do you speak English?	Govorite li engleski?	**goh**-voh-ree-teh lee **ehn**-glehs-kee
Yes. / No.	Da. / Ne.	dah / neh
I (don't) understand.	(Ne) razumijem.	(neh) rah-**zoo**-mee-yehm
Please. / You're welcome.	Molim.	**moh**-leem
Thank you (very much).	Hvala (ljepa).	**hvah**-lah (**lyeh**-pah)
Excuse me. / I'm sorry.	Oprostite.	oh-**proh**-stee-teh
problem	problem	proh-**blehm**
No problem.	Nema problema.	**neh**-mah proh-**bleh**-mah
Good.	Dobro.	**doh**-broh
Goodbye.	Do viđenija.	doh veed-**jay**-neeah
one / two	jedan / dva	**yeh**-dahn / dvah
three / four	tri / četiri	tree / **cheh**-teh-ree
five / six	pet / šest	peht / shehst
seven / eight	sedam / osam	**seh**-dahm / **oh**-sahm
nine / ten	devet / deset	**deh**-veht / **deh**-seht
hundred / thousand	sto / tisuća	stoh / **tee**-soo-chah
How much?	Koliko?	**koh**-lee-koh
local currency	kuna	**koo**-nah
Write it?	Napišite?	nah-**peesh**-ee-teh
Is it free?	Da li je besplatno?	dah lee yeh **beh**-splaht-noh
Is it included?	Da li je uključeno?	dah lee yeh **ook**-lyoo-cheh-noh
Where can I find / buy...?	Gdje mogu pronaći / kupiti...?	guh-**dyeh** moh-goo proh-nah-chee / **koo**-pee-tee
I'd like / We'd like...	Želio bih / Željeli bismo...	**zheh**-lee-oh beeh / **zheh**-lyeh-lee **bees**-moh
...a room.	...sobu.	**soh**-boo
...a ticket to ___.	...kartu do ___.	**kar**-too doh ___
Is it possible?	Da li je moguće?	dah lee yeh **moh**-goo-cheh
Where is...?	Gdje je...?	guh-**dyeh** yeh
...the train station	...kolodvor	**koh**-loh-dvor
...the bus station	...autobusni kolodvor	**ow**-toh-boos-nee **koh**-loh-dvor
...the tourist information office	...turističko informativni centar	**too**-ree-steech-koh een-for-mah-teev-nee **tsehn**-tahr
...the toilet	...vece (WC)	**veht**-seh
men	muški	**moosh**-kee
women	ženski	**zhehn**-skee
left / right	lijevo / desno	**lee**-yeh-voh / **dehs**-noh
straight	ravno	**rahv**-noh
At what time...	U koliko sati...	oo **koh**-lee-koh **sah**-tee
...does this open / close?	...otvara / zatvara?	**oht**-vah-rah / **zaht**-vah-rah
(Just) a moment.	(Samo) trenutak.	(**sah**-moh) treh-**noo**-tahk
now / soon / later	sada / uskoro / kasnije	**sah**-dah / **oos**-koh-roh / **kahs**-nee-yeh
today / tomorrow	danas / sutra	**dah**-nahs / **soo**-trah

In a Croatian Restaurant

English	Croatian	Pronunciation
I'd like to reserve...	Rezervirao bih...	reh-zehr-**veer**-ow beeh
We'd like to reserve...	Rezervirali bismo...	reh-zehr-**vee**-rah-lee **bees**-moh
...a table for one / two.	...stol za jednog / dva.	stohl zah **yehd**-nog / dvah
Non-smoking.	Za nepušače.	zah **neh**-poo-shah-cheh
Is this table free?	Da li je ovaj stol slobodan?	dah lee yeh **oh-vī** stohl **sloh**-boh-dahn
Can I help you?	Izvolite?	**eez**-voh-lee-teh
The menu (in English), please.	Jelovnik (na engleskom), molim.	yeh-**lohv**-neek (nah **ehn**-glehs-kohm) **moh**-leem
service (not) included	posluga (nije) uključena	**poh**-sloo-gah (**nee**-yeh) **ook**-lyoo-cheh-nah
cover charge	couvert	**koo**-vehr
"to go"	za ponjeti	zah **pohn**-yeh-tee
with / without	sa / bez	sah / behz
and / or	i / ili	ee / **ee**-lee
fixed-price meal (of the day)	(dnevni) meni	(duh-**nehv**-nee) **meh**-nee
specialty of the house	specijalitet kuće	speht-see-yah-**lee**-teht **koo**-cheh
half portion	pola porcije	**poh**-lah **port**-see-yeh
daily special	jelo dana	**yeh**-loh **dah**-nah
fixed-price meal for tourists	turistički meni	**too**-ree-steech-kee **meh**-nee
appetizers	predjela	**prehd**-yeh-lah
bread	kruh	krooh
cheese	sir	seer
sandwich	sendvič	**send**-veech
soup	juha	**yoo**-hah
salad	salata	sah-**lah**-tah
meat	meso	**may**-soh
poultry	perad	**peh**-rahd
fish	riba	**ree**-bah
seafood	morska hrana	**mohr**-skah **hrah**-nah
fruit	voće	**voh**-cheh
vegetables	povrće	**poh**-vur-cheh
dessert	desert	deh-**sayrt**
(tap) water	voda (od slavine)	**voh**-dah (ohd **slah**-vee-neh)
mineral water	mineralna voda	**mee**-neh-rahl-nah **voh**-dah
milk	mlijeko	mlee-**yeh**-koh
(orange) juice	sok (od naranče)	sohk (ohd **nah**-rahn-cheh)
coffee	kava	**kah**-vah
tea	čaj	chī
wine	vino	**vee**-noh
red / white	crno / bijelo	**tsehr**-noh / bee-**yeh**-loh
sweet / dry / semi-dry	slatko / suho / polusuho	**slaht**-koh / **soo**-hoh / **poh**-loo-soo-hoh
glass / bottle	čaša / boca	**chah**-shah / **boht**-sah
beer	pivo	**pee**-voh
Cheers!	Živjeli!	**zhee**-vyeh-lee
More. / Another.	Još. / Još jedno.	yohsh / yohsh **yehd**-noh
The same.	Isto.	**ees**-toh
Bill, please.	Račun, molim.	**rah**-choon **moh**-leem
tip	napojnica	**nah**-poy-neet-sah
Delicious!	Izvrsno!	**eez**-vur-snoh

INDEX

Audio Europe

Rick's Free Travel App

Get your FREE **Rick Steves Audio Europe**™ app to enjoy...

- Dozens of self-guided tours of Europe's top museums, sights and historic walks

- Hundreds of tracks filled with cultural insights and sightseeing tips from Rick's radio interviews

- All organized into handy geographic playlists

- For iPhone, iPad, iPod Touch, Android

With Rick whispering in your ear, Europe gets even better.

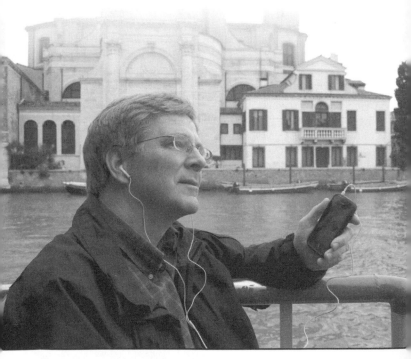

Find out more at ricksteves.com

Join a Rick Steves tour

Enjoy Europe's warmest welcome... with the flexibility and friendship of a small group getting to know Rick's favorite places and people. It all starts with our free tour catalog and DVD.

Great guides, small groups, no grumps.

Start your trip at

Free information and great gear to

▸ Plan Your Trip

Browse thousands of articles and a wealth of money-saving tips for planning your dream trip. You'll find up-to-date information on Europe's best destinations, packing smart, getting around, finding rooms, staying healthy, avoiding scams and more.

▸ Eurail Passes

Find out, step-by-step, if a railpass makes sense for your trip—and how to avoid buying more than you need. Get free shipping on online orders

▸ Graffiti Wall & Travelers Helpline

Learn, ask, share—our online community of savvy travelers is a great resource for first-time travelers to Europe, as well as seasoned pros.

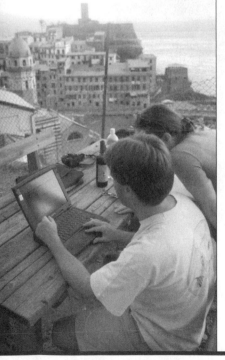

Rick Steves' Europe Through the Back Door, Inc

Rick Steves

www.ricksteves.com

EUROPE GUIDES

Best of Europe
Eastern Europe
Europe Through the Back Door
Mediterranean Cruise Ports
Northern European Cruise Ports

COUNTRY GUIDES

Croatia & Slovenia
England
France
Germany
Great Britain
Ireland
Italy
Portugal
Scandinavia
Spain
Switzerland

CITY & REGIONAL GUIDES

Amsterdam, Bruges & Brussels
Barcelona
Budapest
Florence & Tuscany
Greece: Athens & the Peloponnese
Istanbul
London
Paris
Prague & the Czech Republic
Provence & the French Riviera
Rome
Venice
Vienna, Salzburg & Tirol

SNAPSHOT GUIDES

Berlin
Bruges & Brussels
Copenhagen & the Best of
    Denmark
Dublin
Dubrovnik
Hill Towns of Central Italy
Italy's Cinque Terre
Krakow, Warsaw & Gdansk
Lisbon
Madrid & Toledo
Milan & the Italian Lakes District
Munich, Bavaria & Salzburg
Naples & the Amalfi Coast
Northern Ireland
Norway
Scotland
Sevilla, Granada & Southern Spain
Stockholm

POCKET GUIDES

Amsterdam
Athens
Barcelona
Florence
London
Paris
Rome
Venice

Rick Steves guidebooks are published by Avalon Travel,
a member of the Perseus Books Group.

NOW AVAILABLE:
eBOOKS, DVD & BLU-RAY

TRAVEL CULTURE

Europe 101
European Christmas
Postcards from Europe
Travel as a Political Act

eBOOKS

Nearly all Rick Steves guides are available as eBooks. Check with your favorite bookseller.

RICK STEVES' EUROPE DVDs

11 New Shows 2013–2014
Austria & the Alps
Eastern Europe
England & Wales
European Christmas
European Travel Skills & Specials
France
Germany, BeNeLux & More
Greece, Turkey & Portugal
Iran
Ireland & Scotland
Italy's Cities
Italy's Countryside
Scandinavia
Spain
Travel Extras

BLU-RAY

Celtic Charms
Eastern Europe Favorites
European Christmas
Italy Through the Back Door
Mediterranean Mosaic
Surprising Cities of Europe

PHRASE BOOKS & DICTIONARIES

French
French, Italian & German
German
Italian
Portuguese
Spanish

JOURNALS

Rick Steves' Pocket Travel Journal
Rick Steves' Travel Journal

PLANNING MAPS

Britain, Ireland & London
Europe
France & Paris
Germany, Austria & Switzerland
Ireland
Italy
Spain & Portugal

Rick Steves books and DVDs are available at bookstores and through online booksellers.

ABOUT THE AUTHORS

RICK STEVES

 Since 1973, Rick Steves has spent 100 days every year exploring Europe. Along with writing and researching a bestselling series of guidebooks, Rick produces a public television series *(Rick Steves' Europe)*, a public radio show *(Travel with Rick Steves)*, and an app and podcast *(Rick Steves Audio Europe)*; writes a nationally syndicated newspaper column; organizes guided tours that take over ten thousand travelers to Europe annually; and offers an information-packed website (www .ricksteves.com). With the help of his hardworking staff of 80 at Rick Steves' Europe—in Edmonds, Washington, just north of Seattle—Rick's mission is to make European travel fun, afford-able, and culturally enlightening for Americans.

Connect with Rick:

facebook.com/RickSteves   twitter: @RickSteves

CAMERON HEWITT

 Cameron Hewitt grew up listening to the Polish nursery rhymes of his grandfather, Jan Paweł Dąbrowski. Today, Cameron researches and writes guidebooks for Rick Steves. For this book, he has spent countless hours tracking down Dubrovnik's best *sobe,* disentangling Balkan history, and raving about Slovenia's unique blend of high-mountain scenery and the friendliest locals in Europe. When he's not on the road, Cameron lives in Seattle with his wife, Shawna.

Avalon Travel
a member of the Perseus Books Group
1700 Fourth Street
Berkeley, CA 94710

Text © 2014 by Rick Steves
Cover © 2014 by Avalon Travel. All rights reserved.
Maps © 2014 by Rick Steves' Europe
Portions of this book were originally published in *Rick Steves' Croatia & Slovenia*

Printed in Canada by Friesens. First printing June 2014.

For the latest on Rick's lectures, guidebooks, tours, public radio show, and public television series, contact Rick Steves' Europe, 130 Fourth Avenue North, Edmonds, WA, 98020, 425/771-8303, fax 425/771-0833, www.ricksteves.com, rick@ricksteves.com.

ISBN 978-1-61238-769-7

Rick Steves' Europe
Managing Editor: Risa Laib
Editorial & Production Manager: Jennifer Madison Davis
Editors: Glenn Eriksen, Tom Griffin, Cameron Hewitt, Suzanne Kotz, Cathy Lu, John Pierce, Carrie Shepherd
Editorial Assistant: Jessica Shaw
Editorial Intern: Kim Downing
Maps & Graphics: David C. Hoerlein, Sandra Hundacker, Lauren Mills, Mary Rostad

Avalon Travel
Senior Editor & Series Manager: Madhu Prasher
Editor: Jamie Andrade
Associate Editor: Annette Kohl
Assistant Editor: Maggie Ryan
Copy Editor: Patrick Collins
Proofreader: Janet Walden
Indexer: Stephen Callahan
Production & Typesetting: Tabitha Lahr, Christine DeLorenzo
Cover Design: Kimberly Glyder Design
Maps & Graphics: Kat Bennett, Mike Morgenfeld

Photography: Cameron Hewitt, Rick Steves, Sandra Hundacker, Rhonda Pelikan, Pat O'Connor
Cover Photo: Dubrovnik's Old Town © Cameron Hewitt

Want More Eastern Europe?
Maximize the experience with Rick Steves as your guide

Guidebooks
Rick's Eastern Europe guide makes side-trips smooth and affordable

Planning Maps
Use the map that's in sync with your guidebook

Rick's DVDs
Preview where you're going with 3 shows on Croatia and Slovenia

Free! Rick's Audio Europe™ App
Hear Eastern Europe travel tips from Rick's radio shows

Small-Group Tours
Including the Best of the Adriatic

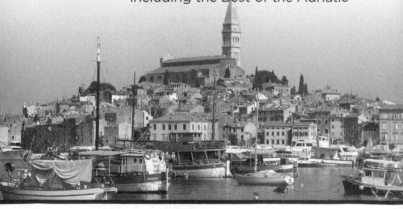

For all the details, visit ricksteves.com

CONTENTS

Rick Steves'
SNAPSHOT

Dubrovnik